Heinrich Bammann

The Bahurutshe

Quellen und Beiträge
zur Geschichte der
Hermannsburger Mission
und des
Ev.-luth. Missionswerkes in Niedersachsen

Band XXVI

Lit

Heinrich Bammann

THE BAHURUTSHE

Historical Events, Culture
and Religion (Traditional and Christian)
in Dinokana/South Africa
from 1857 to 1940

LIT

Cover photo: Missionary Ferdinand Jensen with church-elders.

Translated from the original German book: *Die Bahurutshe – Historische Ereignisse, Kultur und Religion und die Mission der ersten drei Hermannsburger Pioniere in Dinokana/Südafrika von 1857bis 1940* by Klaudia Ringelmann

Bibliographic information published by the Deutsche Nationalbibliothek
The Deutsche Nationalbibliothek lists this publication in the Deutsche Nationalbibliografie; detailed bibliographic data are available on the Internet at http://dnb.d-nb.de.

ISBN 978-3-643-90747-9

A catalogue record for this book is available from the British Library

Klosbachstr. 107
CH-8032 Zürich
Tel. +41 (0) 44-251 75 05 Fax +41 (0) 44-251 75 06
E-Mail: zuerich@lit-verlag.ch http://www.lit-verlag.ch

Distribution:

In the UK: Global Book Marketing, e-mail: mo@centralbooks.com
In North America: International Specialized Book Services, e-mail: orders@isbs.com
In Germany: LIT Verlag Fresnostr. 2, D-48159 Münster
Tel. +49 (0) 2 51-620 32 22, Fax +49 (0) 2 51-922 60 99, e-mail: vertrieb@lit-verlag.de

In Austria: Medienlogistik Pichler-ÖBZ, e-mail: mlo@medien-logistik.at
e-books are available at www.litwebshop.de

I dedicate this book to the three Bahurutshe men **Pontsho Khutswane**, **Moiloa Menyatswe** and **Rapiti Segaloe**, and one Mokwena, **Ramosesane Tladi**

These young men resided with me from 1973 to 1979 in the parsonage of the church at Motswedi, in the northwest of the erstwhile Transvaal Province.

I extend my gratitude towards their parents and siblings, who trusted me with these young men back then and released them from their families.

In July 1977 my wife Giesela neé Röhrs joined our community. After these youngsters had finished high school they left our family and followed their own paths.

To this day, we maintain good contact with all of them.

I want to say thank you to Dr. Werner Jensen, Moshe Mongae and Keitumetse Motsosi for their financial assistance to the translation of this book.

Translated from the original German book: "'Die Bahurutshe – Historische Ereignisse, Kultur und Religion und die Mission der ersten drei Hermannsburger Pioniere in Dinokana/Südafrika von 1857 bis 1940"'

by Klaudia Ringelman

Foreword 1

Dr Rev Heinrich Bammann studied Theology in Germany and, at the completion of his studies, was posted to South Africa by the Lutheran Missionary Society. For several years he served as moruti among the Batswana. He later completed his doctoral studies with the University of South Africa. This book forms a part of his doctoral research studies. He is an artist wishing to make facts and evidence to speak for themselves about challenges and opportunities of life.

While Bammann was stationed at Motswedi near Dinokana in the Zeerust area, I served as a member of his Congregational Committee. My father Paul Diratsagae Legotlo was also member of the Congregational Committee who played a meaningful role in the erection of the Lutheran Church in Borakalalo near Motswedi. During those years we held several meetings over several matters of the church. Bammann demonstrated his leadership qualities and attributes of a successful moruti. He did not only learn Setswana culture and language but also the essential norms and values of Batswana and how to gain respect among the Batswana. In accordance with the policy of the Lutheran Missionary Society, he was obliged to study and know the Batswana because: "*... the Lutheran missionaries were sent out into the world not to return home; when they left Germany they knew there was no chance to come back*".[1]

This book is one of the important documents; in fact, it is a good directional guide that maps out the activities of the Lutheran missionaries among the Bahurutshe. The Lutheran missionaries built a church in Dinokana. In 1871 Thomas Jensen built the first school house of 40 × 15 feet in the Transvaal. It had thick mud walls and a thatched roof. The Bahurutshe attended classes and learnt how to read and write. The main purpose was to convert them to Christianity.

More importantly, the writer traced the movement of the Bahurutshe from Ga-Ditshwene, the old capital of the Bahurutshe in Marico, to Mosega, and from Mosega to Taung and from Taung to Ga-Ditshwene until they eventually settled in Dinokana and surrounding villages. The author notes that the Bahurutshe, like all other tribes and people, passed through the Stone Age to the Iron Age. They mined iron ore around Powe and Poosedumane. In addition, the Bahurutshe are recognized as a senior Batswana tribe and are accorded precedence in ritual and ceremony.

The author emphasizes the following important argument to be considered by the Bahurutshe, readers and other researchers:

1. We should attempt to conceptualize the socio-political factors and circumstances that persuaded the Bahurutshe to move from one place to the other until they settled in Dinokana and surrounding villages. 2. The author has demonstrated the role of the missionaries in providing the foundation of formal schooling. 3.

[1] This changed during the Eighties of the previous century.

Foreword 1

Once more the researchers are reminded of the importance and challenges of documentary analysis and issues of selecting materials to support an argument.

Dr Bammann has demonstrated that he is a scholar. His research work moves from the history of the Bahurutshe to their contemporary socio-political life. This book constitutes an additional source of knowledge in the history of Dinokana and the Bahurutshe of Kgosi Moilwa II.

Prof Marekwa Wilfred Legotlo

Foreword 2

To write a foreword for this book about the Bahurutshe tribe in South Africa by Dr. Rev. H. Bammann is for me a privilege. But I also realised how grateful one should be for people, like the author, who are dedicated spending hours in research, paging through books and manuscripts, visiting libraries in the hope to find just a little bit more information for their task.

Bammann became interested in the culture of several Batswana tribes of which the Bahurutshe interested him in particular. The reader becomes acquainted with the places where the history of the Bahurutshe took place in order to try and visualise the environment in which they travelled and lived their lives through generations, surrounding factors that influenced their behaviour, as well as their living conditions. This book gives one an insight in the areas the Bahurutshe travelled, their living conditions, activities, tribal structures, etc., their role in the region and their problems in society. Information is thereby preserved for generations and is there for everyone to read. All put together in one book by a dedicated man with a purpose.

Pioneer missionaries from different overseas countries came to South Africa in the 19th century. We get to know this by the example of the Bahurutshe tribe at Dinokana. Those missionaries had a dedication to spread the word of Christianity and they lived for it, even in difficult circumstances.

My great-grandfather (Thomas Jensen) and grandfather (Ferdinand Jensen) were sent to Dinokana by the Hermannsburg mission society in Germany and also dedicated their lives for a purpose. They built a congregation among the Bahurutshe and had to send reports to their superiors overseas. Apart from learning the language of Setswana, the customs, rituals and culture of the Bahurutshe people, they also formed friendships with the local chiefs, gathered information from their neighbours on various aspects and made an effort to write many things down in their reports. Theirs was missionary work among the Bahurutshe tribe, including many villages around Dinokana. They worked there for over 90 years.

In the book is also a short history of my forefathers. We gain some insight into their character as well as how they went about their work. Also some facts are mentioned, not yet known to me. They also had their share of difficulties with customs and rituals of the Bahurutshe and also with the political situation in the area. But their dedication is visible.

I want to thank Dr Bammann for his extensive research on the tribe and putting it in book form for us to read, giving us an in-depth view of the Bahurutshe tribe.

"Soli Deo Gloria"
Dr. Ferdinand JW Jensen

Contents

Introduction 1

1 The Bahurutshe 3

1.1 Migrations of the Bantu to the South 3

1.2 Migrations of the Bahurutshe in the Transvaal 7

1.3 Pioneer Missionaries amongst the Bahurutshe 15

1.3.1 French Missionaries 15

1.3.2 American Missionaries 25

1.3.3 A British Missionary 42

1.3.4 The first Hermannsburg Missionary 52

2 Dinokana 65

2.1 The Bahurutshe and Dinokana 65

2.2 Chieftainship and Chiefs, with particular reference to Moiloa II 70

3 The two Hermannsburg Missionaries Thomas and Ferdinand Jensen 83

3.1 Socio-cultural Knowledge 83

3.1.1 Language 83

3.1.2 Construction Style of the Huts and Houses 87

3.1.2.1 Clothing 89

3.1.3 Work and nourishment 91

3.1.4 Celebrations and Days of Rest 98

3.1.5 Taxes and Final Resettlement 105

3.1.6 Succession Quarrels 108

3.1.7 Ikalafeng's attempted Insurrection in the Reservation . . 110

3.2 Knowledge of the Traditional Religion 117

3.2.1 Rites of Passage 117

3.2.1.1 Birth 118

3.2.1.2 Initiation 120

3.2.1.3 Wedding 128

3.2.1.4 Death and Burial 133

4 Harmony and Disharmony amongst the Bahurutshe 139

4.1 Natural Disasters 139

4.2 Cattle Epidemic 144

4.3 Transgression of Tribal Laws 146

4.4 Diseases 148

5 Mission Work in Dinokana 151

5.1 The first Christians 151

5.1.1 Local Converts and those from other Tribes 151

5.1.2 The Problem of Polygamy, as illustrated by the Example of *Tsetlana* 153

5.2 The Work of the two Jensen Missionaries 156

5.2.1 Rites of Passage within the Church and Mission 156

5.2.1.1 Baptism 156

5.2.1.2 Confirmation 162

5.2.1.3 The Problem of Marriage 164

5.2.1.4 Death and Eternity 166

5.3 The Congregation 169

5.3.1 The Sermon 169

5.3.2 The Church Service 172

5.3.3 The Church 175

5.3.4 The School 180

5.3.5 Outstations 187

5.3.6 The First Church Taxes 190

5.3.7 The Foreigners Once Again 193

6 Ferdinand Jensen's Retrospection 199

7 In Conclusion 205

8 Appendix 209

8.1 Personal Observations by the Author 209

8.2 Biographies 211

8.2.1 Thomas Jensen 211

8.2.2 Ferdinand Jensen 213

8.3 Chiefs and Missionaries 215
8.3.1 Reigning Chiefs of Dinokana 215
8.3.2 Pastors and Missionaries in Dinokana from the period 1859–1940 215
8.3.2.1 Stationary Missionaries 215
8.3.2.2 Temporary Pastors and Missionaries 215
8.4 Supplementary Pictures and Picture Credits 216
8.4.1 Additional Pictures from Dinokana 216
8.4.2 Picture Credits 224
8.5 Glossary of Setswana Terminology 224
8.5.1 Terminology of Words in Italics 224
8.5.2 Terminology of Concepts 225
8.6 Church Service Today 226
9 Bibliography 229
9.1 Original Reports by the Missionaries. 229
9.2 Secondary Literature 230

Introduction

The book opens with reflections on the arrival of the Batswana in South Africa. Time and again the *Bantu*[2] reached the south during their migrations from central Africa. As recently as 30 years ago, all Africans in southern Africa, irrespective of their tribal affiliations, be they *Batswana, Bapedi, Zulu, Xhosa* or other tribes, were denoted with the collective term *Bantu.* The only exception are the San people, the original inhabitants of South Africa.

Today the individual tribes are called by their tribal name, which is frequently derived from the first chief of that particular tribe. The chief plays a major role in all tribes. The most prominent chief in this book is *Moiloa II*. He was one of two notable leaders during the tribe's migrations in the Transvaal. By the time that the tribe settled in Dinokana, he had already assumed absolute rule.

After the Bahurutshe had settled in Dinokana and their altercations with neighbouring tribes had come to an end, the oppression by the Boers began. In spite of this they were able to restructure their social, cultural and religious values and restore the cultivation of their traditions. At the same time, a new economic orientation occurred with the appearance of the Europeans, and the traditional religion was challenged by the arrival of the first missionaries. The Bahurutshe had to come to terms with all the various aspects of civilisation and Christianisation if they wanted to survive and not be driven to the brink of despair.

When the Bahurutshe had not yet settled and were still traversing the Transvaal, mission societies from America and Europe concerned themselves with the missionizing of this tribe. With the arrival of the first missionaries it didn't take long for profit-seeking European traders and hunters to appear as well. The missionaries initially remained the first Europeans who lived amongst the Bahurutshe. They were bound to their mission societies whom they were obliged to send regular reports about their work. It is

2 The term *Bantu* is a denotation in the plural. *Ntu* = human being, *Bantu* = humans.

from these reports that my manuscript arose. The texts were gathered from five different archives. Two more archives did not yield what I was looking for.

The first missionaries who came successively to the Batswana from three different mission societies were not able to stay very long. This changed with the arrival of the Hermannsburg missionaries. Two of them stayed for the rest of their lives.

The content of the book has, for the most part, been derived from selected reports and letters written by the missionaries. These missionaries did not only write about their baptismal- and confirmation successes. Especially those Hermannsburg missionaries who had been sent out for the long term learnt Setswana, the language of the Batswana, and studied their culture and traditions. Apart from their missionary activities they also supported the chiefs against the pressure exerted on them by the Boers and helped them to withstand the incipient oppression. They assisted in the transformation of the tribe into a new nation, cured illnesses with homeopathic remedies, thereby lowering the mortality rate, and lived through periods of aridity, drought and viral epidemics with the Bahurutshe.

The reports of the Hermannsburg missionaries are written in the Sütterlin script, which was in use at that time. Capturing these texts was a time-consuming task; the assistance of the ELM archivist had to be frequently enlisted for the transcription of the text.

1 The Bahurutshe

1.1 Migrations of the Bantu to the South

The Bahurutshe constitute a subgroup of the Batswana[3] and live in southern Africa. Today a key area of the Batswana is populated by them, stretching from Marico over Zeerust to the Botswana border; they speak a good Setswana. Over the centuries the various Batswana tribes have developed their own dialect. The Batswana understand one another linguistically, even though they live far apart from each other. Geographically the region of the Batswana encompasses the area of *Johannesburg/Gauteng* and *Pretoria/Tshwane* in South Africa, the entire Botswana, and extending to Windhoek in Namibia.

Before South Africa had boundaries the Batswana populated the erstwhile province of the Transvaal. After the demise of Apartheid, the boundaries in South Africa were redrawn. Four regions turned into nine. The majority of the Batswana in South Africa now live in the North West Province. A great number of young people were drawn to Pretoria and Johannesburg. During the Apartheid era they resided in the townships of these cities. After Apartheid was abolished, many well-to-do families moved into the "white" suburbs, which had previously been reserved exclusively for Europeans. They visited their parents and relatives on holidays. Then they practise their traditional culture with their usual rituals and customs.

All Batswana tribes, including the Bahurutshe, have migrated into the South African region. Their ancestors lived in central Africa. To this day the region and the places in central Africa from where they emigrated can still not be accurately traced. The motives for the emigration, too, remain unknown. The time when this emigration occurred is equally vague. One can only say with some certainty that the emigration began hundreds of

[3] The etymological explanation of the term *Batswana* offers various possibilities: Linguistically, *Ba* is a personal prefix in the plural (singular: *mo), tswana* can be derived from the verb *go tswa* = to separate, together with the diminutive *ana,* meaning: having separated from other tribes; or else *go tshwana* = to be akin to, meaning: to be similar to other tribes; or else derived from the adjective *-ntsho* = black, together with the diminutive *ana,* thus meaning 'blackish'. Conversation of Schapera with Ramoshoana, in Cole 1955 xxf; cf. Bammann 2004 p. 38.

years ago, long before the Boers colonised the Cape in the 17th century. The oral tradition of the Batswana from the old people to the young ones was not only negligent in the exact dates but also in describing the circumstances. Too many other events have since taken place. However, historians have meanwhile begun deliberating and have drawn some conclusions from archaeological findings on the emigration movements.

In the early 20th century, or maybe even a few years before that, an unknown author wrote about the Bahurutshe. Ferdinand Jensen doesn't mention any names, but cites the following words: "Around 200 BC all the Batswana tribes were still united in one tribe. They spoke the same language and revered a common ancestor in their ancestral lineage. Their tribal totem was the eland, and their chief was Keledi I, a Morolong and a great ruler. (…) Around 209 BC they reached and settled in the region to the west of Pretoria, and ca. 300 BC they migrated to the Molopo River near Mafikeng … where Mohurutshe was their chief and where, to this day, the Bahurutshe changed their totem animal to that of the baboon."[4]

There exists no reliable evidence as to the validity of the aforementioned citation. Rather, it constitutes one of only a few oral traditions. The unknown author is interested in the history of the Bahurutshe and is probably a Mohurutshe himself. He writes on the beginnings of the Batswana nation. The dates he proposes can neither be seconded nor refuted, but rather indicate that the time of immigration has to be considerably backdated. The immigration territory in the centre of South Africa can therefore be deemed to be correct. The migration westwards, too, into the area of Mafikeng with the mentioned chief Keledi I, is plausible. And the separation of the Bahurutshe from the Batswana is a reality. Other authors, as we shall later see, have different perceptions concerning this immigration. Of interest is the rendition of the totem. The first totem, before the Batswana split into various tribes, is purported to be the eland.[5] It remains unclear whether the

4 Ferdinand Jensen, File B item 68 *Polelo ea merafe ea Batswana,* p. 1. – "Um das Jahr 200 BC waren alle Batswanastämme noch in einen Stamm vereint. Sie redeten in der gleichen Sprache und verehrten einen gemeinsamen Ahnherrn in ihrer Abstammungslinie. Das Stammestotem war das Eland und der Häuptling Keledi I, ein Morolong und ein großer Herrscher. (…) Sie erreichten die Gegend westlich von Pretoria und siedelten sich dort etwa 209 BC an und ca. 300 BC wanderten sie zum Molopofluss nahe Mafikeng … wo dann Mohurutshe der Häuptling war und die Bahurutshe änderten ihr Totem zum Pavian bis auf den heutigen Tag."

5 The bodily frame of an eland is similar to that of a cow or an ox. The eland was a favourite quarry to be hunted, due to its sluggishness and potential abundance of meat.

eland as a tribal totem was adopted from the San people, who were living in the region centuries before the Bantu settled there, or whether it was already meant to guarantee the cohesion of the Batswana during their migrations to the south.

Before being wiped out by the Bantu and the Boers, the San had also inhabited the North West Province. The only location in this province where the San have left behind their artistic, rock-hewn engravings is on a small hillock on the peripheries of the town of Sione, eighty kilometres to the south of Mafikeng, and only a few kilometres to the east of Khunoane. The eland as well as many other animals are engraved in the weather-beaten stones. The stones lie on the open ground. Compared to the artful paintings of other San families found on the rock faces in Natal, Botswana, the Cape Province and Namibia, these stones are considerably smaller, with equally smaller engravings. Before the arrival of the Europeans the San people were, due to their exclusive nature-related way of life, not considered to be fully human by the Bahurutshe.

The change of the tribal totem from the eland to the baboon heralded a significant new period for the beginning of the Bahurutshe tribe. With Mohurutshe as their chief, a section of the Batswana breaks away and forms a new, independent tribe, the Bahurutshe. The unity of the Batswana is no longer a given, however the name is retained as an umbrella term.

As previously stated, the immigration of the Batswana into southern Africa lies so far in the past that the oral tradition that was carried over many centuries, and was also overshadowed by various civil wars and natural disasters, is no longer able to provide accurate information. Scientific, archaeological research on the immigration of the Bantu into southern Africa has been conducted in recent times, and is still ongoing. Initial findings have, however, allowed certain conclusions to be drawn. Molokoe comments on the archaeological findings: “Although the exact date of the African settlement in southern Africa cannot yet be scientifically confirmed, archaeologists now generally agree that it was between the year AD 200 and AD 450. The Bantu-speaking peoples of which the Batswana are assumed to have formed part were established as far as south of modern Zimbabwe by AD 200 and were expanding through migration southwards beyond the

---

It was the first wild animal to be wiped out. For a detailed description of this tribal totem amongst the San, cf. ‘Eland’, Lewis-Williams/Pears: San Spirituality.

Limpopo River."[6] According to scientific research the Bantu, as Molokoe still refers to them,[7] are said to have advanced into the southern parts of Africa by the fifth century of the Common Era. If this assumption is accurate the ancestors of present-day Africans in southern Africa had already immigrated there more than 1,500 years ago.

It is common knowledge that the Bantu advanced into southern Africa in two separate groups and along two different routes. The *Nguni*-speaking Africans, comprising mostly Zulus and Xhosas, preferred to migrate downwards in the east. They immigrated to the coast along the Indian Ocean. The *Basotho-Batswana* tribes preferred the interior. To this day, the areas of settlement for the large immigration groups remain basically the same.

Schapera concerns himself with the immigration of the Basotho-Batswana tribes. He is of the opinion that their immigration took place in different groups[8] and at different times. During this time of immigration they had not yet separated. The Basotho-Batswana formed a unit. He calls them "Sotho-Tswana".[9] The separation occurred at a later stage. A uniform name is no longer known today. Neither is anything known about the separation. Schapera obtained his information in Botswana. His informants provided further information: according to their statements, though, the Batswana went their own way. It is not unreasonable to assume that the Basotho-Batswana already separated along the way, and then proceeded to move further south as two units alongside one other or chronologically after each other.

In Botswana Schapera furthermore learns that the Batswana separated a second time while migrating south and entered South Africa in different groups. He was told that they immigrated via Zimbabwe in three groups, one after the other. The first immigration group was said to be the *Bakgalagadi.* They settled in Botswana, in the semi-desert of *Kgalagadi* where they live to this day; they are commonly known as the "desert dwellers".

---

6 Molokoe p. 26.

7 The term 'Bantu' is no longer in use. It is being preserved in the history books. The people whose ancestors immigrated to South Africa and who now reside there on a permanent basis are denoted by their tribal names, e.g. Bahurutshe, Bakwena, Bakgatla. If several tribes attest their provenance to one common ancestor or refer to the same heroic chief, the collective tribal name also applies by way of assignation, e.g. Batswana, Basotho, Zulu, Xhosa.

8 Schapera 1976 p. 14f.

9 Loco citato p. 34.

Coertze, who studied the Bafokeng, reached the conclusion that there were only two groups. He leaves out the Bakgalagadi and writes: "The origin of the Bafokeng must be seen in connection with the southward migration of the Tswana tribes. (…) According to the best of our knowledge the Barolong were the first to arrive. (…) The second large group were the Bakwena-Bahurutshe … "[10]

While Coerzte's informants don't mention the Bakgalagadi, they still feature in the writings of Chr. Penzhorn a hundred years earlier. He mentions them in connection with the Bafokeng: "The Basotho (an old name for the Bafokeng, HB) are in all probability not the original inhabitants of this country. (…) The original inhabitants of this country are the Bakhalagare (desert dwellers) … "[11]

Taking Penzhorn's informants into consideration, one is able to effect a connection with Schapera's information. Therefore Schapera's trisection is the more probable one. The semi-desert of Botswana was named 'Kgalagadi' after the original immigrants of the Bakgalagadi group. The second group were the *Barolong* and the *Batlhaping.* They migrated past the Bakgalagadi and settled to the south of present-day Mafikeng. The third group is said to have been the last, but also the largest one. It was comprised of the *Bahurutshe, Bakwena* and the *Bakgatla,* who settled in the region stretching east from the present-day Botswana border to Johannesburg and Pretoria. All these groups then proceeded to divide again several times over the centuries. Schapera reaches the conclusion that, in 1976, the Batswana were already forming fifty or more tribal subgroups. "The Batswana are divided into more than 50 groups."[12]

1.2 Migrations of the Bahurutshe in the Transvaal

During their migration there existed no rivalry amongst the three groups. And the small number of San people who were scattered across the country

---

[10] 'Die herkoms van die Bafokeng moet in samehang met die suidwaartse beweging van die Twanagroepe beskou word … Na ons beste kennis was die eerste van hierdie groepe die Barolong … Die tweede hoofstroom was die Bakwena-Bahurutshe.' Coertze 1971 p. 21.

[11] Chr. Penzhorn 1874 p. 1f: 'Aller Wahrscheinlichkeit nach sind die Basotho nicht die eigentlichen Einwohner dieses Landes. (…) Die eigentlichen Einwohner dieses Landes sind die Bakhalagare (Wüstenbewohner) … '

[12] Schapera 1976 p. 34

were inferior to the Batswana. They were driven away or killed. Back then, the Bantu invaded the open country without encountering any resistance. The different tribes, amongst them the Bahurutshe, migrated from one place to the other. It was a wide open country. It belonged to nobody. As yet there were no Europeans who would divide the country into farms. The country was vast and populated exclusively by Africans. At some point the migrations came to an end; it took many years, however, before that came about.

When the last of the three groups immigrated into southern Africa, the Bahurutshe played a leading role. They retained their leading position for several centuries. Great store was still set on their rank even after the Bakwena and Bakgatla tribes had begun surpassing them in numbers.[13] The Bahurutshe settled at the foot of the Magaliesberg Mountains, between what would later be the town of Groot Marico in South Africa and the border town of Lobatse in Botswana. Cole writes: "The Bahurutshe, situated mainly in the Zeerust (Marico) district of the Western Transvaal, are numerically the least important. However, they are recognised by practically all the others as being the senior Tswana tribe, and, in theory at least, are accorded precedence in ritual and ceremony."[14] This quotation says something about the conditions in those days but has long since become outdated.

The Bahurutshe were able to cite a great progenitor, an ancestor whom the Bakgatla and Bakwena had forgotten long ago. The name of this great progenitor at the end of their ancestral lineage was *Malope*. Breutz comments: "They (his informants, HB) said that Mohurutshe was a female chief, because no male heir had been born to the great wife of Malope, and Kwena, Ngwato, Ngwaketse … and others were sons of junior wives, but all of them … lived at Pogole (between Enselsberg and Rieckertsdam) or on the Crocodile River in the Swartkoppies. These sons and the majority of the tribesmen objected to the female's assuming of chieftainship as this was contrary to custom in those days. Mohurutshe therefore left her adherents, and went first to Ootse (in Botswana, HB) … and from there to Modimong near Taung. This happened about 1440–1480. (…) After the death of Mohurutshe her sons … returned to Sedutlana … Pilanesberg

[13] Schapera 1976 p. 15; Breutz 1953 p. 25.
[14] Cole p. xvi.

district."[15] Three or rather four historical facts contained in this quote will be highlighted here.

It should be noted, first of all, that the Bahurutshe were able to recall a chief from the distant past, a chief whom the tribes related to them had already forgotten their criss-cross migrations. This fact was acknowledged by all the other tribes related to them. All of them adopted Malope into their common ancestral lineage. Because they were able to recall their last great common ancestor, a special kind of respect and recognition for their historically recorded superiority fell to the Bahurutshe. Secondly, the fact that the Bahurutshe were already migrating into the region where they finally settled as far back as the 15th century is worth mentioning. The third fact to consider is the statement that the Bahurutshe formed a new tribe under the leadership of a woman.

It is doubtful or rather unusual at the very least that the tribal name was derived from a female chief. There is no evidence of another female ruler in the patriarchal system of the Batswana. The tradition that holds that the Bahurutshe are descended from a woman remains a contentious one. Ferdinand Jensen writes: "Malope I had two sons, Mohurutshe and Kwena, who separated for unknown reasons after the death of their father."[16]

One may deduce from Jensen's quote that the paramount chief Malope I. had two sons after all, one of whom was *Mohurutshe.* According to this version, Mohurutshe was a man and not a woman. Ferdinand Jensen ascribes his assumption to the break-away of the Bahurutshe from the Bakwena. He suggests that *Mohurutshe* and *Mokwena* were two brothers of the same tribe. They had a quarrel. Each one had their own adherents. Mokwena left the tribe, which had been unified up to that point. Two new tribes arose. The adherents of Mohurutshe subsequently called themselves the Bahurutshe, i.e. they were loyal and answerable to their chief. The Bakwena did likewise. Jeffrey/Jensen are of the opinion that the majority of the tribe aligned themselves with Mohurutshe. "Mohurutshe remained chief of the main tribe, and his people were called Bahurutshe."[17] It was due to this break-away, which resulted in the Bakwena moving away from the Bahurutshe, that the latter were able to retain their superiority for times to come.

---

15 Breutz 1953 p. 25.

16 Ferdinand Jensen, File G item 176, p. 3; manuscript dated 2.3. 1904: "Malope I hatte zwei Söhne, Mohurutshe und Kwena, die sich aus unbekannten Gründen nach dem Tode ihres Vaters trennten."

17 Jeffrey/Jensen 1947 p. 177.

Whether the first chief of an independent Bahurutshe tribe was a man or a woman remains open for discussion until further research might provide a definite explanation in this regard.

A further observation can be made based on the above quote by Breutz. It cites names of places where the Bahurutshe dwelled for a while before moving on to another area. Migrations were a completely natural occurrence. A tribe never stayed in one and the same place for long. It was only through the civilisation and occupation of the Boers and the British in the middle of the 19th century that the Batswana were forced to settle permanently at a specific place.

The above-mentioned place names give occasion to reflect a little on these and other sites that were important to the Bahurutshe. After the Bahurutshe had become an independent tribe, they migrated several times to those places in the Transvaal that they had occupied on previous occasions. A number of places which they only occupied for short periods of time might in the meantime have passed out of mind. Maybe these transitory settlements never had a name to begin with, or they were deemed to be of lesser importance and were not remembered. Of those sites that can be remembered, three of them seem to have been a frequent destination.

The Bahurutshe often remained at these sites for several years. One of the places that they liked to frequent was in the south. It is called *Taung/Thaba-Nchu.* However, other tribes resided in the area around Taung/Thaba-Nchu. The proximity to other Basotho/Batswana tribes prompted the Bahurutshe to not remain there any longer than was necessary. The two places where they felt more at ease and resided for a longer period were *Marico/Ga-Ditshwene* and *Mosega/Dinokana.*[18] The double names Taung/Thaba-Nchu, Marico/Ga-Ditshwene and Mosega/Dinokana bear witness to the fact that they were two different places in each case, which were nonetheless situated in close proximity to one another. The Bahurutshe hardly ever settled in the same place more than once where they had built their huts on a previous occasion. Both Taung and Thaba-Nchu, and Marico and Ga-Ditshwene, as well as Mosega and Dinokana lie in such close proximity to one another that they can be viewed as an entity. At the two consolidated sites Marico/Ga-Ditshwene and Mosega/Dinokana

[18] For a more detailed account of the migrations between these two main stations, armed conflicts with other tribes, as well as smaller groups that stayed behind in various places, I refer to the work of Manson 1990 pp. 37–76.

1.2 Migrations of the Bahurutshe in the Transvaal

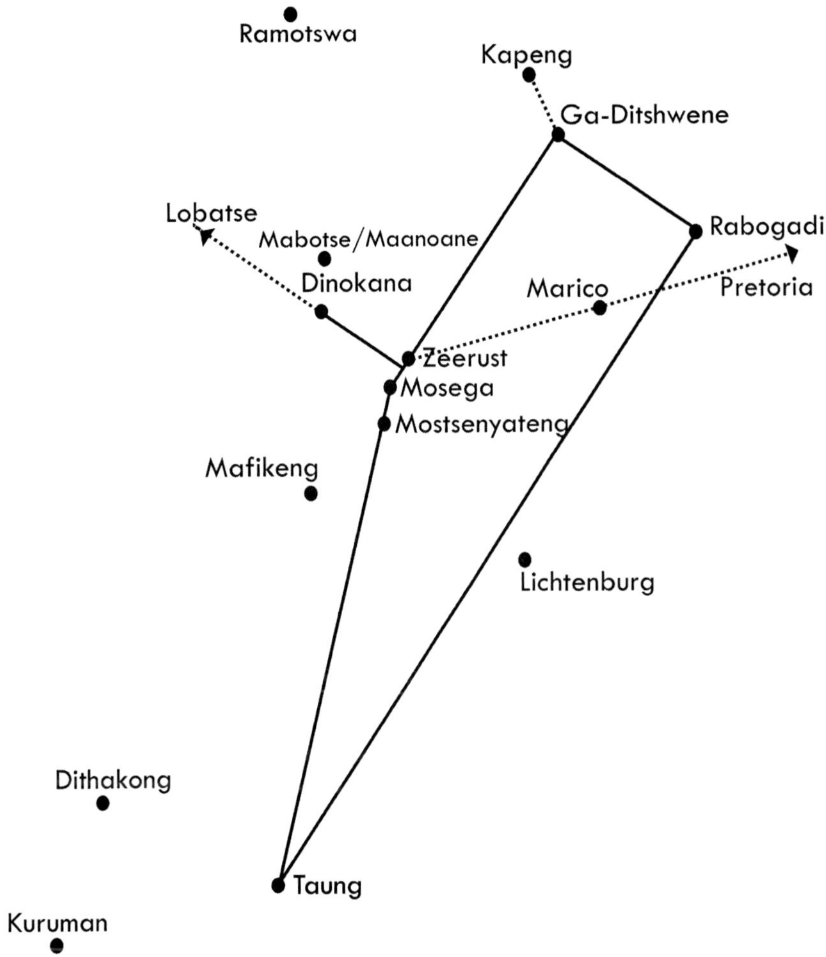

Migrations of the Bahurutshe in the 19th century before settling at Dinokana

there were no immediate neighbouring African tribes. Both these greater regions will be dealt with in greater detail later.

Dinokana was the final place of settlement. The Bahurutshe reside there to this day. After they had settled in Dinokana there was only one occasion when the chief and his tribe moved to another region for fear of the Boers, but never again after that.

During the later migratory periods of the Bahurutshe and before they –

as well as other tribes – had settled permanently, they had their first encounters with Europeans who purposefully sought them out. The Europeans travelled from the Cape in the south into the northern parts of southern Africa. In the beginning these were only individual foreigners who had set out for a host of different reasons.

During their penultimate sojourn at Taung the Bahurutshe had been harassed by neighbouring tribes and had come into conflict with them. That is why they moved back to their old familiar places at Marico/Ga-Ditshwene. There they were visited by the British Rev. J. Campbell. "Campbell's subsequent visit to Kaditshwene in May 1820 is the first written eyewitness account of the last days of this populous town."[19]

Only a few years after Campell's visit, the Bahurutshe were attacked and forced to leave Ga-Ditshwene. The South Sotho had followed them to Ga-Ditshwene from the Taung area. This tribe was comprised of two groups. Chief *Sebetwane* of the *Kololo* tribe had trailed the Bahurutshe. He had been joined by *Moletsane* together with his adherents from a neighbouring tribe. These allies launched an attack against the Bahurutshe from which they emerged victorious. They were able to oust the Bahurutshe from one of their most powerful tribal seats. Von Wimmersperg writes: "The Bahurutshe were defeated by the South Sotho who had followed them. On 12 April 1823 Robert Moffat recorded the destruction of Kaditshwene."[20] The Bahurutshe fled and settled at Mosega. The war with the South Sotho claimed many lives of the Bahurutshe, and many were injured. Campbell had estimated the population figure of the Bahurutshe in Ga-Ditshwene to be between 16- and 20,000. Then, in Mosega, the number of Bahurutshe is listed as being no more than 2,000.[21] Even if these numbers should be drawn into question due to this particularly large difference, the fact remains that the Bahurutshe suffered substantial casualties.

The South Sotho may not have affected the above-mentioned loss all by themselves. In those days there were civil wars all over the region, called

[19] Von Wimmersperg 1999 p. 8: "Die Bahurutshe wurden von den ihnen nachgezogenen Südsotho besiegt. Am 12. April 1823 notierte Robert Moffat die Zerstörung von Kaditshwene." – These days the erstwhile territory of the Bahurutshe in Ga-Ditshwene is divided into four farms. The Boers call this area 'Enselsberg'. Immense ruins of stone-built walls is all that remains of what was once a large settlement. Cf. last two pictures in par. 8.4.1 Cairns at Ga-Ditshwene. Different kinds of smelters can also be discerned at various places. They attest to the forging skills of the Bahurutshe.

[20] Ibid. p. 7.

[21] Von Wimmersperg p. 8f.

difaqane.[22] The different tribes were bellicose; they destroyed and robbed each other with their belligerent attacks. It is possible that the Bahurutshe had previously been weakened by another tribe and that the South Sotho had attacked them during their reconstruction period. The civil wars took place mainly during the years from 1820 to 1832. However, no knowledge exists about the Bahurutshe attacking a neighbouring tribe during this time.

During those times of civil war, the Zulu people in Natal quarrelled amongst themselves. The chief of a small tribe of the Khumalo, *Mzilikazi,* defied *Shaka,* the great chief of the Zulu. That was bound to cause trouble. Mzilikazi assembled around 300 young men from his tribe and, in 1821, fled to the east of the country.[23] The civil war phase proved to be advantageous to him. He began attacking Basotho/Batswana tribes. He attacked the first Batswana tribes in the area to the east of present-day Pretoria.[24] Others followed. He decimated the *Bafokeng* in the Rustenburg area and moved on to the Bahurutshe. The Bahurutshe did not wish to enter into a war with Mzilikazi.

During that time the rightful heir in the line of Bahurutshe chiefs, *Moiloa II,* was still a boy and would only assume his position at a later stage. The tribe had appointed his uncle *Mokgatlhe* to act on his behalf. Mokgatlhe subordinated himself to the conqueror, but was nonetheless in constant fear of Mzilikazi's brutal wars of extermination. When he was no longer able to withstand this pressure, he fled south to the familiar places of the Bahurutshe at Taung. Had he forgotten about the attack by the South Sotho in Ga-Ditshwene? This can hardly be assumed. Would the erstwhile foe now become a friend? This cannot be surmised. On the one hand, several Bahurutshe who had not joined the previous migration had stayed behind in Taung. In the south, on the other hand, Mokgatlhe was more secure against an attack from Mzilikazi. Should Mzilikazi venture there, mustering a combined defence with the South Sotho would put him into a more favourable position, rather than having to defend himself and his tribe on his own.

According to the knowledge he had of these events, Ferdinand Jensen writes: "In 1824 Moselekazi, chief of the Matabele, came and conquered

---

22 *Difaqane* is a term used in literature for various civil wars between the Zulu- and Basotho/Batswana tribes, as well as the Batswana tribes amongst each other. More details in Molokoe pp. 29–31; Tlou/Campbell pp. 101–113; Carruthers p. 225.

23 Carruthers p. 238.

24 Id., pp. 237–242.

the Bahurutshe with hardly any resistance. They were robbed of all their cattle and fled to Taung,[25] where they drove out the Bakgotu and settled in the Maropi ruins of the Batlhaping. Only a few Bahurutshe remained in Mosega under (the leadership of, HB) Ramasega and Seohele. Mokgatlhe was not inclined to relinquish his leadership position."[26]

In the meantime, the young chief Moiloa II had grown up and had many adherents on his side. The escape took up a great deal of time, and the Bahurutshe had been residing at Taung for quite a while. Tensions arose between the two leaders. This prompted Moiloa II to leave Taung. "Moiloa II and his adherents left Mokgatlhe and went to Rabogadi" (Vaalkop).[27]

Their migration would lead them to *Ga-Ditshwene. Rabogadi* constituted an intermediate station. There were other tribes in the same region who did not like the fact that the Bahurutshe were spreading in their area. This prompted them to stay in Rabogadi no longer than was necessary, but to return to their familiar place of Ga-Ditshwene, which was only a short distance from Rabogadi. It is unknown why they didn't move there in the first place. They probably needed an intermediate station to rest for a while. Or maybe they had an inkling of what they would encounter at Ga-Ditshwene. The region where they had previously established themselves was a fertile one. Boers who had been forced to flee from the British in the Cape had meanwhile settled there. They had already encountered the first Boers during their previous sojourn at Taung. They had to find out that the Boers selected arable farmland for themselves, and that, once they had started to cultivate the land, they settled down permanently. It was this experience which leads one to the assumption, amongst other things, that, after having left Taung the Bahurutshe had not immediately relocated to Ga-Ditshwene but had stopped along the way and dispatched scouts. When

---

25 Taung is described as being a region about 70 km to the south and south-east of Vryburg. The flight to Taung did however not occur with the arrival of Mzilikazi. This quote might lead to that assumption. The Bahurutshe humbled themselves under Mzilikazi's rule for eight years.

26 Ferdinand Jensen, File G item 176 p. 6f. – "1824 kam Moselekazi, Häuptling der Matabele, und eroberte die Bahurutshe mit kaum einer Gegenwehr. Sie wurden beraubt von allen ihren Rindern und flohen nach Taung, wo sie die Bakgotu verdrängten und sich in den Maropi Ruinen der Batlhaping niederließen. Nur wenige Bahurutshe blieben in Mosega unter Ramasega und Seohele. Mokgatlhe war nicht geneigt, seine Führung abzugeben."

27 Id., p. 7. This version will later be described in greater detail. – "Moiloa II. mit seinem Anhang verließ Mokgatlhe und ging nach Rabogadi."

they were subsequently harassed at Rabogadi by the tribes in the area, they must have begun contemplating a return to their erstwhile dwelling place. After all, that is where they had already resided before the arrival of the Boers. So that is where they eventually relocated.

However, things should turn out as they had suspected. The Boers increasingly encroached on their territory. They claimed the arable land for themselves. The Bahurutshe were powerless against the superiority of the Boers. They were reluctant to incite a war and risk a showdown. But what other options remained? They were used to relocating. Thus another move was on the cards after a certain period of time. And where to this time? Once again they migrated to an old familiar place in a south-westerly direction, to Mosega.

The final relocations from Taung via Rabogadi to Ga-Ditshwene, and back again to Mosega will be dealt with in greater detail in the following sections. The reason for this is obvious. Missionaries from various mission societies attempted to establish themselves amongst the Bahurutshe. It is thanks to them that this part of the history of the Bahurutshe can be appreciated in greater detail. The missionaries were obliged to submit regular reports to their respective mission societies. These reports facilitate a more detailed depiction of the relocations of the Bahurutshe, describing numerous events during their migrations and their locations of settlement.

1.3 Pioneer Missionaries amongst the Bahurutshe

1.3.1 French Missionaries

During the early 19th century a spiritual awakening took place in Protestant churches. Many mission societies arose in Europe and the United States. They were motivated by the mandate given by Jesus Christ: “All authority in heaven and on earth has been given to me. Go therefore and make disciples of all nations … ” (Matth. 28,18–19). They sent their missionaries all over the world and consequently also to Africa.

The London Missionary Society (LMS) had deployed two Scottish missionaries in South Africa, both of whom attained a high degree of renown: John Philip and Robert Moffat. Philip became the director of the LMS in Cape Town from 1819–1848.[28] During his tenure he not only championed

[28] Davenport in Elpick/Davenport, p. 53.

the cause of abolishing slavery, but also of missionizing the Africans. He asked the Paris Mission Society to send missionaries to South Africa. "The PEMS in 1829 received an invitation from the LMS director in southern Africa, John Philip. It promptly sent three newly ordained missionaries to the Cape."[29]

While Philip held the reins for the LMS in Cape Town, Moffat became the most renowned inland missionary amongst the Batswana in Kuruman. He was stationed there for fifty years, from 1820–1870.[30] He became successful in many different spheres. He became particularly renowned for his translation work. The first Setswana Bible, published in 1857, originated with him.[31] He became furthermore renowned through the mission journeys he undertook to the northern parts of southern Africa. Moffat paid Mzilikazi a visit in his warrior camps, and facilitated the placement of missionaries amongst the Bahurutshe. He for his part missionized amongst the Barolong.

Up to that point no missionary had set foot amongst the Bahurutshe. This might also have been due to the fact that the Bahurutshe were, for various reasons, still in migratory mode. So it came about that, through the facilitation of Philip and Moffat, French missionaries from the Paris Mission Society initially made their way to the Bahurutshe.

The Paris Mission Society dispatched M. Lemue, J.P. Pellissier and S. Rolland as pioneer missionaries per ship to Cape Town. From there they drove overland to Kuruman. Having arrived there, they initially stayed with Moffat for an extended period of time. They learned the Setswana language a little and appointed Rolland to undertake a reconnaissance trip to the Bahurutshe. Rolland was to hold initial talks with them. After his return everybody would then travel to Mosega together. Rolland writes: "When I took my leave from Lemue and our friends Hamilton and Baillie (other missionaries, HB), I was accompanied by even more friends as I travelled towards Mosika, the main seat of the Bahurutzis. Our caravan comprised eight ox-wagons with around 40 people. Six wagons belonged to British merchants and a few Griquas (an autonomous tribe which had settled on the Vaal River, HB), who had (all, HB) embarked on an elephant hunt, also mindful of their own commercial operations. The seventh wagon belonged

---

29 Beck in Elpick/Davenport, p. 110.

30 Elbourne/Ross in Elpick/Davenport, p. 38.

31 Beck in Elpick/Davenport, p. 117f

to an officer of the East India Company who had come to South Africa due to ill health. He wanted to explore the interior of the country before returning to Bombay. The eighth wagon belonged to us."[32]

It is an interesting assortment of travelling companions, comprising Africans and Europeans. What kind of people were they? The reason for the trip was ostensibly an elephant hunt. Hunters, merchants, an adventurer and a missionary had teamed up with one another. The anticipated profit was to the fore where the hunters and merchants were concerned. A British officer who can be described as an adventurer had joined them in Cape Town. He wanted to explore the interior of Africa before returning to India. The route of the travelling party also took them via Kuruman. Their sojourn in Kuruman came at an opportune moment for the Paris missionaries. Rolland had good reason to join the travellers. There were many wild animals along the way, who would rather attack a solitary traveller than a group. The group also provided a certain degree of protection against marauding bandits. A host of dangers lurked along the way when travelling through the bush or desert sand. One simply felt safer travelling with a larger group of people.

Rolland reached *Mosega* on 11 June 1831.[33] The interim chief Mokgatlhe and his nephew Moiloa II received and welcomed him. The Bahurutshe were pleased to see a missionary. Up to that point they had not heard of any European who was prepared to dedicate himself to them. After Rolland had presented his objective, the Bahurutshe assented. However, in doing so, they were hardly interested in the gospel that the missionaries would bring to them. They still feared that they would be killed by Mzilikazi. One of Mzilikazi's warrior camps was situated close to the Bahurutshe. They reckoned that they were more protected from Mzilikazi if Europeans lived amongst them. These considerations encouraged the Bahurutshe to grant access to the Paris missionaries. School education, on the other hand, only played a secondary role during their first encounter with the Europeans.

After the tribe had given its consent to welcome the missionaries, the chief assigned Rolland a site outside the tribe's living areas where the missionaries could pitch their tents. Moffat had selected this site on his previous visit to Mokgatlhe, during which he had announced the arrival of the mis-

32 Paris mission magazine, 1832 p. 10. Rolland's report is dated 5.7.1831 i.e. it was published only a year later, after the Paris missionaries had arrived at Mosega.

33 Rolland, Paris mission magazine 1832 p. 19.

sionaries.[34] After having seen and approved of the site, he for his part concluded a purchase agreement with Mokgatlhe. "We returned to our wagon where we proceeded to hand over five or six pounds of 'beads for necklaces' as payment for the piece of land that he had sold us."[35] As far as Rolland was concerned he had purchased a piece of land. Mokgatlhe had, according to African custom, probably viewed the agreement as a non-binding barter transaction. Rolland was satisfied. He took his leave from Mokgatlhe with a shared "simple meal" and returned to Kuruman to his fellow missionaries.

After the Paris missionaries had received the good news from Rolland that they were welcome in *Mosega,* they immediately began making preparations for the journey and subsequently trekked to the Bahurutshe. They arrived there in January 1832. A mere three weeks after their arrival, Mzilikazi dispatched his messengers to Mosega, calling upon all the missionaries to relocate to him immediately. They decided not to follow this command, but asked Pellissier to pay Mzilikazi a short visit as their delegate. He describes his arrival at Mzilikazi's as follows: "When we were half an hour away from his place of residence where we were supposed to meet him, he sent me two messengers to ask me to unyoke my oxen, climb down from my wagon and come to him on foot. (…) He sat under a tree on an ill-fashioned stool, which constituted his only belonging where seating was concerned. (…) He was surrounded by soldiers, some of whom formed a semi-circle."[36] Pellissier's arrival had been delayed. Mzilikazi put him to the test and expressed his annoyance over the fact that he had come alone. He wanted to see all the missionaries. The general had envisioned the arrival of the Europeans in his realm slightly differently.

Pellissier was obliged to stay for a month. During this time, he had conversations with Mzilikazi and observed the events surrounding the despot. His assessment of Mzilikazi was a negative one. "If he resides at one place for just a moment, he leaves it again to move on to another place. He fears for his life and believes that he is not protected anywhere. It is indeed like Montesquieu once said: 'Despots are slaves of their fear'. (…) He is able to go into action as a criminal while laughing at you at the same time. He promises you one thing and then gives orders to the contrary."[37] The latter

34 Rolland, Paris mission magazine 1832 p. 22.

35 Id., p. 24.

36 Pellissier, Paris mission magazine, 1833 p. 7.

37 Paris mission magazine 1833 p. 13.

will be highlighted by American missionaries at a later stage with a striking example.

One might be able to deduce from Pellissier's assessment the reason as to why Mzilikazi refused the missionaries permission to settle amongst the Bahurutshe on a permanent basis. First of all, they had not introduced themselves to him, only to the Bahurutshe. That is why he had to summon them. According to African culture it constituted an insult if a stranger did not pay a visit to the ruler of the region first. He felt that they had not shown him the proper respect. Secondly, he feared that dissidence amongst the Bahurutshe was looming, something which he wished to nip in the bud. The missionaries did indeed effect moral support amongst the Bahurutshe. Thirdly it might be fair to add that he was not interested in the preaching of the gospel or in school education. His interest was concentrated in his power to defeat other tribes, to subjugate them and to expand his empire. The European missionaries with their objectives constituted an inconvenience to him in this regard.

It was not long after Pellissier had returned to Mosega from Mzilikazi's warrior camp that a new group of messengers arrived. They had been despatched with the command to present all the missionaries to their general. If they should fail to do so they would be killed. They were now faced with a perilous situation that would no longer allow any compromise. The mission director of the Paris Mission Society writes: "M. Pellissier had only just returned and seen Lemue and Rolland, when Mzilikazi's messengers arrived at Mosika yet again with the order to bring the three missionaries and not appear before him without them. Mokatla was justifiably alarmed when he heard this message. (. . .) He came to our brethren, cursing with disgust. That he would be finished if they didn't depart with haste."[38] The missionaries accepted Mokgatlhe's urgent appeal and left the Bahurutshe as fast as possible, did however not follow Mzilikazi's command to come to him immediately.

We don't know what Mzilikazi did to the messengers when they returned to him sans missionaries. We do know, however, that the missionaries spent a mere three months amongst the Bahurutshe before they fled in mid-April 1832.[39] This time they travelled to *Dithakong* (called 'Lattakou'

[38] Id., 1832 p. 19.

[39] Pellissier, Paris mission magazine 1833 p. 6.

by the missionaries), to the north of Kuruman. There they were safe under the territorial rule of the British.

After the Paris missionaries had fled, the Bahurutshe didn't feel safe anymore either. They feared that Mzilikazi would wreak vengeance on them and attack them. Mokgatlhe gave the command to decamp and leave Mosega. And that is what happened. They fled to the south. It was fortunate for them that this had not come to the knowledge of Mzilikazi and his soldiers.

After they had been on the move for a few days, someone relayed the tidings of their flight to the missionaries at Dithakong. This was good news for the Paris missionaries. They set out to go and look for the Bahurutshe. After a week of searching, Lemue and Rolland found the tribe on the banks of a small stream called Hart River. The entire country was in the grips of a drought. The missionaries were nevertheless surprised to find Mokgatlhe and his seven- to eight thousand adherents to be in destitute but stable conditions. The number of those who had fled was very low compared to the total number of residents. Thus the question arose among the missionaries as to the whereabouts of the rest. The reply was: "... that all those who were currently absent had been murdered."[40] An explanation for that could be that Mzilikazi had launched an attack after all. The hungry spears of the soldiers had probably struck out at those who could not make a speedy decision to leave Mosega. They might also have been attacked while they were fleeing; those who were not fast enough had been killed and the rest, marching faster than the others, was able to survive. Another possibility is that the wounded and sick amongst them, as well as those weakened by hunger had perished along the way. Even if a great number of people would have died in this way, these explanations are ultimately unsatisfactory. One may be further assisted in this matter if one takes into account what Ferdinand Jensen recorded, and what the Scottish missionary Moffat experienced and saw at Mosega.

We have learnt previously from Ferdinand Jensen that two leading figures of the Bahurutshe, *Ramasega* and *Seohele,* had not fled to the south with Mokgatlhe and the larger part of the tribe. These two men were probably petty chiefs of the Bahurutshe. For some reason they were not afraid of being killed by Mzilikazi and remained at Mosega with their adherents and a number of individual families.

[40] Paris mission magazine 1833 p. 201.

Moffat saw with his own eyes what Ferdinand Jensen had learnt from his informants. He had visited the Bahurutshe at Mosega for the first time in 1829. Three years later he embarked on another journey to broach the subject of new missionaries with Mzilikazi once more. During this trip he paid a visit to the Bahurutshe who had stayed behind. He wanted to know how many people still resided at Mosega. He had embarked on this trip with a considerable amount of curiosity. The great losses suffered by the Bahurutshe had been reported to him in Kuruman. What would he find at Mosega? He saw Mosega totally differently than he had expected. He comments on this: "We were informed at Kuruman that all, or nearly all, the Baharutshe had been killed, but that report was false, for even here there are four or five towns, or rather villages of Baharutshe, independent of those living farther in the interior."[41] According to Ferdinand Jensen's report, and especially R. Moffat's reconnaissance, the situation of the Bahurutshe at Mosega was not only slightly but significantly different. Even if an event of tragic loss was possibly registered somewhere along the way, the Bahurutshe who remained at Mosega paint another picture. The chief had taken his adherents with him when he fled, but an equal number of people had not taken the hardships of the migration and escape from a possible attack by Mzilikazi upon them.

As a general rule the chief calls the shots in the tribe. If the chief says: "We are under threat and we're moving out", then most of his adherents will obey. In this instance it seems as if a large number of Bahurutshe did not only sympathise with their chief, but also with Mzilikazi. They were at least not afraid of him. They stayed at home. Maybe Mzilikazi had commandeered a number of sons from some of the families, who consequently had less to fear from this despot than the upper class of the Bahurutshe. In a crisis situation like this the leaders are normally those that are most at risk. In this instance those were the chief and most of the petty chiefs with their families. Thus one can imagine that it was predominantly this group of people who fled with their adherents and that the majority of the social substratum did not go with them.

There were other cases, too, where the father of a family did not see eye to eye with the chief. If the tensions between them could not be resolved it sometimes happened that these families then moved to other areas and joined other tribes, if the latter were willing to accept them. And if

41 In Wallis, p. 70.

they subsequently didn't feel comfortable there either they moved on again. Notwithstanding this, they always pledged their allegiance to their tribe of origin. This was the case with *Makgolokoe* and his clan, who moved around an unusual amount of times.[42]

Back to Mzilikazi and the Paris missionaries. It remained uncertain what Mzilikazi had in mind when he called on the missionaries to come to him. The missionaries could have gone and introduced themselves to him. But they didn't. But why didn't they? That was surely a dereliction on their behalf. When they were all subsequently summoned to appear before Mzilikazi, they refused. They obviously feared some kind of escalation if all of them went to encounter Mzilikazi.

Tensions had also reached breaking-point where Mokgatlhe was concerned. Because of the missionaries he had fallen into disfavour with Mzilikazi. Mokgatlhe did not expect a summons to Mzilikazi's warrior camp, but rather feared a brutal attack on Mosega from the despot. To avoid such an attack, he decided to flee immediately. And he had a specific refuge in mind: Taung. He was familiar with this location which lay far south of Mosega from a previous migration. When seeking out a place of refuge he went with a familiar location rather than an unfamiliar one. It was a wide open country and, in contrast to today, unpopulated. He moved along the peripheries of the semi-desert Kgalagadi through an open and wide, but also very arid and unpopulated stretch of land. He could not expect any kind of assistance from anyone along the way. Then, when he temporarily

---

42 Mgadla/Volz, p. 270f: 'It is the tradition of my father, the tradition of Makgolokwe Motlhware Mohurutshe. We are indeed Bahurutshe … We separated from Powe, came down to Molopo valley and eventually settled at Khuis. We then left Khuis and came down the Kudumane River … then we came to Mitlweng. From Mitlweng we came to live at Dithateng. We then left Dithateng and went to build at Diswatlhe. We left Diswatlhe and went to live at Tsineng. We left Tsineng and went along the Mosetsana-Montle stream … and came to build at Khing. We left there and came to Gamohane … We left Gamohane towards Segonyane's place … From there the village left Segonyane's and went toward Ditloung … There the BATLHWARE (Bahurutshe ba ga Motlhware) moved from Ditloung toward Gamosimaneng. Then they moved from Gamosimaneng toward Maje-a-Mokgothu, and Batlhware also went to Khuis and joined together … Then we became divided … These are the words of my father, Makgalokwe' – What these families have taken upon themselves is almost beyond belief. If this verbal tradition should turn out to be the truth, one can look upon these migrations to so many different locations as being the exception. It took place over some generations. The phrase 'tradition of my father' does not only denote the person's own father, but a number of ancestors.

laagered in an area sufficiently distant from Mosega, there was no risk of a marauding tribe in the vicinity. Instead his adherents suffered bouts of hunger. There was hardly anything to eat. The land was not cultivated. The Bahurutshe lived off their cattle which they herded as they went along, as well as off wild animals that they killed, and off grasses and roots. It is hardly surprising that they settled down to rest on the banks of the only small stream in the entire region, the Hart River.

It is at the Hart River that the missionaries Lemue and Rolland found the Bahurutshe with their chiefs, Mokgatlhe and Moiloa II. The latter was the actual heir to the throne but still too young to be able to lead the Bahurutshe. So Mokgatlhe continued in his position as leader. After the missionaries had found the Bahurutshe they suggested that they move to Dithakong with them. They would be safe in Dithakong. No danger of sudden attacks by Mzilikazi. They could ask a tribe of the southern Batswana to accommodate them on a temporary basis. An intense discussion concerning this offer subsequently took place between Mokgatlhe and Moiloa II. While Moiloa II wanted to go with the missionaries, Mokgatlhe rejected their invitation. He prevailed in his tribe, and Moiloa II acquiesced. Mokgatlhe ordered for the tribe to decamp. The missionaries accompanied the Bahurutshe for a few days. "We then walked some days along the Hart River, until we met a group of *Korannas* … "[43]

The Korannas that are mentioned in this quote had already launched a previous attack against Mzilikazi, with the help of *Barend,* the chief of the *Griquas.* Barend was planning a second attack and had motivated the Korannas accordingly. The Korannas were on their way to Barend when they encountered the Bahurutshe and the Paris missionaries in their entourage. Mokgatlhe still bore great animosity towards Mzilikazi. He now saw his opportunity to join forces with the Korannas and Griquas to attack Mzilikazi. He sympathised with the attackers and would have liked to join them, but he could not leave his tribe leaderless. But the majority of the tribe was not interested in being drawn into a war. It is likely that a few of his young tribesmen were incited and participated in the attack on Mzilikazi with Mokgatlhe's consent. All the others moved on towards Taung.

The missionaries left the Bahurutshe at this point. A few Bahurutshe went with them. They left their tribe because they were not prepared to

[43] In Wallis, p. 204.

go to Taung with the others. That was the end of the work of the Paris missionaries among the Batswana. They returned to Dithakong.

The Bahurutshe reached Taung and settled in the area. Ferdinand Jensen writes: "In 1832 the Bahurutshe fled from their homeland, the Marico district, before the Zulu tyrant Moselekazi to Maamuse, the present-day Schweizer-Reinecke."[44] *Maamuse* and Schweizer-Reinecke are towns in the region that the Bahurutshe call Taung. Had the Bahurutshe forgotten about the attacks by the *Bakololo* in Ga-Ditshwene, seeing that they moved back into close proximity to them? Maybe they accepted this risk, too, simply to feel safer from Mzilikazi's unpredictable and radical attacks. Their calculations paid off. They were in fact much safer in Maamuse and they stayed for twelve years, an unusually long period of time.

An increasing number of Boers[45] began to flee before the British and settled, amongst other places, in the vicinity of Taung. The Bahurutshe had their first encounters with the Boers. They learnt that some Boer families had been attacked by Mzilikazi, and that more Boers were advancing who planned to defeat Mzilikazi and banish him from the country. This appealed to Mokgatlhe. Once again there were probably a number of young Bahurutshe men who joined the Boers in their fight against Mzilikazi. Mokgatlhe received regular updates about the progress of the Boer attacks on Mzilikazi's camp. One day he received the news that the Boers had attacked and defeated Mzilikazi's soldiers at Mosega, and that Mzilikazi had moved to Botswana shortly afterwards.[46]

A few years had gone by. Meanwhile tensions with neighbouring tribes flared up now and again at Taung. Moiloa II had become more mature and many of his adherents now expected of him to assume his inherited chieftainship. A sizeable group had gathered around him which was now so large that the Bahurutshe who pinned their hopes on him outnumbered those who supported Mokgatlhe. Mokgatlhe had fulfilled his task. A new era was on the horizon and the Bahurutshe were contemplating the specifics of a renewed exodus from Taung. It was to be their final migration from Taung to

44 Ferdinand Jensen, File D item 152 p. 1. – "Im Jahre 1832 flohen die Bahurutse aus ihrem Heimatland, dem Marico-Distrikte, vor dem Zulutyrannen Moselekazi nach Maamuse, dem heutigen Schweizer-Reinicke."

45 'Throughout 1836, parties of Boers, dissatisfied with life under British administration in the Cape, began to migrate from the colony.' Carruthers, p. 259.

46 The battle of Mosega is mentioned by the advancing American missionaries.

Ga-Ditshwene. But before they could put their plans into action, something else happened in Mosega.

While the Bahurutshe were still residing at Taung under their two leaders Mokgatlhe and Moiloa II for a period of time, some American missionaries had taken an interest in the South African interior. From Cape Town they established contact with the English-Scottish missionary R. Moffat in Kuruman and appealed to him to make recommendations for a new field of work.

1.3.2 American Missionaries

In the United States of America, too, the interest in mission work had been awakened. While the Hermannsburg missionaries went ashore in the harbour city of Durban in later years, the American missionaries, just as the Paris missionaries, were sent to Cape Town. From there they were to embark on their journey into the interior. The plan of the mission society in America had been for the missionaries to establish a mission station amongst the Zulu people along the Indian Ocean. That plan failed. The Zulus were ruled by their powerful but also ruthless and unpredictable chief, *Dingaan.* This acted as a deterrent to the Americans. While they were sojourning in Cape Town they got into conversation with Dr Philip, who had previously assisted the Paris missionaries. Philip advised them to take up contact with Moffat.

This was welcome news to Moffat. He was glad to assist with the facilitation of American missionaries to the African tribes. He was contemplating the possibility of replacing the Paris missionaries with the Americans. But he was also aware of the tensions between the Paris missionaries and Mzilikazi. And since Mzilikazi was still the ruler of the Transvaal who subjugated all the other tribes during this time, Moffat was obliged to set out on yet another trip to Mzilikazi. Moffat and Mzilikazi were acquainted with each other from a previous encounter. Briggs mentions that the arrival of the Americans in Cape Town prompted Moffat to visit Mzilikazi a second time: "Their arrival was Moffat's main reason for his second visit to Mzilikazi."[47]

So Moffat drove to Mzilikazi. It is a little surprising that he was not snubbed by Mzilikazi. The Paris missionaries had disappointed Mzilikazi beyond measure. Now the American missionaries would act differently and

[47] Briggs/Wing 1970 p. 62.

conduct themselves better? Moffat was able to influence Mzilikazi and the American missionaries obtained the permission to go to the Bahurutshe at Mosega. After they had received this welcome news from Moffat, they set out from Cape Town to Kuruman. "After the PEMS's brief sojourn the American Board of Commissioners for Foreign Mission sent out three missionaries."[48]The three American missionaries D. Lindley, H. Venable and the physician Dr A. Wilson left Cape Town in 1835. They were married and their wives accompanied them. They described their stopovers along the way. About halfway along their journey they were forced to put in a prolonged period of rest in Beaufort-West, where they required a new team of oxen. Six of them had perished on the first stretch of their journey. Their next stopover was in Griquatown, where the British missionary Wright was stationed. They learnt from Wright that Mzilikazi had, apart from his mother tongue *Setebele,* also learnt to speak *Setswana* while living amongst the Batswana people, and that this language would prove to be very important where they were concerned. The British missionary Grant writes: "While most of Mosilikatse's people are subdued Bechuanas who retain their own language, so much so, on the authority of the English missionary Mr. Wright at Griquatown, is this the case that Mosilikatsi has learned the Bechuana language and must soon be the only language among his people, though some of them are Zoola [Zulus]."[49] It now became apparent to the Americans that they, too, would have to learn Setswana in order to be able to communicate with Mzilikazi since he didn't understand any English. They decided to learn from the mistakes made by the Paris missionaries and to initiate a more successful introduction.

Their next stopover was at Kuruman, which constituted the central point of the mission amongst the Batswana. It is also frequently referred to as the "Moffat Mission".[50] In Kuruman it was pointed out to the Americans once again how important it was to learn the language of the Africans. Setswana was the most important one amongst these, but they were advised to also learn a bit of Setebele so that they could greet Mzilikazi. And Afrikaans was also important, so that they could communicate with the Boers. All

48 Manson 1990 p. 83f.

49 Grant report 21.05.1835 p. 1.

50 There was a small gathering of several British missionaries at Kuruman. David Livingstone would also be part of this group at a later stage, who is generally known to have been the first European to cross the African continent from east to west, and, in doing so, discovered the Victoria Falls in the Zambezi River for the Europeans.

this was however not possible during their short sojourn at Griquatown and Kuruman. The result was that they didn't learn any of those three languages particularly well and were unable to communicate in them. Therefore they required the services of an interpreter with every conversation. That was not a good beginning for their work.

After a few days an inspection trip was planned from Kuruman to the Batswana at Mosega. Venable and Lindsay were to take them there. They set out from Kuruman at noon on the 22nd of January 1836. They required local people who would show them the way and perform other necessary tasks. Lindsay writes: "Our company consists of Br. Lindley and myself, and nine natives, two of them are Hottentots and the others are Bechuanas."[51] He mentions the two Hottentots by name: Adolph and Friederich. Adolph cooked and served the food while Friederich had to yoke the oxen and goad them on. Of the Batswana he mentions *Baba, Leselo* and William, who acted as interpreters. The other four Batswana not mentioned by name worked as cow herds and messenger boys.

On their journey from Kuruman to the north Lindley and Venable, who had set out with their African companions, stopped over at *Motito,* which lies roughly seventy kilometres north of Kuruman. In Motito the French missionary Lemue had taken over the mission station from the Paris mission society, after his mission work amongst the Batswana had failed. Lindley reports: "The population of this place may be five hundred. We were here very kindly received by Br. Lemue and his lady ... He has been at this place (Motito) about three years."[52] They stayed there for an entire weekend, celebrated communal church services and listened to Lemue telling them about Mosega. Then they continued on their journey.

This preparatory journey was to fulfil two objectives: firstly, they wanted to pay Mzilikazi a visit, and secondly they wanted to have a look at the site where the Paris missionaries had lived amongst the Bahurutshe in Mosega. On this exploration trip they were, for the time being, not particularly interested in the Bahurutshe themselves. Both the above-mentioned objectives had their own focal points. Under no circumstances could they neglect to pay Mzilikazi a visit, and the site was important to them as a residential place for their families. It would be a good start for the families if they could find a couple of huts that the Paris missionaries had erected.

51 Venable Journal, January 22nd to May 18th 1836 p. 5.

52 Lindley Journal 23.01.1836.

When they had reached the vicinity of Mzilikazi's southernmost camp, they despatched their Batswana messengers to announce their impending visit. They returned with the message that Mzilikazi was absent. They said that he had several camps and that he was residing at another place. A petty officer had however indicated to them that they should travel to and see *Kalipi*[53] who would be able to provide them with more information as to Mzilikazi's whereabouts. Kalipi was in charge of a camp which, although it was still within the southern region of Mzilikazi's domain, was situated considerably closer to the main camp at Motsenyateng.

The journey continued through a more populous region. The group passed through two villages before reaching Kalipi's settlement, Motsenyateng. Venable calls the villages towns. "The first town we saw had about 75 houses, the next 50, and Kalipi's may contain 90."[54] Before the travellers were granted permission to enter *Motsenyateng*, gun salutes were fired. Their arrival must have been previously announced. A messenger of the neighbouring camp must have been faster than the travelling party with its entourage and cattle. When they eventually entered the settlement they were warmly welcomed by Kalipi, with his soldiers forming a guard of honour. After their encounter Kalipi granted them permission to travel three kilometres northwards to Mosega, their travel destination. He also granted the missionaries permission to visit the site of the Paris missionaries and to repair the houses they had left behind for their families who would arrive later.

After they had arrived at Mosega on 10 February 1836, Lindley and Venable first of all searched for several hours for a suitable place to live.[55] They asked the Bahurutshe who resided there to point out the former houses of the Paris missionaries to them. After they had inspected them they decided that it would be worth their while to restore the old houses during the following days and weeks.

Kalipi presently paid them a visit in Mosega, and this first meeting proceeded amicably. He discerned an affection that the Bahurutshe held for the missionaries. This perception caused him to pay a second visit after two days. This time he observed something that he didn't like. Batswana women, as well as a number of Zulu women, had cut some grass and had

---

53 Kalipi was one of Mzilikazi's highest ranking officers. The missionaries call him "Induna" = petty chief, a term that would denote a camp commander in this case.

54 Venable Journal, January 22nd to May 18th, p. 23.

55 Lindley Journal, 29.08.1836.

taken it to the missionaries so that they could thatch the roofs of their houses with it. The women had received the instruction to do so from the missionaries. As a matter of fact, Kalipi could have endorsed this work, but he didn't. Lindley writes: "This morning Kalipi brought us a fine large sheep as a present from Moselekatsi". He goes on to say: "A considerable number of women began to bring us grass but Kalipi made them all desist, except a few Bahurutshe women who are regarded and treated as slaves."[56]

The above quote highlights the fact that the Bahurutshe women were treated differently to the Zulu women. The women did not make this differentiation amongst themselves when interacting with one another socially. Was it Kalipi's intention to show the Batswana women how worthless they were, something that Lindley had understood to be the case when he used the term "slaves"? Were the conquerors of the region obliged to demonstrate their dominance and to ensure that the defeated tribes were being made aware of their humiliation? Or should the slight towards the Bahurutshe women be interpreted in yet another way? An attempt at humiliation can certainly not be denied. However, the other aspect is the singling out, the difference in status of the Zulu women. Kalipi had brought a sheep as a welcoming gesture to the missionaries. The significance of this welcoming gift was bolstered by the fact that he prohibited the Zulu women to perform any demeaning work. He viewed any additional deference towards the missionaries expressed in this regard as being inappropriate.

The denotation of the Batswana women as being servants of the missionaries looking for work does not necessarily mean that the term "slave" would have been appropriate. Slavery was a common practise amongst the Boers and the British. It was openly denounced by the British missionaries, however. In Kalipi's case the more appropriate term for the disparagement of the Batswana women is obviously that of humiliation.

On one of the following days Kalipi visited the missionaries yet again. This time he came with the message that Mzilikazi wished to see the missionaries. They were to make an appearance in his main camp. So this was to be their big moment they had hoped for, to meet the ruler in person and to obtain his consent for their mission work amongst the Bahurutshe.

After they had been waiting for word from Mzilikazi for two months, they set out from Mosega on 09 April 1836,[57] travelling via Motsenyateng to

---

56 Lindley Journal, 14.03.1836.

57 Lindley Journal 09.04.1836.

Kapeng. They reached Mzilikazi's residence two days later. Mzilikazi came out from his kraal and approached the missionaries. The missionaries, too, left their ox wagon and walked up to Mzilikazi. Venable writes: "The king came out to meet us, and we advanced towards him. We shook hands, and he gave us the Dutch salutation 'goen dag'[58] ... Kalipi immediately went on to make an oration in praise of his master."[59]

Apart from the salutation, the entire conversation was translated. Venable goes on to say: "We held some conversation with his majesty, which had to go first to Baba, from him to Leselo in *Sichuan,* and as Leselo cannot directly speak to the king he must tell it to Kalipi, and he to the king. And what the king said came back through the same line, but in the reverse order."[60] One can imagine that the multiple translation of the same words into various languages took quite some time. It might also have happened now and again that what was said did not come out at the other side as the speaker had intended. But nobody seemed to be bothered by this. The most important thing was the meeting in and of itself. Nobody queried anything. Therefore one can assume that the essential parts of the mutual encounter were understood and accepted.

Gifts were exchanged on both sides. This is an indication of the fact that preparations had been made for the meeting, and from both sides at that. The missionaries were presented with a cow, some food and indigenous beer. They for their part presented Mzilikazi with tobacco and beads. Lindley mentions the amount of tobacco: "We now, in return, made the king a present of about thirteen pounds of tobacco."[61]

Kalipi had told Mzilikazi that the missionaries were building their houses in the European style and that they planned to build a church. Mzilikazi's reaction to this was that he also wanted a European-style house as well as a church. He wanted the missionaries to erect both these buildings for him. Lindley reports: "The king said we must build him a house like the one we were building for ourselves; and spoke about other small conveniences with which we must furnish him. In so doing he betrayed an expectation that we had come to do him considerable worldly service. He

58 Lindley writes loc. cit.: "goeden morgen".

59 Venable Journal, January 22nd to May 18th 1836, p. 36.

60 Loco citato, p. 37.

61 Lindley Journal, 09.04.1836. Venable however writes: "We brought for him four rolls of tobacco, each weighing five or six pounds." Venable Journal, January 22nd to May 18th 1836.

also said we must build him a church, of which we were better placed to hear than a house for himself."[62] The missionaries declined; they were not prepared, beyond the exchange of gifts, to indulge Mzilikazi's every whim. Neither did they believe that he was serious in his intentions and would be a man of his word. They had heard too many reports of his arbitrary actions.

Maybe the king of the Zulus, Dingaan, also still played a role in the background. It had been their original intention, to wit, to go to the Zulu people of Dingaan. Due to the brutal warfare carried out by the latter, however, they had been strongly advised to abandon this plan upon their arrival in Cape Town. Mzilikazi was a Zulu fugitive, and he did indeed share similar character traits with Dingaan.

The missionaries could also have come to a different conclusion. If they would have complied with his demands and responded to him with Christian charity, this matter would probably have taken a better turn. But they had approached the matter with their preconceived ideas and their own notions about how they wanted to take up the mission work amongst the Bahurutshe. Mzilikazi did not fit in with these ideas. It would at least have been worth a try to give Mzilikazi an understanding of the Christian message of the salvation in Jesus Christ, and for them to bear witness in this regard. Maybe they could have taken a leaf out of Moffat's book. He had paid Mzilikazi several visits. Even though his responsibility was towards the Batswana at Kuruman he maintained contact with Mzilikazi for many years. He seemed to know how to deal with a despot. He succeeded in preserving his own opinion while respecting that of the other, even if that other person thought and acted contrary to his belief.

Even before their departure from Kapeng, the decision not to agree to Mzilikazi's wishes proved to be the correct one, albeit in a terrible way. Mzilikazi was well-disposed towards his American guests, but where his own subjects were concerned he could be profoundly inhumane in meting out punishment at even the smallest of incidents. The following incident unfolded itself in front of the missionaries' eyes. Lindley witnessed the king performing a merciless act: "Witnessed today an act of barbarity that chilled my blood. A poor herder came with the report that one of his flock had died. The king ordered him to be beaten, and immediately 12 to 18 men fell on him with large sticks and in less than one minute beat the unfortunate fellow so much, that he reeled as he walked away, and seemed half deprived of

62 Lindley Journal 09.04.1836.

sense."[63] What a contrast and an infamy this posed to the foreigners! On the one hand the amicable reception, but simultaneously the severe punishment of an innocent cow-herd.

The honest cow-herd was punished for something that was not his doing. He would have gotten off much better if he had not mentioned the loss of livestock. A herd consisted of many animals. If one takes into account that the Africans could not count much in those days, one animal more or less in the herd would have gone unnoticed. Thus he was punished for his honesty. Maybe also for his naivety, that he didn't anticipate such punishment.

Upon their arrival in Kapeng the missionaries had informed Mzilikazi that they would depart again after five days. They cited their families as a reason for this, who had remained at Kuruman. They would then return to Mosega with their families. Mzilikazi was in agreement with these arrangements, but had also thought of something special for his guests. On the eve of their planned departure they waited in vain for Mzilikazi to come to them one last time, or at least despatch a messenger who would tell them that he wished his guests a speedy journey back home. Nothing happened.

Instead, something out of the ordinary took place on the day of their departure. Mzilikazi celebrated a traditional, religious feast in front of their eyes. What was the meaning of this? Was he intent on showing the missionaries that he, too, was a praying and believing person just like them, but in his own way? Or did he want to entice them to share his companionship and extend their visit? Or was the feast even supposed to be one of heathenish thanksgiving for the visit of the guests? The hastily arranged feast might speak for the latter. The huge amounts of tobacco and the pretty beads had possibly also contributed to the surprise feast. Mzilikazi did not cultivate any tobacco himself, but his soldiers smoked the tobacco of the Europeans; they had no idea how to cultivate it themselves. The same was the case with regard to the beads. Mzilikazi could not manufacture any beads himself. Therefore a gift of beads for his many wives was considered to be an extraordinary one indeed.[64]

But what events unfolded right in front of the eyes of the missionaries?

---

[63] Lindley Journal 10.04.1836.

[64] One of Mzilikazi's many wives was given permission to visit the missionaries on one occasion. Lindley writes: "Today one of the king's wives, a great fat thing, came to see us – she is the first who has been permitted to pay us this respect. He has, it may be, a hundred wives, may be more … " Lindley Journal 03.04.1836.

Two heads of cattle[65] were presented to the crowds. Then Kalipi stood in front of the king and held a speech dictated to him by the king. The speech was addressed to *Machaubane,* the deceased father of Mzilikazi. Venable observes the following: "Kalipi began a speech … He walked forward and backward near the king. While walking from the king he spoke, but while returning, the king dictated what he should say."[66] In another report Venable refers to the two mentioned heads of cattle. He writes: "Kalipi … spoke about an hour, apparently to the two oxen."[67] In his speech, which can be viewed as being a public invocation by Mzilikazi, he addressed Machaubane on behalf of Mzilikazi. In this invocation the king's deceased father, i.e. the spirit of Machaubane, was entreated to give rain for crops and livestock, and to provide weapons for the warriors. "William informed us that Kalipi was asking Machaubane to give rain, assegai etc."[68]

The two heads of cattle were slaughtered as sacrificial offering. They were consecrated to the deceased spirits and ancestors. Because Machaubane was closest to the living, it was he who was called by name in this case. Kalipi directed his eyes towards the two oxen. He wanted to know how they would react. If they remained calm, that would be a sign that Machaubane had accepted Mzilikazi's pleas with this offering.

In the afternoon Mzilikazi paid the missionaries a visit. Venable writes: "He was more familiar than he has been on any former occasion."[69] On the following day was still friendly. After they had packed their things they informed him that they were about to leave. He walked up to them and told them that nothing was standing in their way. He climbed onto the wagon with them and accompanied them for a while. Then he climbed off the wagon, bade them farewell once more and walked back.

The missionaries continued on their journey to Mosega, albeit via another route. Kalipi had suggested that it would be in their own interest to drive past Ga-Ditshwene[70]. This suggestion appealed to them, and so they

---

65 Two of "… more than a thousand oxen", ibid. 13.04.1836.

66 Venable Journal 13.04.1836.

67 Id., January 22nd to May 18th 1836 p. 43.

68 Loco citato, p. 44.

69 Venable, January 22nd to May 18th 1836 p. 44.

70 In this context, an additional comment regarding Ga-Ditshwene. As has been previously indicated, Ga-Ditshwene has now been integrated into the toponym of Enselsberg. The town lies about 40 km to the north-east of Zeerust. The distribution of the ruins of Ga-Ditshwene over four different farms once again highlights the size of the tribe that once dwelled there. One of the four farmers, Mr. Scheepers, collected a vast array of utensils

drove past the oldest settling place of the Bahurutshe. They came upon the cattle kraals, old houses, ruins, superimposed stone walls and many other signs of an abandoned settlement.[71]

After the missionaries had arrived at Mosega they stayed there for a few days. They established contact with the Bahurutshe and continued with the building of the houses for their families. They longed to be back with their families again. Kalipi visited them repeatedly during that short time, before they departed to travel back to their families. They set out from Mosega on 05 May 1836.[72] It took them fourteen days to travel back to Kuruman, where they arrived on 18 May 1836. In Kuruman, immediate preparations were made for the group to move to Mosega.

Six weeks later everything was ready. The missionary families, including the Wilsons, travelled to Mosega together. They arrived on 15 June 1836.[73] After they had moved in they immediately started laying out a garden. They sowed and planted and cultivated a piece of land with their oxen. Initially they kept themselves to themselves as much as possible, but did have a few guests now and then who came over from the village.

After they were of the opinion that they had finally settled in, they invited the Batswana to their premises. Regular meetings took place once a month. They cautiously made their intentions known as to why they had left America to come to Africa and to the Batswana people. They had to be cautious and show restraint as far as their mission work was concerned, seeing that Mzilikazi had not yet given them permission to hold public meetings and preach the gospel. They were, as yet, only allowed to reside at Mosega. During those conversations where they only alluded to the Christian message, they met with a response ranging from meagre to hostile. That was not very encouraging. They saw their patience being severely tried and were of

---

on his farm, which he found lying about on the ground, or which he discovered while ploughing his fields. On his farm Bloemfontein he opened quite a respectable little private museum with all the things he found. H. Langwieder has captured the farm and the museum in various illustrations. In his binder, Attachment D, Langwieder includes the article 'In Search of Kaditshwene' by J. Boeyens. Boeyens writes about the settlement at Ga-Ditshwene: "Careful consideration of both oral and archaeological evidence suggest that Kaditshwene was established no earlier than the seventeenth century, and became the capital of Hurutshe probably only towards the end of the eighteenth century." Boeyens p. 4.

71 Venable Journal, January 22nd to May 18th 1836 p. 45.

72 Venable Journal, May 31st to August 2nd 1836 p. 4.

73 Venable Journal, May 31st to August 2nd 1836 p. 4.

the opinion that the interest of the Bahurutshe in the Christian message would be awakened once Mzilikazi had given his consent for the gospel to be preached openly. They waited, patiently hopeful.

Then, one day, Kalipi despatched a message to Mosega. His scouts had told him that a military commando was moving up from the south into a northerly direction.[74] He said that he himself had gone on a reconnaissance trip to see for himself whether this information was just a rumour or whether there actually was an impending danger. Rumour had it that Dingaan and his Zulu warriors might be on the move to subjugate the secessionist Mzilikazi.

Another rumour did the rounds, according to which the Griquas, together with the Korannas, planned to launch a series of attacks onto Mzilikazi. The Korannas were already armed with rifles, which they had obtained from the Boers. This frightened Kalipi. Mzilikazi's soldiers only had a few rifles. The vast majority continued to fight with spears and shields.

A backward glance to Kapeng may be appropriate at this point. During the ritual feasting Kalipi had looked at the oxen while making his speech to invoke the ancestors' help. The ancestors were entreated to place strong assegais into the hands of the soldiers, so that they could defeat the enemy. Was this already an indication that the enemy would possess numerous firearms against which the spears of the warriors would be of no use? And why had Mzilikazi gone out of his way to be so friendly towards the missionaries? Was it already his intention back then that he might use the missionaries as mediators who could procure firearms from the Europeans for him?

When Kalipi returned from his reconnaissance trip he brought with him the insight that there was, for the time being, no threat from any advancing enemy.

A short while later, another reason as to why Mzilikazi had been so well-disposed towards the missionaries in Kapeng became apparent. He had received a present from the governor in Cape Town. He wanted to give thanks for this but could neither read nor write. It was important for him to express his goodwill to the ruling British in the Cape. Seeing that the missionaries had come from Cape Town, he had two reasons why he thought that they might be the best mediators. After Reverend Moffat had shown him a Bible, to wit, Mzilikazi knew that the Europeans not only transmitted

74 Loco citato, p. 38f.

their communications orally via messengers, but were also able to communicate with each other by means of a written piece of paper. Thus they were also able to draw up a letter on his behalf. A messenger did indeed presently arrive at Mosega, asking the missionaries to write a letter on Mzilikazi's behalf. They were willing to oblige and sent Wilson to Kapeng.[75] This visit also provided Wilson with the opportunity to introduce himself to Mzilikazi. This undertaking did however not succeed. Mzilikazi's letter of thanks never arrived in Cape Town. The reasons for this will be dealt with at a later stage.

With Wilson's visit to Kapeng the missionaries probably also expected that the time had come that they would be granted permission to openly preach the gospel. But Mzilikazi didn't mentioned this at all and Wilson, for his part, did not broach the subject because he was reluctant to provoke him.

While they continued to wait for permission to teach and preach in Mosega, time began hanging heavy on their hands and they contemplated what they could do. Their attempts to approach the Batswana and have a conversation with them once a month did not satisfy them. Even the newly laid-out garden contributed little to tide them over. So they began writing down everything they saw and observed in their surroundings and also what the people with whom they came into contact told them. In addition, they wanted to explore their immediate surroundings.

One day they climbed onto a hill[76] and looked down over the surrounding land. While doing so, they made a surprising discovery, which enabled them to have a totally different perspective. They saw, virtually all around them, numerous small and larger settlements. They had hitherto not been aware of the extent of the settled population. Lindley/Venable/Wilson writes: "By ascending a small mountain in the near of our house, we may count 10 or 12 towns, and in the basin there are 18 or 20. Within 5 miles of

---

75 Venable Journal, May 31st to August 2nd 1836 p. 7f.

76 There are small ridges in Mosega, which are the foothills of the Magaliesberg Mountains towards the west. The Boers had also occupied this stretch of land. They gave the highest mountain in their area two names: 'Mosegas Koppie' = Mosega's Hill', aligning it to the Setswana culture, and 'Antjie se Kop' = Antjie's Hill, a name that is tied up with the dramatic love story of two Boer children. A boy and a girl were in love with each other. The parents of the girl were opposed to the relationship. The girl rebelled against her parents. She ran away and hid herself in the mountains. They found her after three days. The story goes that she gave up her love in the solitude of the mountains. Because she had a change of heart in those mountains, the Boers named that koppie (hill) after her.

us there are four or six averaging from 60 to 70 houses, and as many more smaller places."[77] They had not realised up to that point just how many people resided at Mosega, and this realisation took them aback.

The first rain of the season had fallen during the short period of time in which they tried to find their feet in Mosega. That was a good omen. When visitors or, in this case, new residents come to Africans, and it rains, this will always be a sign of goodwill. The spirits of the deceased, who watch over everything, bid the strangers welcome in this way. If sufficient rain fell during periods of drought, as happened occasionally at Mosega, this constituted a great blessing for humans and animals, for nature in general. The inhabitants suffered no want during this time. If the conquerors and oppressors also stayed away during this time, the indigenous people lived in contented peace for a while. Lindsay/Venable/Wilson write: "The people are generally cheerful and have the appearance of living well."[78] Even though there was no chief – or maybe because of that – the Bahurutshe who had remained behind conveyed the impression to the missionaries that they were not subject to any repressive measures.

It is the chief's role to see to it that order is maintained in an intact community. The Bahurutshe at Mosega were temporarily able to get by without their chief. Where was he located at that particular time? The American missionaries seem to know: "Mokgatla, chief of the Baharutsi, who held this district six years ago, is on the Hout River,[79] another branch of the Orange, which is west of the Fall."[80] Mokgatlhe and Moiloa II were afraid of Mzilikazi. That is why they had already moved away from Mosega six years previously. They could not return to their home territory as long as Mzilikazi ruled the region.

Then it came to pass that the American missionaries fell ill. Almost all of them were stricken by a terrible fever.[81] They were all able to recover after a period of suffering, except for the wife of the doctor, Mary Jane Wilson, who died of this fever on 18 September 1836 and was buried in Mosega. Before she died she told her husband: "Tell my mother, sister and friends, that I never regretted coming to Africa."[82]

77 Lindley/Venable/Wilson, 18. 08. 1836 p. 5
78 Id., p. 10.
79 What is meant is the Hart River.
80 Lindley/Venable/Wilson, 18. 08. 1836 p. 15.
81 The region was infested with malaria in those days.
82 Lindley/Venable/Wilson 06. 5. 1837. – Many years later, South African women of Euro-

For the duration of the fever the missionaries couldn't even contemplate paying Mzilikazi another visit to finally attain his consent to preach the gospel openly. It was not only their illness, however, which prevented them from seeing Mzilikazi. Mzilikazi was repeatedly embroiled in fresh wars against the Boers. This situation finally culminated in the end of what had been a hopeful mission endeavour of American missionaries amongst the Bahurutshe. All three missionaries had already approached Mzilikazi, and had hoped for his permission to teach and preach the gospel to the Bahurutshe. Meanwhile several local individuals had indicated that they were open to the new Christian message. But since they feared Mzilikazi and Kalipi, they, too, waited for permission from their conqueror. Without the consent of this ruler they were not prepared to embrace the new teachings of the American missionaries. Until such time that Mzilikazi gave a sign in this regard, the missionaries had to exercise patience. In the end they came away empty-handed.

It has been mentioned previously that the Boers moved into the Transvaal. To recap, the reasons for this: The British sought to take over power in the Cape. The Boers not only felt under pressure because of this, but also experienced a sense of inferiority in the light of the increasing immigration of British people with their political know-how and position of advantage where world trade was concerned. After the first Boers had retreated from the Cape, had migrated into the interior and were feeling at ease there, others followed.

The first immigrants to the Transvaal had been killed by Mzilikazi.[83] Mzilikazi enriched himself with their possessions and cattle. When other Boers heard of these attacks they refused to let them go unpunished. It had pleased Mzilikazi to get the better of individual Boer families. Now the Boers clustered together in groups. Mzilikazi attacked one such group of Boer immigrants. This time round, however, the group had been forewarned by the original inhabitants of southern Africa, the San people.[84]

---

pean descent erected a memorial stone to this first missionary woman who died amongst the Bahurutshe. The memorial stone was erected along the railway line between Zeerust and Mafikeng.

83 "In August 1836, when a Boer hunting party under Stephanus Erasmus ventured into the Magaliesberg ahead of the main trek, the Ndebele ambushed it and killed all but three ... During the next few days other Voortrekker families who had crossed the Vaal were also attacked and many were killed." Carruthers, p. 260.

84 In the past, the San people have been referred to as "Bushmen". This term is outdated.

A violent battle ensued. Even though the group under attack was not very large and was up against a military force far superior in numbers, a huge number of Mzilikazi's soldiers were killed.[85] The mighty gunpowder had defeated the myriad of spears, which Mzilikazi had still imagined at his ritual celebration in Kapeng would be able to defeat the Boers.

Mzilikazi retreated. A small group of Boer families had, under cover of their laager – ox wagons chained together in a circle –, defeated the African warriors, killed many of them and had put the rest to flight. Other Boers, who were trekking around the Transvaal independently of one another, got news of this. They began to rally. Africans from various tribes, too, who wished to repulse Mzilikazi, joined them. Together they deemed themselves to be strong enough. The Boers took over the leadership. Mzilikazi was to suffer a crushing defeat and be driven from the region. Several attacks took place in different areas of the Transvaal. One battle took place at Mosega, where Mzilikazi's soldiers had insinuated themselves into the civilian Bahurutshe population, seeking protection amongst them against the attacking Boers.

The Boers were well aware that three missionary families resided amongst the Bahurutshe. They wanted to protect the Americans and sent them an early-morning message – before sunrise – on the day of the planned surprise attack on the Bahurutshe. The information they received was to the effect that an attack would imminently be launched on their settlement, in a few minutes' time. This came as a complete surprise to them. There was no time to flee. Mzilikazi was residing at a different camp, and his soldiers who had insinuated themselves at Mosega were about to suffer a crushing defeat. During the battle the Boers had no regard for the civilian Bahurutshe who lived there. "The Boers use guns of large calibre, the common size carrying 12 balls ... They load fire from their horses, hence they can easily keep out of the way of footmen armed with only a small spear."[86]

The course of events during the attack is described by the missionaries as follows: "The people of the kraal fled towards our house ... This brought us in midst of the carnage. Several balls passed over our house, some struck it, and one passed through Br. Venable's chamber window ... many lives were destroyed ... there were 107 Boers accompanied by about

85 "At the famous battle of Vegkop in October 1836, about 40 families successfully defended their laager against an Ndebele impi of 3,000." Carruthers, p. 260.

86 Lindley/Venable/Wilson 06. 05. 1837.

50 Griquas and about as many Bechuanas[87] … The Boers took away with them six thousand head of cattle and made our field of labour an awful desolation."[88] After this battle the American missionaries abandoned their mission endeavours at Mosega.

The Boer commando, together with local African men, had destroyed Mosega within three hours. The missionaries were given the alternative either to stay or flee with the Boers. They had a hasty discussion about their chances and decided to flee under the protection of the Boers. It was a decision they subsequently questioned. Within hours they were ready to leave: "At one o'clock P.M. of this trying day we set out in company with white men, black men, footmen and horsemen, some armed with guns and others with assegais, shields, bows and arrows, and driving before them 6,000 head of cattle. We endured much hardship for fifteen days, when we arrived (on 31. 01. 1837, HB) at Taba Unchu (i.e. black mountain), a station of the Wesleyan Missionary Society of England."[89]

Thus the work of the American missionaries amongst the Bahurutshe, and their hopes for their mission, came to an end before it had even started. They had merely established contact with the indigenous people. It did not extend further than that. They were unable to carry out their intention to spread the gospel amongst the Africans, and more specifically amongst the Bahurutshe. The Americans had after all given up so much when they left their prosperous, civilised country. Had all their efforts been in vain? Hardly. We can reiterate the Apostle Paul's words – and the same applies to the Paris missionaries who were working amongst the Bahurutshe before them: "He who plants and he who waters are one, and each will receive his wages according to his labour" (cf. 1 Cor. 3,5–8). Although not even a trace of a planted seed could be discerned from either the French or the Americans, we will see later that their mission was not in vain.

The American missionaries had previously not mentioned once that they wanted to leave the Bahurutshe. They were well aware of the fact that their French colleagues had been forced to take their fate into their own hands five years before, and under similar conditions. They thought that they could do better, and had taken a great deal of trouble in the process.

---

87 Amongst the 'many Bechuanas' were probably also a number of Bahurutshe volunteers who had been hired by the Boers to fight against Mzilikazi. If this was indeed the case, this battle can be construed as having been a war of brothers.

88 Lindley/Venable/Wilson 06. 05. 1837.

89 Id., 08. 05. 1837.

They had brought along great and valuable gifts to please Mzilikazi, and had always endeavoured to obey him. There was nothing they had to fear from him. They had buried their mission sister, Mary Jane Wilson. They now had to bid her farewell for ever. It would be almost impossible to ever visit her grave again. There might have been various reasons for their eventual decision to abandon their mission and leave the Bahurutshe and go with the Boers.

One reason might have been the damaged house and destroyed fields. And the impatience of repeatedly having to wait and asking themselves how long it would still take before they could preach the gospel openly probably also played a role. Maybe they had seen through Mzilikazi and had reached the conclusion that they would never obtain the permission to missionize. And their hearts had probably also filled with a certain amount of fear and frustration. The liberation by the Boers and the prospect of immersing themselves back into civilisation within a few days might also have been a contributing factor in their hasty and maybe not sufficiently pondered decision. Later, when he was already living far away from Mosega, Lindley subsequently considered their unexpectedly hasty departure to have been a mistake. From Grahamstown on the shores of the Indian Ocean he writes: "Did the cause of our failure lie solely between us and Moselekatsi, then we should fear that we have failed for want of wisdom: but we were not in any case a party either with Moselekatsi, or with the Boers; nor had we an opportunity of acting even as mediators between them. In looking back at the past our only consolation is in conscience void of offence, and in resignation to God's will. If we erred in anything, it is leaving so abruptly."[90]

It has to be acknowledged that the situation at Mosega was not an easy one. The population consisted of various tribes. There was a war raging. The Bahurutshe were leaderless, since they were short of a chief who would have been able to provide direction. The missionaries were at the mercy of a foreign culture. They were still not able to communicate with the local people, neither in Setswana nor in Setebele. This, too, will have contributed towards their insecurity. This earlier dereliction might have been the cause for their subsequent lack of confidence in establishing their mission work at Mosega.

While fleeing with the Boers the missionaries had no opportunity to call on the main tribe of the Bahurutshe at Taung. They first of all had to

[90] Lindley 10. 05. 1837 p. 1.

come to rest. During their sojourn at Mosega there had been no contact between Mokgatlhe and Moiloa II and themselves. Connections possibly existed between the Bahurutshe on both sides, but the missionaries were not aware of them and thus also received no information. During their short sojourn in Mosega the Americans had other things on their mind than to deal with the Bahurutshe at Taung.

Another missionary, neither Frenchman nor American, but an Englishman turned his attention to the Bahurutshe at Taung. This Englishman, Inglis, established contact with them before he even knew where they had come from or what locations they laid claim to as their actual living area.

1.3.3 A British Missionary

Over the years, tensions had developed at Taung with neighbouring tribes. Taung had become a familiar place for the Bahurutshe, one which they repeatedly frequented during their migrations. The last "migration" was the flight from Mosega to Taung. Ferdinand Jensen estimated the distance between Dinokana and Taung to be "roughly a seven day's journey from here".[91] When the Bahurutshe covered this distance with their women, children and livestock, they needed weeks and months to accomplish this.

The time had arrived to leave Taung once more. An old woman could, during the tenure of the Hermannsburg missionary Thomas Jensen, recall Taung and the final departure to the north. However, due to her old age, she was no longer able to provide details. She was known amongst the Bahurutshe at Dinokana to be the last survivor who had taken part in the migration from Taung to Ga-Ditshwene.

On the flight to and during the early days of Taung, Mokgatlhe retained his chieftainship. The Bahurutshe had settled at Taung on numerous occasions and for several years at a time. However, during the final years of their sojourn there, Moiloa II had increasingly gained in reputation and recognition. He was the future chief in the line of succession, and Mokgatlhe had merely acted as substitute. After he had reached maturity, more and more Bahurutshe favoured him. Mokgatlhe was initially not comfortable with this situation. They both had their adherents. The number of Moiloa II's adherents began to increase. It seemed as if the tribe would split while it was still on foreign land and that one or even two new tribes might come

91 Ferdinand Jensen 1909 p. 1.

about by seceding from the main tribe. That did not happen. Even under extreme tensions and temporary segregation the tribe's unity was preserved. The tribe did nonetheless move out of Taung in two, or rather three separate groups.

Tensions arose in Taung, not only with neighbouring tribes, but within the tribe as well. These tensions prompted Mokgatlhe and Moiloa II to leave the communally occupied area together with their adherents. This was opposed by *Motlaadiile,* a respected petty chief of royal lineage, who had also gathered his own adherents around him. Motlaadiile was Moiloa II's half-brother who made demands on the position of heir to the throne. Mokgatlhe rejected this claim. This probably constituted the real reason as to why he refused to take part in the collective exodus.

All three leaders finally made their decisions independent of one another. Mokgatlhe and his adherents moved out first, followed shortly afterwards by Moiloa II. Motlaadiile remained for a longer period of time, and little is known about his subsequent departure. He reconciled with Moiloa II after the death of Mokgatlhe. He is later mentioned one more time in Dinokana.

Motlaadiile was so angry about Mokgatlhe's refusal to be the tribal chief that he urged the neighbouring Koranna tribe to chase after his half-brother and debilitate him with a raid. This appealed to the bellicose Koranna. They followed behind Moiloa II and embroiled the Bahurutshe in a war. Ferdinand Jensen comments: "In 1844 a chieftainship quarrel brought about a division in the tribe, and the main section of the people … moved away. (…) Motlaadiile, the chief who stayed behind, resented their departure and would have liked to have prevented it, but he was not strong enough to do that and therefore plotted his revenge in order to inflict damage. In those days a Hottentot tribe, the Koranna, resided on the banks of the Vaal River and called 'Bakgothu' or 'Makgotu' by the Batswana. Motlaadiile drew their attention to the cattle herds of the tribe members who were moving away and successfully induced them to launch an assault on them. Fortunately Mokgatlhe was alerted by one of his peers, the chief of the Batlhasing, and the attack did not happen unexpectedly.[92]

The reasons as to why Mokgatlhe and Moiloa II moved out might have been the same for both. After they had resided at Taung for quite a considerable period of time, new quarrels broke out with the South Sotho. And

[92] Ferdinand Jensen *'Das Heldenlied'*, p. 375.

the Boers had in the meantime driven Mzilikazi out of their former areas of residence.[93] One can but guess as to the reason why Mokgatlhe moved out first, followed by Moiloa II. The question as to which one of the two acted more wisely also remains open. Tensions had escalated over a period of time to such a degree that a secession seemed unavoidable. Both had understood the dangerous nature of the situation and wanted to avoid the looming quarrel. Mokgatlhe had aged and was, probably for that reason alone, not interested in conflict and moved out first. Was he therefore the wiser of the two? Moiloa II, on the other hand, didn't want to leave anybody behind and, as future chief, he was concerned about the larger part of the Bahurutshe tribe, stayed put for longer and risked being persecuted. Was this the wiser move?

Moiloa II, who had the larger part of the tribe on his side, and was therefore also probably not able to move quite as fast as Mokgatlhe with his smaller group, was left standing. As mentioned above, the Koranna had been persuaded to follow him and rob the cattle. Moiloa II had been informed about Motlaadiile's betrayal, however, and was consequently prepared for a raid and was able to defend himself sufficiently. A number of people were wounded and killed.

Let us briefly return to the period before the exodus and reflect on a memory of the above-mentioned old woman. She told Thomas Jensen that, when they were on the move under Moiloa II, a missionary had moved out with them. She had admittedly forgotten his name but one can assume that this missionary was Inglis. He had already attended to the Bahurutshe when they were still residing at Taung. Moiloa II had brought him in during the period when Motlaadiile's claims to succession were being discussed at length in the tribe. Ferdinand Jensen writes: "When Mokgatlhe paid no heed to his nephew (to put him on the throne, HB), a fierce discussion developed in the settlement. During this time Moiloe embarked on a

93 When Mzilikazi's soldiers had been defeated after numerous attacks, he gathered them from all the various camps and fled across the border into present-day Botswana. But the Boers could have pursued him there, too. So he chose to move even further north to conquer yet another area. He moved to Zimbabwe. There were enough survivors with whom he was able to build a new empire. Amongst those who had fought in his army and moved to Zimbabwe were quite a number of Bafokeng tribesmen. Cf. Bammann 2010 p. 34f.

journey to Kuruman with the desire to ask for a missionary who could teach his tribe, and God answered his plea. He returned with Reverend 'Inglis'."[94]

The reason remains unknown as to why Moiloa II took a missionary from the London Missionary Society with him, and not one from the Wesleyan Missionary Society[95], which was already active in the area around Taung and which had established its mission station at Thaba-Nchu. It may be assumed, however, that he principally found it to be of advantage to have a missionary in his midst. One may further assume that the teachings of the gospel appealed to him personally. He will once more have approached Moffat in Kuruman, who had sent the Paris missionaries to the Bahurutshe at Mosega.

A chief never takes a decision all by himself; he has to obtain the approval of his adherents for his course of action in each case. One can assume that this also applied to his intention of acquiring a missionary from Kuruman. Moiloa II embarked on the journey to Kuruman, something that did not escape the notice of Motlaadiile. He gathered his supporters around him and rejected Moiloa II's plan on the grounds that this required his approval, seeing that he was the rival candidate for the position of heir to the throne. Notwithstanding this, Moiloa II embarked on his journey to Kuruman, thereby demonstrating his superiority to the tribe.

Inglis had accepted Moiloa II's invitation. He had moved to Taung. Being a young missionary, he attended more to the interests of the younger Moiloa II and his adherents as he did to those of the older Mokgatlhe with his smaller group of sympathisers, and even less to those of Motlaadiile. As a consequence, Inglis, together with Moiloa II and his supporters, subsequently moved out of Taung. It was his objective to be the exclusive missionary to those people who followed Moiloa II, and accordingly went where they went. Unfortunately these good intentions came to nought, since a war broke out shortly after the exodus.

The *Bakgothu* had trailed Moiloa II. As previously mentioned, Moiloa II was prepared for the raid and was not only able to avert the attack but also to emerge triumphant from the confrontation. Inglis was an observer

---

94 'Mme ka Mokgatlhe le ene a gana go utlwa ngwana oa ga mogolooe, kgang e e botlhoko ea tsoga mo gae. Ka shona sebaka seo sa likgang, Moiloe a etela koa Kuruman ka keletso ea go bitsa moruti, eo o ka tlang go ruta morafe oa gag abo, mi Modimo oa mo thusa, a boa le moruti "Inglis" teng.' – Ferdinand Jensen, *Moshupa-Tsela* No. 8, 1910 p. 60.

95 'Wesleyan missions ... existed in Transorangia from the 1820s ... ' Beck, in *Christianity in South Africa*, p. 128.

to the war and describes the outcome of the attack: "The Bakgothu left 25 dead on the field and lost about 20 guns – the Bahurutshe left one dead."[96] After the battle had ended, Inglis and Moiloa II parted company. Inglis returned to Kuruman and didn't accompany the Bahurutshe further on their migrations, but did however, seven years later and under different circumstances, become the first missionary of the Bahurutshe at Dinokana for a short while.

The direction that the two Bahurutshe groups took under Mokgatlhe and Moiloa II was the same for both. They moved towards Ga-Ditshwene. Along the way Mokgatlhe, who was ahead, stopped over at Rabogadi. Maybe he had heard of the bellicose attacks of the Bakgothu, and was waiting for Moiloa II and his followers. Manson writes: "Here a few hundred people under Mokgatlhe had now moved from Motlabastad (i.e. Taung, HB). In September 1838 Moiloe finally arrived."[97] That Manson mentions only a few hundred people who accompanied Mokgatlhe should be a clear indication of the fact that the majority of the Bahurutshe had moved out under Moiloa II's leadership, thereby unofficially assigning the chieftainship to him. In Rabogadi the Bahurutshe were united once again. They remained there for a while and then migrated further towards Ga-Ditshwene, which was not very far away. One can assume that they used the time of recuperation in Rabogadi to investigate as to how far the Boer settlement in Ga-Ditshwene had advanced, before making the decision to return to their familiar haunts.

But the Bahurutshe could not stay in Ga-Ditshwene for long. They were increasingly put under pressure by the Boers who had appropriated the fertile land and had begun settling their families in greater numbers. After two years the Bahurutshe moved yet again. After a long interval, Inglis re-established contact with them. He had resided very far away from them but had nonetheless kept track of their movements. He visited them twice at Ga-Ditshwene before they left again.

The Boers in the areas around the Bahurutshe called Ga-Ditshwene "Zendelingspost",[98] even though they were only vaguely aware of what took place there. Translated from Afrikaans, Zendelingspost means mission station. How did they arrive at this name? The British and the Boers

96 Inglis report 31. 03. 1840 p. 3.

97 Manson 1990 p. 85.

98 To the various localisations of 'Zendelingspost', cf. Ferdinand Jensen 1909 p. 1f; Breutz 1953 p. 95f.

were at loggerheads. It is unknown whether Inglis, the Englishman, visited the Boers on their farms. It may however be assumed that a number of Bahurutshe men and women were employed on the fields, in the gardens and kitchens of the Boers. It amounted to a sensation to these people when the Reverend Inglis paid them a visit in their village. They could probably have told the Boers that he was planning to come and live amongst them. Even though Inglis had made no statements to this effect, it was probably in accordance with what the Bahurutshe had in mind. He had after all already stayed with them at Taung.

Since the Boers were certainly a very religious people, one may presume that they embraced the considerations of their labourers and subsequently gave Ga-Ditshwene the name of Zendelingspost. This name was not unique, however. Roughly three to five hours to the west, another two British missionaries were missionising amongst the Batswana. Edwards was working amongst the Bakgatla in Maanoane, and Livingstone had moved to the Bahurutshe Bo-Manyana at Kolobeng. Even though these two British mission stations were a long distance away from the Boers at Ga-Ditshwene, they nonetheless knew about them.

On his second visit Inglis was taken to the "Ruins of Kurrechene".[99] Hence the Bahurutshe had settled not far from their previous settlement area and had not taken up their old decaying dwellings. The ruins of the large stone walls that had been put up in Ga-Ditshwene had however remained. In spite of this, the Bahurutshe proceeded to erect a similar settlement right next to it.[100]

It has been mentioned that an increasing number of Boers moved to Ga-Ditshwene. In their drive towards colonisation the Bahurutshe stood in their path. The pressure from the Boers increased daily. The threat of the Boers intimidated the Bahurutshe so much that they considered moving again. The Bahurutshe outnumbered the Boers by far. They could have defended their fertile land and their settlement. Especially considering that they had

99 That is to say, the ruins of Ga-Ditshwene, Inglis report, 31.01.1847 p. 3.

100 The ruins of Ga-Ditshwene cover a large area. The Bahurutshe of Dinokana are interested in reclaiming their old places of residence. They are however not in accord as to how this should come about. Several of the Boers in that area put up resistance. The Bahurutshe lack the financial means if they should be obliged to purchase the farms from the Boers. They have been offered the farm Bloemfontein for sale. A buyer has hitherto not emerged. It may be that, to some extent, the collective soul of the Bahurutshe is still burdened by fear towards the Boers of the past.

erected several forgeries in Ga-Ditshwene and could therefore easily have manufactured a sufficient amount of weapons. But war was not uppermost in their minds. They had neither prepared themselves for an armed conflict, nor did they contemplate in any way to fight against the Boers.

During his second visit to Ga-Ditshwene, Moiloa II informed Inglis that he was thinking of moving again, but that the elders were opposed to this idea.[101] On his way back, Inglis travelled to Edwards in Maanoane, from where he had undertaken his journey to the Bahurutshe. He stayed with Edwards for an extended period of time, and undertook reconnaissance trips to two other tribes from there. Inglis was in search of a tribe with the objective to begin with new missionary work. He had admittedly not committed himself to the Bahurutshe but nevertheless showed a clear sympathy towards this particular tribe. He had also spoken to Moiloa II about his objectives. There would have been no obstacle as far as the Bahurutshe were concerned if Inglis would decide to move to Ga-Ditshwene. But for some reason he was reluctant to move into the proximity of the Boers. So it was conducive to him that Moiloa II had spoken of a possible exodus of the tribe. This may have induced Inglis to prematurely decide in favour of the Bahurutshe. He would welcome a move on the part of the Bahurutshe. He would no longer have to deal with the psychological strain of being an Englishman living at close quarters with the Boers. The conversation between Moiloa II and Inglis seemed to have created a good starting point.

A few months later, after the two men had met at Ga-Ditshwene, Moiloa II travelled to *Maanoane*, where Inglis resided with Edwards. "In the beginning of May, Moiloe came from the Bahurutshe to see me, and to arrange their removal."[102] They discussed the same issue: Where should they go? A section of the tribal elders had in the meantime become sympathetic to Moiloa II. The way had been cleared for a renewed change of location. When it became clear to Inglis during the conversation that the Bahurutshe might relocate after all, he communicated his proposals to Moiloa II. He wanted to settle outside of Mosega, seeing that other Bahurutshe continued to live there. That was also not that far away from Edward's place of residence and the Bakgatla who stayed there. Moiloa II then proceeded to put forward his proposal and told him that he planned to move into the same region. Inglis wrote: "I told Moiloe that I wished to plough at a stream

[101] Inglis report 15.10.1847 p. 2.

[102] Ibid., p. 1

about 2 miles from the Bakgatla. He told me that the Baharutsi would in all probability settle at the Maineloe River."[103]

Inglis regularly drove from Maanoane to the piece of land he had selected, cultivated it, built a house for himself and moved in with his family towards the end of August 1847.[104] A number of indigenous people resided in his immediate vicinity who had not relocated previously, and additional families who had seceded from Kuruman had come to settle there. A small number of Boers also resided close by. While Inglis had visited the Bahurutshe in Ga-Ditshwene, it had not crossed his mind that he should go and see the Boers even once. But now, seeing that he had settled in on a more permanent basis, he was obliged to do so. On this visit to the Boers he also wanted to establish if they were hostile towards him, and if so, the extent of such hostility. Of the British missionaries he was after all the one who had settled in closest proximity to the Boers. He decided not to go to any of the Boers but to approach the District Administrator directly. "The new Landdrost was rather shy at first. We came to understand each other – had a very interesting conversation – found him a respectable religious man. He told me to go ahead with the mission – that I would meet with no opposition."[105]

Only a year after Inglis had arrived at his mission station, Moiloa II began with his departure from Ga-Ditshwene. It was however not the entire tribe that initially followed him in August 1848. The rest followed in various migrations at a later stage. Moiloa II settled at the location that he had previously described to Inglis during his visit to Maanoane. It was at a certain distance from Inglis' house, but not so far that possible church attendance where Moiloa II was concerned could be out of the question. And so it came about that he regularly attended the church services. Inglis rejoiced in the fact that he Moiloa II never came alone but was always accompanied by a small flock of his adherents. "He used every means to bring out the people. Often we had above 50 men from the village 3 and 4 miles distant."[106]

Inglis' delight due to the Bahurutshe's attendance did not last very long, however. Disappointment soon set in. His mission work ended sooner than he had anticipated. His assumption that most Boers would settle around Ga-Ditshwene or elsewhere proved to be an erroneous one. The Boers also

[103] Inglis report 15.10.1847 p. 1

[104] Ibid., p. 2

[105] Ibid., p. 2

[106] Inglis report 06.09.1849 p. 1

settled in Zeerust, which subsequently developed into a European-style city, and its surrounding areas. And they also had plans to move to *Dinokana*, as it was later called by the Bahurutshe, where Moiloa II had settled. The reason for this was obvious. The Boers required water for their farmland. There was a spring at Dinokana that provided ample water. It was for this reason that the entire region was so coveted by the Boers who continued to move up from the Cape. "the Boers ... came into Bahu – like a flood – occupying the last fountain."[107] Even though he didn't have to endure any reprisals, Inglis developed an inner resentment towards the Boers.

Ever since the Boers had been driven out of the Cape, their sentiment towards the British was one of hostility. A certain political accord was however reached with the Sand River Convention of 1852.[108] The Boers were awarded the right to found their two provinces north of the Vaal River, the Orange Free State and the Transvaal. This agreement did however not bring a resolution to the actual conflict, which continued to smoulder beneath the surface on both sides. The Boers were still angry that they had been driven out of the Cape, whereas the British wanted to unite the entire country under their dominion. They begrudged the Boers their own republic. British missionaries sympathised with their political leadership.[109] Livingstone was alleged to have supplied the Batswana with guns and ammunition.[110] This in turn increased the rancour of the Boers. Inglis, too, had criticised the Boers. He could not tolerate the harshness with which they treated their African workers. This again displeased the Boers. Thus that which seemed to be unavoidable finally happened. The three British missionaries, who had begun working amongst the Batswana in the domain of the Boers, were ordered to leave their stations. The Boers had come up with a plan to bring this about.

All three British missionaries, Inglis in *Mathebe,* Edwards in *Maanoane* and Livingstone in *Kolobeng* were to be expelled from the Boer territory of what was then the Transvaal. A Boer commando of sixty horsemen was mustered for this purpose.

But first the Boers wanted to remove another obstacle. There is no precise information as to what had actually happened, but certain conjectures can be made. Motlaadiile, who had already aspired to the chieftainship in

---

107 Inglis report 06.09.1849 p. 1

108 Carruthers, p. 271 f.

109 "British missionaries increasingly threw their support behind the British Government." Mills, in *Christianity in South Africa,* p. 340.

110 Strauss, in *Christianity in South Africa,* p. 116.

Taung but which Mokgatlhe had denied him, had arrived at Dinokana with his adherents. It is possible that he no longer felt at ease all alone at Taung, and that he had also come into conflict with the South Sotho and the resident Boers. Maybe he was also sympathetic towards the British. At some point the Boer commando, for reasons unknown, carried out an act of revenge and mercilessly drove out him and his kinsmen. "A commando of 60 Boers – who took him away from Matebe by force ... located him three days south east from here."[111] The crackdown on Motlaadiile terrified all the other Bahurutshe to such an extent that they assumed that they were next in line to be so brutally beaten and driven out. To escape this presumed terror, they fled westwards into the semi-desert of the Kgalagadi. There they suffered great hardship and poverty, pushing them to the limits of their survival.

Inglis remained behind alone after the Bahurutshe had fled. The Boers now had nothing to fear from the Bahurutshe. Their commando advanced to the mission station. They took Inglis captive and, taking him with them to Maanoane, they took Edwards captive there as well. Their campaign led them on to Kolobeng, where they intended to capture D. Livingstone, their greatest adversary. But Livingstone was on an exploratory expedition in Central Africa at that time. Because they didn't find him at home they destroyed all his belongings. They took Inglis and Edwards to Potchefstroom, the seat of government of the Boers in those days.[112]

After the situation had calmed down and the Bahurutshe realised that the Boers had not confiscated their abandoned Dinokana for farmland, they returned from the semi-desert of the Kgalagadi. But Inglis was no longer there. That was one more reason why they decided to settle on the Pooe

[111] Inglis report 06.10.1852 p. 1

[112] In 1863, eleven years after the deportation of the British missionaries, the Hermannsburg superintendent A. Hardeland pays the Boer government a visit in Potchefstroom. It was Hardeland's intention to send new Hermannsburg missionaries into the Boer Republic of the Transvaal. From the opposing camps he writes about the Boers: "After the experiences they (the Boers, HB) have apparently had with the British missionaries, especially with Livingstone, they could and would not allow British missionaries to ever settle there again. Filled with hatred and animosity towards the Boers, they were purported to have instilled their sentiments in the heathen tribes as well." – ['Nach den Erfahrungen, die man (die Buren, HB) mit den englischen Missionaren, besonders mit Livingstone gemacht habe, könne und werde man nie zugeben, dass sich englische Missionare wieder dort niederließen. Von Hass und Feindschaft gegen die Buren beseelt, hätten sie auch den heidnischen Stämmen ihre gesinnung eingeflößt.'] – In Schröder, p. 173.

Mountain. They reckoned that they would be able to scan the vast plains of the Transvaal and catch sight of the advancing, ruthless Boers. The mountain would simultaneously afford them better protection against a Boer attack than a settlement in the valley.

After the Bahurutshe had erected their huts on the mountain and also on the slopes, but rather provisionally as we shall see later, the Hermannsburg missionaries began showing an interest in the Bahurutshe. A period of seven years had passed once more.

1.3.4 The first Hermannsburg Missionary

The missionaries from Hermannsburg went ashore in Natal in 1854. The missionaries who had previously arrived from the Berlin – and Norwegian mission societies assisted them in finding a suitable mission station amongst the Zulu people. The Hermannsburg Mission Society purchased a farm for its missionaries, called "Perseverance" by the British. The missionaries named it "Neu-Hermannsburg" (New Hermannsburg) to emphasise its relationship to their homeland.[113]

In Germany, the Hermannsburg Revival had proliferated under Pastor Louis Harms. An increasing number of young men signed up to do missionary work all over the world. Most missionaries from Hermannsburg were sent to South Africa. It was not possible to deploy all of them amongst the Zulu people; they soon had a sufficient number in place. A call from the Transvaal in 1857 arrived in Neu-Hermannsburg at an opportune moment. In those days there existed no border between Botswana and South Africa, and a section of the Batswana-tribe fell under the jurisdiction of the Boer Republic of the Transvaal. There, in present-day Botswana, the Hermannsburg missionaries were to take up their work in the South African interior.[114]

[113] Voges, in Lüdemann, p. 233. The town of Hermannsburg exists to this day, with currently 84 descendants of the Hermannburg mission residing there. Its German boarding school has become renowned far beyond its local borders.

[114] Since the abolition of Apartheid, the province of the Transvaal no longer exists. In 1994 the Africans assumed political power. The erstwhile four provinces of South Africa were re-divided into nine. This was, if one should choose to view this in a sarcastic light, exactly what the Homeland policy of the Boer regime had envisaged. The Africans declared their new provinces to be those that the Boers had set up and planned. After the Boers had already done the groundwork, the naming of the provinces constituted a mere formality. The process was concluded within nine months without any complications. Land was separated from the previous Transvaal to become the provinces of Gauteng,

Dinokana is situated in the west of the present-day North-West Province. Pretoria/Tshwane and Johannesburg/Gauteng lie ca. 350 km to the east, while Lobatse in Botswana is about forty kilometres to the west of Dinokana. Before the Hermannsburg missionaries began their work in Dinokana, they first of all travelled to Botswana to the Bakwena tribe that resided there. *Setshele* was chief of the Bakwena in Botswana. He was baptised and, what's more, he had himself appointed as preacher for church services, which is rather unusual for a chief. After the British missionaries had left, he was on the look-out for new assistance, as he was fully aware that the time for an autonomous church had not yet come. Setshele dispatched a letter to the Boers. He was a firm believer in the message of the gospel and demanded new missionaries. The Boers took cognisance of his letter, but had no missionaries at their disposal. In a roundabout way, a letter from the Boers with Setshele's invitation reached the Hermannsburg missionaries in Natal.[115]

M.W. Pretorius, the President of the South African Boer Republic, had written the letter. The advancement of spiritual ministry amongst the Batswana was important to the Boers. This was just not to be done by British missionaries. They were looking for men for the orphaned mission stations who were sympathetic to them. As mentioned previously, this came at an opportune moment for the Hermannsburg missionaries. They had no knowledge of the conflicts that had gone down between the Boers and the British, which had resulted in an expulsion of the British missionaries from Boer territory. Marée writes: "The district officer GJ Coetzee wrote a letter in October 1856 to the President MW Pretorius that he had advised Setshele, and Setshele instantly requested the President, replacing Livingstone, to send him another missionary."[116] After this letter had arrived in Natal, the missionaries at Neu-Hermannsburg discussed who of them should be sent to Botswana.

Since Louis Harms had not only sent missionaries but also catechists and artisans, who, right from the start, would proceed to constitute an exemplary little congregation, three missionaries were accordingly earmarked for the new mission endeavour with these various focal points in mind.

Limpopo, Mpumalanga and the Free State. The Transvaal was renamed "North-West Province". Since the dissertation of this book is as a result of history, the name Transvaal is being retained.

115 Bammann, 2004 p. 39, footnote 23.

116 Maree, p. 28.

They were the Reverend J. Schröder with his wife Dorothea, the catechist H. Müller and the artisan J. Herbst. They departed from Natal and, after a journey of about a thousand kilometres, arrived with their ox wagon in Dithejane on 16 July 1857.[117]

There were enough missionaries available in Natal, and other tribes amongst the Batswana had not yet acquired any missionaries. An additional number of Hermannsburg missionaries was therefore dispatched to Dithejane. Chr. Schulenburg, F. Zimmermann and Chr. Backeberg, as well as the colonist Meyer and the fiancée of colonist Herbst, Lena Meyerhoff, were earmarked for this endeavour.[118] The missionaries were to expand their mission work to the surrounding tribes. This was not what Setshele initially had had in mind. He welcomed the arrival of the missionaries and wanted to keep them all in his tribe. The Hermannsburg missionaries discussed this possibility, but arrived at the conclusion that they should split up. They conveyed the outcome of their discussions to Setshele, and he eventually agreed with them. He then gave them the advice to station some of them with his friend, Sechulathebe, who resided along the Ngami River in Zimbabwe. The Hermannsburg missionaries gladly accepted this proposal. They prepared for a long journey through desert-like, arid land.

While they were making preparations, a Boer stopped over to rest. He had returned from an elephant hunt in Zimbabwe and wanted to adjourn for a while in Dithejane. The missionaries were familiar with this hunter. His name was Jan Viljoen, and he came from the Transvaal. They had encountered him on their journey to Dithejane. Viljoen advised the missionaries not to embark on the arduous journey to the north, but to first have a look around in their own area. Zimmermann writes that he told them "to not overlook the tribes nearby".[119] Viljoen recommended that they should call on the Bahurutshe. This idea appealed to them, especially since they had already met the chief of the Bahurutshe, Moiloa II, on a previous occasion, the details of which will be gone into again later. F. Zimmermann was designated to undertake an exploratory trip to the Bahurutshe.

Zimmermann set out for Dinokana: "… accordingly, I was despatched in Oct. (1858, HB) to travel back to the land of the Boers and look for a suitable site amongst a larger tribe."[120] He presented the request of the Her-

[117] Voges, in Lüdemann, p. 239.

[118] Zimmermann, 1874 p. 1; Bammann 2004 p. 39.

[119] Zimmermann 1874 p. 1

[120] Loco citato – "… ward ich demgemäß im Oct. ausgesandt, um nach dem Wege rück-

mannsburg missionaries to the Bahurutshe. The reply was long in coming, however. An immediate response was out of the question anyhow, since the chief was obliged to summon the tribe for a decision of this nature. It could take several days for the tribe to rule on the matter. Zimmermann decided to spend the time of waiting on Viljoen's farm.

The farm bordered on the territory of the Bahurutshe. It took him four hours to reach the farm, and he stayed for two days.[121] Viljoen loaned him a horse for the way back. Zimmermann had never ridden on a horse before and had his misgivings about surviving unharmed. But the horse was well-behaved and the trip went well. The Bahurutshe gave him a warm welcome and invited him to attend the meeting of their council of elders. His linguistic skills were however not adequate enough for him to understand more than just a few words.

Meanwhile, a number of foreigners from other tribes had settled at Dinokana. They were granted permission to also attend the tribal council meeting. Amongst the foreigners was a teacher who gave private lessons, as well as "several Hottentots who were able to speak some Dutch".[122] These people tried to translate the essence of what was being said in *Setswana* into Dutch (Boer language = Afrikaans). Zimmermann observed the speakers who were present. Not all of them were in favour of his plans to reside with them, but the majority must have nonetheless been in favour thereof. One old man in particular caught his attention "... who illustrated his recommendation very vividly with metaphors and parables, the way the Batswana love to speak in metaphors anyhow and also have a special talent in doing so".[123] After the long speech had been concluded, the chief gave a summary of what Zimmermann had hoped for, namely that he would be welcome. Chief Moiloa II went on to say, as Zimmermann noted, that he should be "... his (the chief's, HB) and the people's teacher, with the request that I would never leave them again for as long as I lived, as other teachers were always wont to do, leaving again straightaway. Moiloa II spoke from

wärts nach dem Baurelande nach einem passenden Platz bei einem größeren Volke zu suchen".

121 Loco citato.

122 Zimmermann 1874 p. 2 – "... etliche Hottentotten, die etwas Holländisch sprechen konnten".

123 Loco citato – "... der seine Empfehlung sehr lebhaft in Bildern und Gleichnissen deutlich machte, wie denn die Betschuanen überhaupt gerne in Bildern zu sprechen lieben und darin auch eine besondere Gabe besitzen".

experience, seeing that his, Setshele's, Moseleli's and other chiefs' British teachers had soon left again."[124]

This quote from Zimmermann's report, written in 1874, leads to the assumption that he was privy to more information at that time than in 1858, when he heard these words from Moiloa II during the tribal council. When Zimmermann lists "Setshele's, Moseleli's and other chiefs' British teachers" who had worked amongst the Batswana, he means British missionaries like Inglis, Edwards, Livingstone and others. Zimmermann is referring to British missionaries in general, who had left not only the Bahurutshe, but the Batswana with their various tribes as a whole. Moiloa II, on the other hand, was better informed about all the teachers[125] who had tried to preach the gospel in his tribe, even though he will probably not have been personally acquainted with all of them. He had become acquainted with the Paris missionaries as well as the British missionary Inglis, but he never met the American missionaries. The latter were working at Mosega when he had fled with his tribe to Taung, where he had subsequently resided for several years. Moiloa II however had additional information of which Zimmermann had received no knowledge.

When the Boer commando had taken Inglis and Edwards away to Potchefstroom, the British mission was reluctant to cease its work amongst the Bahurutshe unconditionally. It had already trained Africans to be evangelists, amongst them a Mohurutshe by the name of Paul. The British mission sent him to Dinokana. Paul belonged "... to a small group of Bahurutshe who had fled to Kuruman in the 1820s."[126]

Paul was not the only Mohurutshe who had been deployed as evangelist by the British mission. Other Bahurutshe who had also been separated from the main tribe had been baptised by the British and subsequently been appointed as preachers: "John Mogwere ... was a Mohurutshe, separated from his people by attacks during the Difaquane."[127] Another Mohurutshe

---

[124] Loco citato – "... sein und seines Volkes Lehrer, mit der Bitte, sie nie wieder zu verlassen, solange ich lebe, wie andere Lehrer immer thäten und sobald wieder davon zögen. Moiloa sprach aus eigener Erfahrung, da sein, Setchelis, Moselelis, und anderer Häuptlinge englische Lehrer bald wieder davon gegangen waren."

[125] In 19th-century Setswana, "teacher" and "missionary" had the same meaning. They were both called *moruti.* These days they are separate terms. There is no Setswana word for 'pastor = minister, religious counsellor'. The pastor is the *moruti,* one who teaches or instructs, and a teacher is a *moruta-bana.* He teaches the children.

[126] Volz, p. 167.

[127] Ibid, p. 149.

was Paul's brother *Mebalwe:* "While Mebalwe spent a total of about twelve years at interior missions before returning to Kuruman, his brother Paulo devoted most of the last thirty years of his life starting new congregations among various northern Tswana groups."[128] The two brothers had been baptised by the British missionaries and trained as evangelists by the London Mission Society. They were deployed in Kuruman. Of the two, Paul served the longest period of time.

Paul remained in the service of the British mission society for about thirty years. Amongst his various assignments was also a three-year service with the Bahurutshe after Inglis was no longer located there. Volz writes: "Paul ... in early 1854 accepted an invitation from *kgosi* Moiloa to teach the Bahurutshe at Pooe."[129] Moiloa II was also referring to this relatively short deployment when he spoke to Zimmermann about the teachers who continuously left the Bahurutshe. Of course Zimmermann could not have any knowledge of this. He had not been told anything about Paul's work in Dinokana, even though it had only happened fairly recently. Paul was in Dinokana from 1854 to 1857. The Bahurutshe wanted a teacher who would stay with them for the rest of his life, who instructed them and preached the gospel to them. Moiloa II had expressed this clearly in his discussion with Zimmermann: He should not leave them for as long as he lived.

Moiloa II's invitation spoke exactly to the way he felt. Louis Harms had sent out his missionaries with the stipulation that they should not return to Germany. Now an offer of life-long service had just been made to him by an African chief. That suited him well. After the tribal council had come to an end, Moiloa II took Zimmermann to the place where Inglis had lived. A tumbled-down "pole hut" with a grass thatch could still be seen. Zimmermann was content. He travelled back to Dithejane via Viljoen once again, feeling "... thankful towards my Lord and God".[130]

Zimmermann's report of his encounter with the Bahurutshe and their consent to take up his services was received favourably by the missionaries in Dithejane. He had probably also mentioned in Dinokana that, upon his return to the Bahurutshe, he would bring other missionaries along as well. On 3 January 1859 F. Zimmermann, Chr. Schulenburg and colonist Meyer left Dithejane with eleven shillings in their communal cashbox. They

128 Ibid, p. 169.
129 Ibid, p. 172.
130 Zimmermann 1874 p. 3. – "... dankbar gegen meinen Gott und Herrn".

reached Dinokana on 7 January 1859.[131] Referring to their eleven shillings, Zimmermann observes: "We lived very austerely. We had no cow; our nourishment consisted almost exclusively of black coffee and dry bread, meat on rare occasions."[132] After the missionaries had arrived in Dinokana, they immediately began laying out a garden. Water was available for the garden. Their piece of land was situated next to a small stream, outside the settlement area of the Bahurutshe.

During this pioneer period the missionaries did not reside in the villages.[133] The tribes with their traditional belief systems would frequently settle them on the village peripheries. Dinokana followed suit, even if the reason was a different one in this case. It had started with Inglis, who had been able to select a place since there was no resident chief at that time. As peripheral residents, the missionaries received the name *batswantle* from the Batswana, meaning people (humans) who live outside. This emphasises the fact that they also spoke about them in an impersonal manner.

The Bahurutshe eventually also moved there, and Moiloa II settled his tribe in close vicinity to the mission station.

The Hermannsburg missionaries had moved during the South African summer months. The summer was hot. After the heat had subsided, Zimmermann and Meyer began with the construction of a house.[134] They didn't construct a house similar to the African round huts but rather a European-style rectangular one – and a big one at that. The missionaries and the colonist were unmarried. Louis Harms was of the opinion that missionaries had to stay single in order to be of better missionary service to the Africans. An expectation existed in Dinokana that more single men would move up presently. It is for this reason that a house with eight single rooms was constructed. Louis Harms' notion of this Hermannsburg "Communism" of single missionaries living together, sharing a household and representing the beginnings of a Christian fellowship in a pagan country had to be aban-

[131] Loco citato.

[132] Loco citato – "Wir lebten sehr dürftig. Wir hatten keine Kuh; schwarzer Kaffee und trockenes Brot, sehr selten Fleisch, war unsere fast ausschließliche Nahrung."

[133] Motswedi, Maanoane, Pella, Mahanaim, Phokeng, Hebron, Phalane and other erstwhile mission stations also bear witness to this fact.

[134] Schulenburg was no longer around to help. The Bangwato had asked Schröder to send them a missionary. Schulenburg had heeded that call. Zimmermann 1874 p. 6.

The missionary house
Constructed in the style of early Hermannsburg Communism

doned only a few years after his death.[135] This stipulation did not prove to be worthwhile beyond the first years of its implementation.

In Dinokana, the colonist Meyer later bade farewell to the missionaries over there. When Thomas Jensen replaced Zimmermann in Dinokana after four years, he reduced the size of the missionary house from eight rooms to four.[136]

135 Schröder writes: "The end of our bachelor existence – During the month of October in 1856 the long-awaited 'Kandaze' came into the harbour of this country again (Durban, KZN, HB). Amongst others, the ship presented the Brothers – with female assistance. The 'Golden Age of Bachelorhood' thereby came to an end, never to return again. The combined wedding celebration took place on 25.11.1856." – "Ende des Junggesellenlebens – Im Monat Oktober des Jahres 1856 kam die ersehnte 'Kandaze' wieder in den Hafen dieses Landes. Die brachte den Brüdern – auch weibliche Hilfe. Das 'goldene Zeitalter des Junggesellenlebens' hörte damit auf und ist nie wieder zurückgekehrt. Der 25.11.1856 war der gemeinschaftliche Hochzeitstag." Schroeder, p. 71.

136 Thomas Jensen 1874 p. 20.

Zimmermann began his work in Dinokana by erecting a school. Seeing that he had an inadequate understanding of the language, however, he proceeded to appoint one of the Batswana who had moved there from Kuruman, who had already been baptised by and received instruction from Moffat. The name of this Motswana was *Sehuneloa.* More will be said about him regarding Thomas Jensen.

As opposed to Paul, Sehuneloa had not become an evangelist after his baptism. It is unlikely that Sehuneloa was a Mohurutshe who had returned from Kuruman to his tribe of the Bahurutshe. There was probably another reason why he had chosen to move to Dinokana. Sehuneloa initially gave instruction by himself, under Zimmermann's guidance. Later, after his knowledge of the language had sufficiently improved, Zimmermann himself also gave instruction.

Meanwhile, Zimmermann maintained a good relationship with Moiloa II. He regularly attended the tribal council meetings, thereby not only learning Setswana from the mouths of the local people, but also learning about their socio-cultural behaviour, and, in the hearings of the court, the laws, penalties and taboos of the Batswana. Commenting on Moiloa II's invitation to attend the tribal council meetings, he later wrote: "I have subsequently taken part in many a tribal council meeting and was always awarded my place amongst the elders next to the chief."[137] About Moiloa II he decreed: "He had an amiable disposition and good judgement".[138]

School was initially conducted out in the open. When Zimmermann began to be more proficient in the language and could start to hold church services, he constructed the first congregational building. It was a dual-purpose building which was utilised as church on Sundays and as school during the rest of the week. Because he endeavoured to get closer to the people he erected this thatch house amongst the Bahurutshe and not on the mission station. The majority of the Bahurutshe, still out of fear of the Boers, continued to live on the *Pooe* Mountain. However, a few had meanwhile moved to the foot of the mountain. He found a site in their midst where he erected the large thatched building. The construction was supported by sturdy poles. The house was said to have been able to accommodate a large number of people, provided protection from rain, wind and sun. Just as he had done with Inglis, Moiloa II now regularly attended Zimmermann's church ser-

137 Zimmermann 1874 p. 3.

138 Loco citato, p. 13. – "Er hatte ein gutes Gemüt und viel Verstand."

vices. Thomas Jensen called this building a church even though it was not discernible as such, seeing that it had neither an altar nor a pulpit as visible church features. No watch was kept on the church in the village. There are no reports from Zimmermann dating from Dinokana, and therefore one can only surmise that he feared acts of vandalism from the traditional believers, and therefore did not put up an altar and a pulpit. Thomas Jensen, to whom the building did not appeal to for a number of reasons, describes the church as follows: "The church is a very poorly one, it is a pile building with the walls having collapsed in places. It is so big that surely around 300 people have room inside."[139]

The good cooperation between Moiloa II and Zimmermann once led to the circumstance that they both received a citation to appear in court. They had been summoned to the Supreme Court of the Boers in Potchefstroom. The reason for this was Zimmermann's criticism of the Boers' harsh treatment of their labourers. Many Bahurutshe men were employed a farm hands by the Boers. The Boers ruled the land after they had repulsed Mzilikazi. They were in need of workers on their fields. If the Africans did not do this willingly, they were compelled to do so by force. If their performance did not live up to expectations the men were beaten, in some cases extremely brutally. The duress under which the Boers placed the workers, as well as the severe punishments were abhorrent to Zimmermann. He admonished them on this behaviour and lodged a complaint with the Boer landowners. The Boers were not amused. Manson writes: "In 1860 Zimmermann mounted resistance … to the compulsory labour system".[140] Zimmermann comments on the inhumane treatment by the Boers, adding his own perspective when he writes: "The Boers … despise the black people, take pleasure in their ignorance and abuse and deceive them in all kinds of ways. (…) Because the missionary educates the black people, thereby awakening their intellect and leading them to an understanding of themselves … these people observe this with great chagrin … ."[141] Zimmermann not only registered his protest with the Boers. He also encouraged the Africans not to put up with the Boers' behaviour and to become aware of their own dignity.

139 Thomas Jensen 04.08.1864 p. 3.

140 Manson 1990 p. 143.

141 Zimmermann 1874 p. 17. – "Die Buren … verachten die Schwarzen, freuen sich ihrer Dummheit und missbrauchen und betrügen sie auf alle Weise. (…) Weil der Missionar die Schwarzen lehrt, dadurch ihren Verstand weckt und sie zum Bewusstsein ihrer selbst (hinführt, HB) … das sehen diese Leute mit Grimm."

The Boers were of the opinion that they were justified in their conduct. Africans had to be educated with harshness. They would therefore not tolerate Zimmermann's criticism. He refused to back down, however. Several court cases ensued. Zimmermann had the following to say: "I had the good fortune to have appeared before their court several times. On one occasion in earnest."[142] He goes on to describe this dramatic case in a packed courtroom in Potchefstroom, which turned out to be the last. "It was in 1860 that several Boers took me to court, amongst them a field cornet (District Administrator). (…) The chief and I were summoned to appear in the capital, and with great haste at that. Our case came up. The entire hall was filled with officials, and even the President … the District Administrator, and the commander of the region sat at the green table; our accusers were also present. The inquiry went on for hours, but the accusations lacked evidence. The whole denunciation was one of malice and enmity."[143] After several hours, when the charge failed to produce a successful outcome, the President, in his capacity as counsel for the accusers, was the first to leave the court, followed by all the others. The only people left were Zimmermann and Moiloa II. A court decision was never handed down. The hall was totally deserted. This episode in court was a lesson to the Boers. They had to concede that the missionary had asserted himself. No further charges were brought against Zimmermann in Dinokana.

Zimmermann did good work in Dinokana. Unfortunately, structural changes within the Hermannsburg Mission Society had some unpleasant consequences for him. He was forced to abandon his work in Dinokana after four years. Once again Moiloa II, and the Bahurutshe with him, were disappointed; they had placed great trust in him. As far as the various mission attempts within their ranks was concerned, this proved to be their last disappointment, however. What had led to the termination of Zimmermann's service in Dinokana?

---

[142] Zimmermann 1874 p. 17 – "Ich habe das Glück gehabt mehrere Male von Ihnen vor Gericht verklagt zu werden. Das eine Mal sehr ernstlich."

[143] Loco citato – "Es war im Jahre 1860, als eine Anzahl Bauern, unter ihnen ein Feldcornet (Landrat), mich bei der Regierung verklagten. (…) Ich ward mit dem Häuptling nach der Hauptstadt zitiert, und das sehr eilig. Wir kamen vor. Der ganze Saal war voll Beamte, und auch der Präsident, … der Landrat und der Commandant des Ortes saßen am grünen Tisch; unsere Verkläger waren auch da. Stundenlang hielt die Untersuchung an, aber es fehlten für die Klagen die Beweise. Die ganze Denunciation war eine Art der Bosheit und Feindschaft."

Louis Harms, the founder of the Hermannsburg Mission Society in the Lüneburg Heath was the pastor of the local congregation, which kept him fully occupied in itself. Over and above that, the revivalist movement had increasingly gained ground. After the mission centre had been established in 1849 and the first missionaries had been sent out, Harms' workload, assistance and responsibilities had taken on such proportions that it was impossible for a single person to take care of it all.[144] A division of responsibilities was therefore agreed upon. The majority of missionaries had been deployed in South Africa and Louis Harms wanted to cede the responsibility of this division. He found a capable missionary for this position who had been in Borneo/Kalamanta in Malaysia for nineteen years. His name was August Hardeland.

Harms appointed Hardeland as superintendent of the Hermannsburg missionaries in South Africa. He took up residence in Natal. His leadership style was rather authoritarian. Whoever failed to comply with his directives had to face the consequences. The missionaries in the Transvaal were a thousand kilometres away. Modern means of communication were non-existent in those days, and the news that Hardeland was now their superintendent had not reached them in the Transvaal.

When they reached the first directives from Hardeland they refused to submit to them. This induced the superintendent to take an immediate, extreme decision. He removed all the missionaries from office who had failed to submit to his directives. Zimmermann was amongst those who were dismissed. Consequently, Zimmermann was compelled to leave Dinokana. Negotiations and discussions were not an option. Hardeland did also not take into account the valuable groundwork done by the missionaries whereby they had already gained a great deal of trust from the local people. He had enough other missionaries at his disposal. The work done by the pioneer missionaries was not acknowledged. They could be summarily dismissed and replaced. If Hardeland had not had substitute missionaries at his disposal, he might not have ordered the immediate dismissal of the Transvaal missionaries.

After an initial period of resistance, Zimmermann resigned himself to Hardeland's punishment. He was suspended from his duties for one year

[144] Everything that is nowadays managed by over 50 staff members at the headquarters of the Hermannsburg Mission Society rested on the shoulders of a single man in those days.

and subsequently redeployed in the mission society; he was however not allowed to return to Dinokana. He was replaced by Thomas Jensen. Both lived together at Dinokana for three months and Zimmermann acquainted Jensen with his work without any reservation before handing the station over to him. Thomas Jensen remained at Dinokana for the rest of his life, and is also buried there.

2 Dinokana

2.1 The Bahurutshe and Dinokana

The Bahurutshe not only lived off their livestock, their gardens and hunting. They also cultivated the land and had a reputation for being a prosperous and industrious people. Two reports attest to that. Moffat, who had undertaken yet another exploratory journey, drove past the fields of the Bahurutshe near Mosega. He was taken aback by the vastness of their agricultural lands. "We passed over a considerable space of the country in the vicinity of Mosega and everyone was surprised at the immense cornfields."[145] The second report is by Zimmermann. He makes his observations about the Bahurutshe twenty years after Moffat. Moffat made his observations when the Bahurutshe were still living in Mosega, whereas Zimmermann observes them in Dinokana. He draws the same conclusions in his own way. "The Bahurutsi are generally wealthy, in some cases even rich, because they do a great deal of agriculture apart from their animal husbandry. They are one of the most industrious of the Betshuana tribes."[146] Compared to other Batswana he thereby rates the Bahurutshe as being particularly industrious.

Is this prosperity that is attested to by both reports also in evidence at all as far as their building culture or their livestock are concerned? One is not able to answer this question in the affirmative. The way in which they constructed their houses and homesteads, as well as the size of their livestock was definitely in line with what other tribes had to show. One can however assume that the Bahurutshe had more food and were able to tide themselves over periods of drought more efficiently than their neighbouring tribes.

Today Dinokana is a large town, due to the by now large number of inhabitants. It assumed a typical African structure with numerous rondavels (round huts) and front yards. European influences cannot be discerned. The head of every family built his house on a site that he had selected himself. His choice of site had to be approved by the chief, however. Then as

[145] In Wallis, p. 67.

[146] Zimmermann 1874 p. 8 – "Die Baharutsi sind im Allgemeinen vermögend, zum Theil gar reich, weil sie neben der Viehzucht viel Ackerbau betreiben. Sie sind eins der arbeitsamsten Völker der Betshuanen."

now, the site in the centre of town is reserved for the chief. The huts of the petty chiefs are close to his site. It was only later that the various families constructed houses from clay- or cement bricks next to their huts. Situated directly in front of the present-day massive town council building with its offices is the *lekgotla,*[147] the erstwhile public gathering place. Tribal meetings still take place there. In the town itself many of the original rondavels have been preserved. On the homesteads the door of the main house always faced the tribal gathering place. The door was always open. If a message was proclaimed from the tribal gathering place it could be heard in all the rondavels.

The town is protracted into its length rather than its width. A road that connects Zeerust in South Africa with Lobatse in Botswana goes through the town. In the old days, when the settlement was laid out 160 years ago, many people preferred to build their dwellings next to the road. The settlement is situated in a fertile valley at the foot of the Magaliesberg Mountain. This mountain range stretches from the east of Pretoria through to Botswana. The Bahurutshe adopted one of the mountain springs as their own. The previously mentioned Pooe Mountain is an individual mountain situated opposite the Magaliesberg Mountains. Ever since the Bahurutshe came down the Pooe Mountain and moved into the valley – something Thomas Jensen will still report on at a later stage – they utilised the spring water. They channelled it to their houses, gardens and fields with canals that they had constructed themselves. It is possible that they had adopted this canal system from the Boers, whom they had encountered in the Taung area during their previous migration.

The etymological explanation for the name Dinokana has to do with water. Dinokana means "little rivers". If one should dissect the word, the prefix *di* denotes the plural. The root word *noka* in its singular form means river, and *ana* suffixed to a noun turns it into the diminutive. Zimmermann writes: "Before Br. Schulenburg left we discussed a name for our station, and named it Linokana.[148] (…) The stretch of land behind the mountain range on the left is hundreds of feet higher than the Linokana valley, this probably being the reason that the mountain range has so many springs that

[147] Daily meetings took place in the *lekgotla.* A large tribe has always something to discuss. These are often complaints that are dealt with by the men. In the old days, women did not participate in the tribal councils. The petty chiefs' input is valued higher than that of other men. After a lengthy discussion the chief pronounces his irrevocable verdict.

[148] A linguistic, orthographic development turned 'Linokana' into 'Dinokana', for instance.

provide such a vast amount of wonderful water, making the whole valley with its good farmland so rich and fertile, this being the reason why the locals refer to this mountain range as Linokana … below Linokana all rivulets and furrows converge into one river that is about half the size of the River Oertze near Hermannsburg."[149] We learn from Zimmermann that the Bahurutshe had already chosen the name "Dinokana". The missionaries call their mission station Dinokana as well, seeing that it is situated about a kilometre from where the tribe resides. Inglis had still called it Mathebe. The entire region was, over and above the settlement and the mission station, sometimes referred to by this name. Louis Harms had read Zimmermann's bi-annual reports. Summarising, he writes in the *Hermannsburger Missionsblatt* (Hermannsburg Mission Journal): "There is good water available over there, flowing through the valley by several conduits. We can therefore see that the Bahurutse already know how to make use of water conduits."[150]

Zimmermann's successor Thomas Jensen mentioned the name of the stream into which all the canals and smaller rivulets enter. He also mentions that Inglis did not refer to the station as Dinokana, but rather as *Mathebe,* after the stream. "The British called this station Mathebe after the stream … I was unable to ascertain why the stream has this name."[151] Inglis himself was also not able to provide an explanation for the name of the stream. He thought that the Boers had come up with this name. "Mathebe is the name of the stream, hence the place is usually called Mathebe by the Boers."[152] Neither Inglis nor Jensen had an explanation for the name Mathebe. Köller, another Hermannsburg missionary, was also at a loss as to an interpretation of the meaning of the name. It is surprising that there is no explanation for the term "Mathebe". It is also out of the question that Mathebe is a loanword that was integrated into Setswana.[153] Seeing that the Bahurutshe not

149 Zimmermann 1874 p. 6f.

150 *Herrmannsburger Missionsblatt* 1864 No.7, p. 99.

151 Thomas Jensen 1874 p. 1. – "Die Engländer nannten diese Station Mathebe nach dem Fluss … Warum der Fluss so heißt, habe ich nicht erfahren können."

152 Inglis report 06.09.1849 p. 2.

153 Nowadays, if one asks the Bahurutshe for an explanation, they also have no answer. A possible explanation would be the following: Mathebe can be linked to Mzilikazi's soldiers. *Thebe* =shield. *Lesole* = soldier, *masole* = soldiers. *'le'* and *'ma'* are prefixes that can, as an exception, allow for an inversion in linguistic constructs. Even though the soldiers were deemed to be intruders they were nonetheless part of the country's rulers. When they washed themselves in the stream, cleaning their shields, they were

only resided at Dinokana – many families had settled on the peripheries as well – Köller moved to where those people lived. He named his station Mathebe, in contradistinction to Dinokana. "This is therefore a secondary station which I call Mathebe (after a stream that flows close by)."[154]

Compared to other tribes like the Zulu people in Natal, for instance, the Batswana did not live together in family clans but rather in villages. A number of authors refer to large settlements like Dinokana as being cities. But they cannot in any way be compared in to European cities that are enclosed by city walls and boast double-storey houses. The difference can be clearly demonstrated by taking the Bahurutshe as an example.

The main tribe remained an undivided entity throughout its migrations, with the chief as their ruler. We see their large settlements at Ga-Ditshwene, Mosega and Taung, and finally in Dinokana. That is where the migrations of the Bahurutshe came to an end. The civil wars were over and Mzilikazi had been banished. The Bahurutshe were united once again. The tribe comprised those who had not been part of the migrations, as well as the main tribe with its two chiefs who had fled before a possible subjugation by Mzilikazi. Zimmermann estimated their numbers to be as follows: "10,000 souls is not too high an estimate, not counting their relatives who reside elsewhere and are just as multitudinous.[155] Around the middle of the 19th century, "10,000 souls" constituted a quite considerable crowd. What does Zimmermann mean when he refers to the "relatives who reside elsewhere"? One can assume that the Bahurutshe, during their tribal assemblies, told him about their relatives who had stayed behind on the various stations along the way. The implication of this would be that he could not possibly estimate the numbers of all those Bahurutshe who had been assimilated into other tribes.

The Bahurutshe had always extended a welcome to the large number of missionaries who passed them in transit, they had never turned away a missionary. All missionaries had been important to the tribe. They were open to the new challenges that the missionaries brought with them. The Paris missionaries had their first attempt at Mosega. Then the Americans came and took over the ruins of the French. Both groups lived amongst the Bahurutshe, the Paris missionaries when the tribe still had a chief, the

observed by the local people; thus the configuration *masole* and *dithebe* could have been converged to *Mathebe*. The stream thus received its name from the foreigners.

154 Köller 04.06.1871 p. 2.

155 Zimmermann 1874 p. 9.

Americans during the time when it was leaderless. The time spent by both groups was too short, however, for them to begin with the task with which they had been sent there: to do mission work. Then Inglis came. He didn't need permission to proclaim the gospel. Mzilikazi had moved away and Moiloa II had not arrived yet. Inglis gathered the foreigners and Bahurutshe families who lived scattered in the area. He held the first church services in the tribal territory of the Bahurutshe. He was therefore the first missionary who preached the gospel on Dinokana's soil. Inglis did however also not perform any baptisms.

While the Bahurutshe resided at Rabogadi and Ga-Ditshwene, the first Boers settled at Mosega. After the move from Ga-Ditshwene had been contemplated, Moiloa II knew that he could not move back to Mosega. He found a new place to stay not far from Inglis, a site he had been allocated by the Boers, about twenty kilometres to the east of Mosega. The entire area where Inglis and Moiloa II had settled was later called Dinokana. After Inglis came Zimmermann, a Hermannsburg missionary, and it was he who performed the first baptisms on 27 November 1859.[156]

The Bahurutshe settled down in Dinokana. The fact that they stayed there for ever was not due to the influence of the missionaries, but rather due to the Boers, and this for two reasons. The Boers arrived as conquerors and colonists. They were European and had a European mind-set. They distributed the land they had invaded amongst themselves, calling the individual pieces of land "plots". These plots could be privately purchased. The British called these plots "farms". These distributions of land, be they called plots or farms, and the transition to private property were completely alien concepts to the Bahurutshe. In the minds of the Batswana, all land on which their ancestors had already migrated from one place to the next belonged to the tribe, with the chief as its head. The Boers did not concern themselves with this notion, they transferred European conditions onto the African territories they had invaded. The Boers were of the opinion that they had rid the region of Mzilikazi's oppression, therefore it now belonged to them. The control of the region remained in their hands, thinking that they were thereby doing the Batswana a favour. Instead they have deprived the Batswana people of their land.

After twenty years of Boer rule the Hermannsburg missionaries came

[156] Cf. the baptisms listed in the first baptismal register of the Dinokana congregation. Their names will be mentioned later.

to the Bahurutshe. Even though they were not able to bring about a fundamental change in the political situation, they contributed their share towards the moral support of the Bahurutshe in their struggle for freedom and individual rights, the best example of which is offered by Zimmermann.

2.2 Chieftainship and Chiefs, with particular reference to Moiloa II

When the first Hermannsburg missionaries were on their way to Botswana they also travelled past Dinokana, without any stopover, however. They only had a rest and pitched their tents for the night shortly after Dinokana. While driving through Dinokana, Dorothea Schröder had taken a look at the settlement. She saw the rondavels and observed the people who had come onto the road in their traditional clothing. She wrote down some of her observations. She sent her letters to relatives, one of which has been preserved in which she also mentions Moiloa II. He had received word that Europeans had passed through his settlement and had camped out for the night outside of town. The Hermannsburg missionaries had not deemed it necessary to pay Moiloa II a visit. The chief for his part was however interested in the European passers-by.

The following morning Moiloa II paid the Hermannsburg missionaries a visit. Dorothea Schröder writes: "On the evening of the 10th (of July 1857, HB) … we arrived at the great chief Mohilo. (…) We drove straight through the populous settlement. (…) On the 11th the chief himself arrived also. He was well-dressed and looked like a Boer. (…) This is a wonderful place to do mission work. Mohilo stayed and drank coffee with us, and when we held our morning devotion he voluntarily knelt down with us."[157] This quote contains various pieces of information.

When D. Schröder writes: "We drove straight through the populous settlement" she not only refers to the fact that the Bahurutshe were a large tribe. We can also gather from her description that the tribe no longer lived

[157] In Schütte, p. 157 – "Am 10. (Juli 1857, HB) … kamen wir abends bei dem großen Häuptling Mohilo an. (…) Wir fuhren mitten durch den volkreichen Ort. (…) Den 11. Kam den auch der Häuptling selber. Der war gut gekleidet und sah aus wie ein Bauer. (…) Ein sehr schöner Missionsplatz ist dieser Ort. Mohilo blieb bei uns und trank Kaffee mit uns, und als wir unsere Morgenandacht hielten, kniete er freiwillig mit uns nieder."

a closed existence on the Pooe Mountain, therefore no longer fearing a further attack by the Boers. Several families had already moved into the valley and had begun growing. The wish uttered in the words: "… a wonderful place to do mission work" was to come true at a later stage. The call to the Hermannsburg missionaries had gone out from Setshele. Her wish could therefore not be granted as yet. She points out that Moiloa II visited them in the morning. The small missionary family shared its breakfast with him and they prayed together.[158] Mrs Schröder goes on to say that Moiloa II was not clothed like a traditional tribesman, neither was his demeanour that of a traditional believer. He had discarded his leather apron and had adopted the Boers' way of dressing like civilised people do. And that he knelt down with them is testament to the fact that he was aware of the Christian message and was open-minded about it. At that time the missionaries were totally unaware of all the other mission societies who had already attempted to find their way into the Bahurutshe tribe, and who had abandoned their attempts.

Moiloa II's visit with the Hermannsburg missionaries is indicative of the fact that he had now finally taken over tribal reign. Mokgatlhe is no longer in the picture. There is another point that is mentioned and that speaks for Moiloa II. Normally a chief will not visit strangers. He sends tribal delegates who find out and report what has happened and, in this case, why the strangers have pitched their tents outside his settlement for the night. The personal encounter that took place between Moiloa II and the missionaries was not only because he needed to know about the things that went on in his tribal territory. He approaches them because he is sympathetic towards them. Maybe the Hermannsburg missionaries had, while passing through the settlement, announced themselves as missionaries. Moiloa II is interested in these missionaries, since he has previously had positive experiences with all the other missionaries. His appearance and demeanour where the missionaries are concerned leads one to the assumption that Moiloa II also had good leadership qualities as chief.

A chief *(kgosi)* is not elected. He succeeds his ancestors and rules his tribe *(morafe)* for as long as he lives. The tribe comprises families and extended families. The extended families are under the control of a petty

[158] The common prayer is a Hermannsburg prayer ritual, a custom that is practised to this day in Hermannsburg circles. The kneeling prayer as well as the mealtime prayer form part of Hermannsburg piety.

chief *(kgosana).* Men who have proven their natural leadership qualities over many years become petty chiefs. They, too, cannot be elected. They are appointed by the chief and are subject to him in all matters. Schapera writes: "The chief, however, is served by several different wards, whose original headmen were specially selected for their loyalty and their devotion."[159]

In the old days the clan members lived together as a unit on a site of their choosing. The clan size of a petty chief can be compared to that of a neighbourhood. These days, families can also belong to a petty chief who do not share a common ancestry with the other families. All petty chiefs, together with their own subjects, answer to the chief. The chief is the head of the petty chiefs and the entire tribe. The petty chiefs assist the chief with their families. The chief is where all the threads come together. He consults his people, he listens when the daily tribal- and council meetings in the *lekgotla*[160] take place. In the tribal councils, judicial cases are argued, socio-cultural concerns discussed and ceremonial matters of the tribe debated. All decisions are reached by consensus. If a matter has been debated long enough and at least each and every petty chief has had his say, the chief has the final word. In doing so, he takes all contributions made towards the issue at hand into appropriate consideration. His ruling is binding and cannot be reversed. When making his final ruling the chief has no recourse to any laws or ordinances or the like. There is no written code of law that he can refer to. The only help he can possibly get is from the orally transmitted traditions of his ancestors that he is able to recall.[161] The enforceability of his ruling rests solely on his authority.

In the Bahurutshe tribe Mokgatlhe had acted as temporary ruler. During the period of war and unrest Moiloa II had handed over regency to Mokgatlhe. And Mokgatlhe took no decisions without first having obtained

---

[159] Schapera 1976 p. 28.

[160] The *lekgotla* denotes the gathering place in this instance. When this term is used, context matters. When someone says: "The *lekgotla* has decided", it is not the gathering place that is referred to, but the gathering itself. Mulemfo substitutes *lekgotla,* meaning gathering, with 'palaver'. He writes: "A big gathering is convened to find ways and means to acknowledge or remedy the situation. Such big gathering is called palaver." – In Missionalia, Aug. 1996 p. 133.

[161] These days, even though it is deemed to be advantageous for a chief to have completed high school or obtained a diploma and occupational experience outside of the tribe, all this does not contribute towards the decision that he chooses to make. He must be a legitimate heir of royal lineage. Ultimately that is the only thing that counts.

Moiloa II's advice. Mokgatlhe is not listed in the genealogy of Bahurutshe chiefs as being a direct heir. According to Breutz there are five names of chiefs that the Bahurutshe can remember who feature amongst the Batswana before the great split. Their names are: *Mogale, Mhete, Melore, Masilo* and *Malope*[162] The question as to when they reigned and whether there were other chiefs that can be added to this list remains open. A great split ensued, dividing the Batswana into different tribes: *Bahurutshe, Bakwena, Bangwato* and others. After these splits the succession of Bahurutshe chiefs appears to have remained intact. Up to the time that the Hermannsburg missionaries arrived, Breutz lists the following chiefs: *Mohurutshe, Motebele, Motebyane, Melore II, Malope II, Mohurutshe II, Pule, Menoe, Thekiso, Tiroe, Moiloe I, Sebogodi* and Moiloa II.[163] Mokgatlhe was not included in this line of succession. Breutz only mentions him in passing. – Ferdinand Jensen, who will be dealt with in greater detail later, has compiled a genealogy of the Bahurutshe. According to his research the succession of Bahurutshe chiefs is as follows:[164]

The chief of a tribe was awarded great authority by his people. He was the most revered and powerful person in a tribe. Every imaginable function was united within his person. Over and above the rulings pertaining to human relations within the tribe, the priestly functions were also transferred to the chief. Nobody was permitted to work the fields, sow or harvest before the chief had not consulted the ancestors. They had to give their approval for all situations of life. Who had the authority to call on the ancestors? That could only be the person who held the highest office in their community, their chief.

If no rain fell in years of drought the chief had to take on the function of medicine man and attract rain with magical enactments. His father had taught him how to do this. The function of rainmaker was transferred to the heir apparent when he took over office from his father. Schapera writes: "In principle, the ruling chief was supposed to see that his heir learned how to make rain."[165] If the chief was successful in conjuring up rain he was deemed to be a powerful chief. If he was unsuccessful or if he failed in other important judicial functions he stood to lose his reputation and power. His people looked to him in all respects. Life was viewed in its entirety. The

[162] Breutz 1953 p. 123.

[163] Breutz 1953 p. 123f.

[164] Ferdinand Jensen, File B p. 60; cf. Breutz 1953 p. 123f; 142f, 1989 p. 299.

[165] Schapera 1871 p. 43.

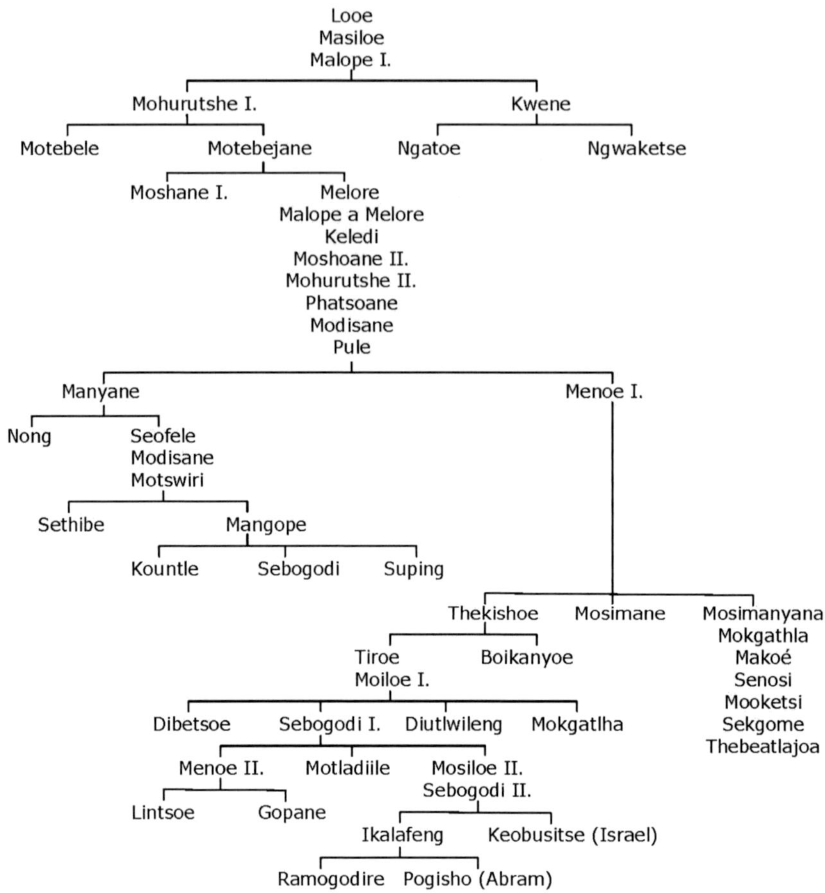

Genealogy of the Bahurutshe chiefs

purely mundane things and those of a spiritual nature were just inextricably linked with one another. Thus the chief was also responsible for the superordinate religious functions. Schapera once again: "Apart from worshipping their own ancestors, all members of the tribe acknowledged those of the chief as a source of welfare and prosperity … Hence on all important or critical occasions, he would sacrifice and pray to them on behalf of the tribe as a whole. The role he thus played as tribal priest … helps explain the great reverence with which he was regarded by his people."[166]

[166] Id., p. 60.

Pogiso II, Abraham Moiloa

One is able to discern from this quote that the tribal hierarchy was reflected in the world of their ancestors. Just as the petty chiefs accepted a subordinate role to the chief, the family ancestors of these petty chiefs did also not play any role in the tribal ceremonies. They did not feature whatsoever. The chief addressed his ritual offering exclusively to the tribal ancestors, and, in such superordinate matters, the Batswana awaited help from them alone.

The people revered their chief in various ways. When he held a speech at a large tribal gathering or at public festivities, someone would always step on the podium before him. The chief was praised in the preambles by addressing him with the tribal totem on the one hand, and by revering him with songs of praise made up of numerous strung-together proverbs on the other.

The tribal totem – possibly comparable to European flags or coat of arms – was usually a powerful animal. It symbolised a tribe's power. This tribal totem animal enjoyed special protection. It was forbidden to hunt or kill it. The Bahurutshe had originally revered the eland *(phofu)* as their tribal totem.[167] After that it was the baboon.

[167] Breutz 1953 p. 19.

Oral tradition regarding the baboon has the following story to tell: *Motebele* and *Motebeyane* were two brothers and descendants of Mohurutshe. Motebele, being the older one, was the ruler. Motebeyane caught a young baboon while herding the cattle. He took the little baboon to his brother, the chief, who commanded him to look after it and not to let it escape. One day, when Motebeyane was herding the cattle again, the baboon ran into the bushes and did not return. Motebeyane went and informed the chief. The chief was angry, scolded him and ordered his younger brother to be punished. A quarrel ensued between the two brothers, culminating in a war during which Motebeyane, together with his adherents, defeated chief Motebele. The largest part of the tribe allied itself with the victorious Motebeyane. Motebele was forced to flee.

Motebeyane's followers did not forget the root of the separation from Motebele. It was Tshwenyane, a "little baboon" who had brought about the tribal split. Since Motebeyane had come to power because of a quarrel about a baboon, he instituted the baboon as the new totem and named the new settlement to which he had meanwhile moved *"Tshwenyane"*, after the little baboon. "He adopted the baboon as totem and founded a new village at Tshwenyane … at some time between 1470 and 1520."[168] Breutz not only reports the historical tradition pertaining to this split that was caused by a little baboon, but also dates the first settlement of the Bahurutshe at Ga-Ditshwene to have been established around 1500.

The episode with Tshwenyane is said to have occurred outside of the familiar migration areas of the Bahurutshe, further to the north of Ga-Ditshwene in the proximity of the North-Sotho. The incident with the little baboon accompanied them on their migrations until the Bahurutshe settled in Ga-Ditshwene, where the name Tshwenyane was transferred to the new settlement and used as a new or an additional name. The renaming or additional naming occurred soon after the Bahurutshe had arrived. After the Bahurutshe had come across a countless multitude of baboons that they were unable to dislodge, they not only called the settlement Tshwenyane, but, due to the large baboon colonies, subsequently also "Ga-Ditshwene" = Dwelling of the Baboons. The name Tshwenyane was also retained as it had already been internalised. Today it is used synonymously for the Boer town of Enselsberg.

Boeyens is of the opinion that the correct name for Ga-Ditshwene is

[168] Id. Cf. Ferdinand Jensen: The Bahurutse, translated into English by M. Aalburds p. 2f.

Kaditshwene. "Kaditshwene is indeed the correct name and it is most probably derived by ellipsis from the idiomatic Tswana expression *Ga se ka ditshwene!* This can be translated roughly as 'what an incredible number of baboons'."[169] Boeyens' explanation might be open to scrutiny. There are other versions as well. One shouldn't be compelled to adopt the name Kaditshwene. The name Ga-Ditshwene can be equally substantiated.[170]

So the Bahurutshe revere the baboon. It was elevated to serve as tribal identification and, to this day, tribe members are forbidden to shoot it.[171] They not only revere their baboon during their orations on the chief, but also during special greetings. When the chief is present the main orator might address him as *motshwaneng,* which is equivalent to a nature-orientated declaration of solidarity. If the chief is not present during a larger ceremony, those gathered can be addressed with *batshwaneng.* Literally translated this means "dear baboons". This address is not seen as an affront in any way. It should be understood to mean "dear friends/dear Bahurutshe".[172]

When the chief's praises are sung in a preamble during a large gathering, as described above, this praise takes on many variations. The praise singer incorporates the line of ancestors. In doing so, a familiar ancestor who has done great deeds is mentioned by name.

In earlier times the chief was praised because he had slain wild animals with his spear. The praises of his heroic deeds that he had performed during times of war were also always sung. The vanquished enemy was mentioned by name as this underlined tribal pride. Breutz published four songs of praise for the chiefs Diutlwileng, Moiloa II, Gopane and Sebogodi. In the preface he writes: "Here follow the praise songs of some of the best-known Hurutshe chiefs and regents. The songs were collected by the Hermannsburg mission at Maanwane in 1906 and were translated by Levy

169 Boeyens in Langwieder/Scheepers p. 4.

170 The prefix *ka* has a linguistically instrumental meaning. The prefix *ga,* on the other hand, signifies locality. A noun with the prefix *ga,* in this instance the baboons, is therefore *Ga-Ditshwene* = Dwelling of the Baboons, or else possessory *ga tsone* = their places, which is synonymic with Dwelling of the Baboons.

171 I was repeatedly reminded by my neighbours that a baboon is revered and may not be shot under any circumstances, when I attempted to banish the 25-strong horde of baboons with my voice from my small maize garden in Motswedi.

172 The address *motshweneng* or *batshweneng* only applies to the Bahurutshe. It cannot be assigned to strangers. In some cases, missionaries who have lived amongst the Bahurutshe for a long time have been accepted into their oral culture. They will subsequently be welcomed with the baboon greeting at special events.

C. Moumakwa M.B.A."[173] The praise song *(loboko)* of Moiloa II shall serve as an example:

> *Thou mighty man with a thick stick,*
> *A man who carries a striped shield*
> *does not walk behind the people.*
> *He dashes in front with the shield,*
> *To show himself to his father Sebogodi*
> *who says: 'I did not beget a child (weakling, HB),*
> *I begot a hurricane, a storm wind on massive legs.'*
> *Spring to your feet: We shall give battle,*
> *The tribes east live in fear;*
> *For a long time they have tormented us.*
> *The cow has dropped her afterbirth before the enemies,*
> *The afterbirth which is Kontle and Mookotedi,*
> *Thou the mighty one of Maota, the son of Matswe,*
> *Who never eats in hidden places but in the open.*
> *Spear of Mogotlodise, the son of Sebogodi,*
> *How did the spear pierce the zebra?*
> *It struck and broke his spine.*[174]

The person reciting this praise song addresses his praise to Moiloa II, having the chief as a younger man in mind. Moiloa II had proven himself to be a hero in a civil war. That is being emphasised, and his leadership style alluded to. He is thereby in line with his ancestors centring on Sebogodi. The chiefs of neighbouring tribes, *Kontle* and *Mookedi* are portrayed as enemies. They are scornfully described as afterbirth.

We can gather from the following quote by Ferdinand Jensen that not only were the chiefs praised, but other heroes as well. "Praise was given to especially war heroes, but also men who had proven themselves to be particularly courageous and skilful when fighting off wild animals like lion, leopard and rhinoceros. (…) The victorious man deserved to be praised, and this was bestowed on him during the *dipoko* (plural of *loboko*, HB)."[175] Those days are gone. Huntable wildlife, as mentioned in the quote, no longer exists, neither are there civil wars. Nevertheless: the praise songs

---

173 Breutz 1953 pp. 28–35.

174 Id., p. 31.

175 Ferdinand Jensen 1929 p. 372. – "Gepriesen wurden vor allem Kriegshelden, aber auch Männer, die sich im Kampfe mit wilden Tieren, wie Löwe, Panther und Nashorn, als besonders tapfer und gewandt gezeigt hatten. (…) Der Sieger hatte Lob verdient und das wurde ihm in den *Dipoko* gespendet."

have survived to this day. However, the content now incorporates historical events, with an absence of contemporary relevance. Heroic deeds performed in dangerous situations hardly feature any more. The praise songs, along with the scores of proverbs, are amongst the first recorded literary works of the Bahurutshe.

Praise songs and proverbs have a history and continue to have their place in the modern-day life of the Batswana. They are often quoted in speeches and orations. Ferdinand Jensen was the first to compile a collection of the proverbs commonly used by the Bahurutshe. Initially there were only eighty-eight.[176] As regards content, they reveal something about their socio-cultural life. There are also a number of proverbs that arose from observing animal behaviour. They transfer latent animal behaviour onto that of humans. No. 31, for instance: *Mogogoro wa phuthi o tshosa phuduhudu* = The sound of the duiker alerts the steenbok. In other words: When one matter is exposed, others will appear. Most proverbs pertain to interpersonal relationships, for example No. 53: *Segoagoa se nwa metsi se itekanya le kgomo* = the frog drinks water and compares himself to the ox. In other words: It is not wise to have an exaggerated opinion of oneself. A small number of proverbs pertain to the chief. In Ferdinand Jensen's first collection, only three relate have reference to the chief, numbers 25, 35 and 88. No. 25: *Tiro ya kgosi e bolaya lesilo* = the chief's work/action kills the fool. Here, killing doesn't necessarily mean "ending someone's life", but rather: The chief will not give the obstinate dimwit a chance. No. 35: *Bana ba kgosi mono kana o sele, se kaeya baneng ba kgaoganya* = The chief's children become estranged to one another. No. 88: *Lentswe la kgosi le agelwa lesaka* = The chief's word emboldens the community. In other words: What the chief says is something positive/builds confidence. Numbers 25 and 88 attest to the chief's authority with regards to his people. Number 35 refers to his descendants who will not always stay loyal to the tribe. In subsequent years Ferdinand Jensen's collection grew to contain over six hundred proverbs.[177]

A chief had more children than the ordinary man. Polygamy was permitted amongst the Batswana, with prosperous men usually having more wives than ordinary men. Since the chief was the wealthiest man of the tribe he also had the most wives, something the tribe expressly desired. A

[176] Ferdinand Jensen, in Haccius 1913 p. 147; 152.

[177] Ferdinand Jensen, File D item 165–166; File E item 172; File F item 173.

love match was not on the cards for the chief. He married women from influential families, and a recommendation to that effect was almost always put forward by the tribal council. Such marital unions always gained him special sympathies and a great amount of respect from all sides. The possibility of oppositional influences by individuals who sought to harass or dethrone him was significantly smaller if he had a large number of wives from eminent families. His relatives by marriage would stand by him in critical situations. Moiloa II married eleven wives. Thomas Jensen gives their names, as well as the names of all his children.[178]

Kgosi Moiloa II's family:

1. Mojanku, no children
2. Lekgathunyana, with Gaborone, Mmanoaneng, Makgotha, Lesang, Tshose le Bogatsu
3. Kgetsing, no children
4. Phore, with Ramatu, Nkgabe le Gareoloele
5. Moroka, with Mosimanegape, Seamung, Seamunyaneng, Gaonakala, Sekaoarane, Makame, Phakedi le Matlale
6. Mmakgorapedi, with Mokgatle, Mokalekoma, Mogari, Sebe, Tshikamma, Kotane, Letlhaku le Mmamodibane
7. Kebotlhokile, with Thomas, Godirwang, Motswabatho, Malope, Ntutu le Mmoniemang
8. Mmapole, with Bogatsu le Ngwanyawatshipi
9. Dikeletsane, with Diutloileng, Matlapeng le Letlhoa
10. Kethibetsoe, no children
11. Sebokolodi, with Rratauagae

Christianity does not allow polygamy. All missionaries of the different denominations were in agreement about this matter. Moiloa II regulalarly attended the services of his missionaries. He heard the gospel and accepted it. He could not receive baptism, however, because he could not simply dismiss his wives and keep only one. Zimmermann discussed baptism with him, upon which he replied: "I believe in God and the Lord Jesus Christ, but how can I dismiss the mothers of all my children? They have all grown up with me. No, I cannot."[179] His decision was unequivocal and well-founded. He valued his wives and children. He had lived with them for so long.

[178] Thomas Jensen 04.08.1864 p. 2.
[179] Zimmermann, 1874 p. 13.

Where should they go? Back to their families? That would have caused great upheaval, leading only to discord and animosity. The chief, being far outnumbered by the traditional believers, would have been persecuted, chased away and poisoned. He was aware of all of that. He therefore opted for the unity of the tribe and a continued existence in polygamy. He was not the only one to do this, other chiefs, too, were reported to have done likewise.[180]

So Moiloa II remained unbaptised. He bore testimony to his Christian faith by other means, showing by his conduct that he had accepted the gospel of the redeeming Good News of Jesus Christ. The gospel had changed him. On previous occasions during tribal court cases he had, in severe cases, frequently pronounced the death penalty on the offender. The last two cases where he handed down the death penalty was when Thomas Jensen had already assumed his service at Dinokana. Thomas Jensen writes in 1866: "Since I arrived, Moiloa has for instance ordered two such preparers of poison[181] to be shot dead."[182] But then he had been overcome by the gospel. The condemned men were severely punished with beatings, but their life was spared.

In the Christian congregation, Moiloa II lent his support to the construction of the church building and the missionaries' school system. If tensions arose between Christians and traditional believers, he had a conciliatory influence. The first small group of Christians was not neglected in any way. Shortly before his death, and when he knew he was about to die, Moiloa II asked Thomas Jensen to see to it that he was not buried according to traditional custom. Thomas Jensen kept his promise.

---

180 The chief at Phokeng constituted an exception in this regard. Towards the end of his life the resident chief of the Bafokeng, Mokgatle, made a proposition to Chr. Penzhorn, the Hermannsburg missionary stationed in Phokeng, that he regard his wives as his children, thereby releasing them from their marital duties. The missionary accepted this rather strange proposal, and Mokgatle was baptised. Cf. Bammann 2010 p. 54f.

181 These preparers of poison were medicine men where poisonings resulting in death could be proven.

182 Thomas Jensen 28.06.1866, p. 2. – "Moiloa hat z.B. während ich hier bin, schon zwei solcher Giftmischer totschießen lassen."

Missionary Thomas Jensen (1829–1908)

Missionary Ferdinand Jensen (1871–1941)

3 The two Hermannsburg Missionaries Thomas and Ferdinand Jensen

3.1 Socio-cultural Knowledge

3.1.1 Language

Primarily there were three reasons why the Hermannsburg missionaries learnt the indigenous languages. The first reason had to do with the sending out of missionaries. Louis Harms sent them out for life, with no financial means to even visit their homeland again. So they had to proceed from the assumption that they would, for several decades, live in a language region that was foreign to them. The second reason was also directly linked to Hermannsburg. Hermannsburg was a small town on the heath, away from large cities. Most of the missionaries came from the rural area surrounding Hermannsburg. They received missionary training, initially for four, later for five, and eventually for seven years. The 19th century as a whole, and a rural area in particular, was characterised by authoritarian structures. To lead a rural life, to respect authoritarian structures, all this was particularly true for people living in Hermannsburg. And they found the existing conditions in Africa with their chief-oriented social order to be similar to those in their homeland. The third reason is the natural implication of the first two: If they were to live and survive on the land it was absolutely vital to learn the indigenous language for the purpose of neighbourly communication and the translation of the gospel into the African language and culture.[183]

They acquired the new language orally. Learning aids like language textbooks, -courses, -cassettes or exams did not exist. The pioneer missionaries had to rely on the most primitive means. A good opportunity to learn the language presented itself with the servants who were employed in house and garden. Seeing that the pioneer missionaries weren't paid a salary in order to obtain food, it stood to reason that a garden and agricultural land was established as soon as possible. They needed assistance in doing so, and this was readily available in the local community. They

[183] This was not always the case with the British missionaries, who frequently sought the services of a translator/interpreter. Cf. Bammann 2010 p. 116f.

acquired words and phrases from these workers. The situation was similar with the missionaries' wives. They employed a domestic worker. The missionary couples exchanged and augmented the vocabulary each one had learnt. Different words and phrases were used in the church and home than on the fields and in nature. As previously mentioned, Zimmermann also regularly attended the tribal gatherings and practised his communication skills on those occasions. Thomas Jensen took this welcome opportunity to make good language progress. He, too, attended the tribal gatherings. One can also imagine that these two missionaries noted down their new vocabulary in the evenings and, in the community, subsequently ascribed the correct meaning to the new words.

Thomas Jensen was slightly better off than Zimmermann. While he was still stationed in Natal the suspension by Hardeland of the four Transvaal missionaries took place. If they wished to be readmitted they were obliged to spend one year of obedience under the mission administration in Natal. Zimmermann, just as Chr. Schulenburg who had moved to Natal earlier, had accepted the burden of this humiliation. When Thomas Jensen already knew that he had been transferred to the Transvaal he took this opportunity to receive an hour of instruction in Setswana from Schulenburg every day.[184] This hour of instruction could not have been much more than a mere introduction. Even so, he developed an early feeling for the language; much more was needed to understand it.

Upon Thomas Jensen's arrival in Dinokana, Zimmermann made a request to be able to stay on for another three months before the mission station was finally handed over.[185] That suited Thomas Jensen, seeing that he was able to learn from Zimmermann. After Zimmermann had left he came to an agreement with the teacher Sehuneloa, whom Zimmermann had appointed in the school. With Sehuneloa's help he was able to advance his knowledge of Setswana. They both taught at the little school.

Sehuneloa had received payment from Zimmermann. Thomas Jensen had to continue doing so, even though he deemed the amount to be inappropriately high. But continuity was his first priority for the time being. "I began teaching in the school [at Dinokana] and let the old school master who had served under Zimmermann help me for the time being, seeing that I could not speak the language. I was obliged to pay him one pound sterling

[184] Thomas Jensen 1874 p. 25.

[185] Loco citato p. 17f; 25.

per month, as Zimmermann had done. I also let him preach on Sundays since he had occasionally done that for Zimmermann as well."[186] In the mornings he taught in school together with Sehuneloa and learnt from him, and on Sundays he sat under his pulpit to try and understand the sermon. There are no records of Sehuneloa's sermons.

In early February 1864, while Zimmermann was busy preparing for his departure, W. Behrens and K. Lohann returned from Botswana. They had been sent to the Batswana together with Thomas Jensen. But they had been refused permission to work there by the Bakwena, the resident tribe. They stayed with Thomas Jensen at Dinokana, from where they looked for new mission opportunities. They, too, were in need of a greater proficiency in Setswana. Thomas Jensen writes: "In the afternoons I and the other Brothers would read as much Secuana as time allowed."[187] Right from the beginning it was obvious how hard not only he but also the other Brothers tried to grasp the language of Setswana. Zimmermann can also be included in "the other Brothers". He stayed for another month at Dinokana with the Brothers who had returned from Botswana. If Zimmermann was really part of this group then it cannot be ruled out that Behrens and Lohann took the initiative to be instructed by Zimmermann, and Thomas Jensen joined in.

Thomas Jensen made good progress in learning the language of the local people. He delivered his first sermon roughly ten months after his arrival at Dinokana, on the 17th Sunday after Trinity.[188] He dismissed Sehuneloa from his services roughly at the same time. He did not get along with him very well. Sehuneloa acted too independently for his liking. Zimmermann had allowed Sehuneloa free scope. Was it this autonomy of action that was a problem for Thomas Jensen?

Another Motswana by the name of *Moremi* had offered his services for the school. He was one of the first people to have been baptised in Dithejane. He felt himself drawn to the Hermannsburg missionaries, and since there was no Hermannsburg missionary in Botswana for the time being,

---

[186] Id., 04.08.1864 p. 4. – "Ich fing daselbst an, die Schule zu halten, ließ aber den alten Schulmeister, der für Zimmermann die Schule gehalten hatte, mir noch helfen, weil ich die Sprache nicht konnte. Ich musste dafür ein Pfund Sterling im Monat geben, wie Zimmermann auch getan hatte. Ihn ließ ich des Sonntags auch predigen, da er es für Herrn Zimmermann auch bisweilen getan hatte."

[187] Thomas Jensen 1874 p. 25. – "Des Nachmittags aber las ich mit den anderen Brüdern soviel ich nur Zeit hatte Secuana."

[188] Thomas Jensen 1874 p. 26.

he had come to Dinokana. Thomas Jensen appointed him as teacher in the school. He also assigned the Sunday sermons to him and, in order to facilitate this, had introduced a regular preparatory discussion with Moremi on Saturdays. Of course this made it much easier for him to understand Moremi's sermons. This probably gave him courage to present his own sermons to the little congregation on a more regular basis. Moremi also acted autonomously, but in a different way to Sehuneloa. On one occasion he had gone hunting for a protracted period of time. He had probably joined a European hunter and had travelled far away. During this time Thomas Jensen was obliged to prepare his own sermons, something that took him the whole week.[189] But the preparation for the sermon was simply a part of the process to improve his language skills more and more.

Zimmermann writes, and this may have applied to Jensen as well, that they received much praise from the Batswana for their first attempts at their language. But a couple of years later they realised how many mistakes they had nevertheless made despite their good intentions and the great trouble they had taken in the beginning. After the missionaries had realised this "… even the praise that the Betshuana people were only too keen to generously strew as frankincense on their teachers was no longer effectual."[190]

It had not been easy for Thomas Jensen to learn Setswana. His son Ferdinand, on the other hand, was able to grow into the language. After Ferdinand Jensen had returned from his studies in Germany and was obliged to spend two years in Dinokana due to his illness, he assisted his father in the school. "My son, who has learnt the language since he was a little child, and has now settled back into it, is better able to make himself understood than I am. It is for this reason that the people prefer to attend his instruction classes rather than mine."[191] The father noticed and realised that his son, due to his superior language skills, was better received by the pupils. Another reason for this may have been that the young missionary, having newly arrived from Germany, was more attractive to the pupils. Other missionaries with

[189] Referring to Moremi's hunting trip and the preparation of his first sermon, Thomas Jensen cites extracts from his second report dated December 1864 in his station chronicles of 1874 p. 26. This second report is non-existent in the files of the ELM archives, the only file that is missing.

[190] Zimmermann 1874 p. 6. – "… wollte auch das Lob nicht mehr haften, das die Betschuana nur allzu bereit sind, ihren Lehrern als Weihrauch reichlich zu streuen."

[191] Thomas Jensen, July 1896 p. 6. – "Mein Sohn, der von Kind auf die Sprache gelernt hat und sich nun wieder hinein gelebt hat, kann sich besser verständlich machen als ich. Darum gehen die Leute lieber bei ihm in den Unterricht als bei mir."

whom he interacted at conferences and conventions also recognised Ferdinand Jensen's superior language skills. Pape writes: "He was a formidable authority in matters of mission relations and black people, and could speak their language like only a few others, and had knowledge of innumerable African proverbs. Reports by his contemporaries state that the Reverend and Superintendent had, at all times and every occasion, a suitable proverb on hand."[192]

3.1.2 Construction Style of the Huts and Houses

Dorothea Schröder described the houses of the Bahurutshe. During the Hermannsburg missionaries' first trip through Dinokana in 1857 she had caught a glimpse of the settlement. She called the dwellings of the Bahurutshe huts. "Their huts are round, tapering towards the top, the roof is made of grass, the walls of clay, with a veranda all around them."[193] This description of the exterior of their houses is succinct and accurate. She does not say anything about the interior of the rondavels or whether one family had built several dwellings or whether they had a yard. Neither could she have done so. If the missionaries had stopped over in the settlement and had sought to enter into a discussion with the residents, D. Schröder would probably have produced a more extensive description. The travellers had only their destination in their sights and were reluctant to tarry unnecessarily along the way.

One can nonetheless already deduce from the simple description of the huts that the Bahurutshe were neither familiar with fired bricks for the walls of their houses, nor with corrugated iron or roof tiles. So the houses were round. This construction style owed its origins to the cyclical world view of the Batswana. The world was round. This pre-Copernican view of the world was dominant amongst the Batswana. In nature, summer and winter made their cyclical return. The cycle of the traditional belief system had no end. The life force that the ancestors had bestowed at birth returned to the ancestral collective as spirit. All life and everything that happened on earth was part of a cycle. The pointed roof, too, fitted into this circular perception

[192] Pape 1986 p. 85. Due to his superior language skills Ferdinand Jensen could have compiled a language textbook or grammar book of Setswana. He did not dare to do that. This humility probably stems from his training in Hermannsburg. The subjects that were presented were pre-specified. They did not include anthropological- or linguistic studies.

[193] In Schütte, p. 157. – "Ihre Hütten sind rund, oben spitz zulaufend, das Dach von Gras, die Wände von Lehm und um dieselben her eine Veranda."

of the world. The roof tip pointed upwards. The sky covered the earth with its canopy. The almighty God (*modimo mothatayotlhe*) resided up above and, in his proximity, the spirits (*badimo*). The sun and rain came down from above. The forces of nature were under the control of Modimo.

A possible etymological explanation of this term lies in the adjective *godimo* (above). The entire world view resembled a circle, was circular in its dimensions.

D. Schröder also mentions the veranda, which can serve a twofold purpose. Propped up with poles above the entrance door it can be an awning, protecting the arriving visitor in inclement weather. The veranda may also denote the front yard. Equipped with a low clay wall meant for receiving guests, it is also a playground for children and an open space for eating. It is on this veranda that the nocturnal conversations take place during which the stories, folk tales and traditions are handed down to the next generation. The children were born in the hut and, if the weather was unpleasant, it served as sleeping place. If the weather was fine, everyone slept on the veranda. There were no beds, only animal skins to lie down on. Everybody slept on the ground. Thus everyday life in its entirety took place on what D. Schröder called the veranda.

The term hut is also the correct one in another respect. It was easy to build, speedily constructed and just as speedily demolished. A hut did, for the most part, not have a long lifespan. Until the time that the Hermannsburg missionaries arrived the Bahurutshe had been a migratory tribe. If they felt harassed or oppressed and the chief gave the order to decamp, everybody had to move out of their huts. Frequent migrations meant that they constructed their huts as simply and plainly as possible. Ga-Ditshwene, with its many ruins, was an exception in this regard as the Bahurutshe had probably resided there for a longer period of time and had had many stones at their disposal to use as building material. Due to the forced decampments the tribe had gained a wealth of experience in demolishing and constructing their dwellings. With their final move from the Pooe Mountain into the Dinokana valley, "over 2,000 huts" had to be demolished one last time.[194]

The change in building style from a round hut to a rectangular house occurred with the immigration of the Boers who didn't build rondavels, and also with the missionaries who took up residence with the tribes. The missionaries, by way of assimilation to and sympathy for their neighbours,

194 Thomas Jensen 29.06.1865 p. 2.

erected one or two rondavels alongside their massive residential houses. They used these rondavels as store room, study- or guest room, or to house their employees.

The chief took the lead in all matters pertaining to the tribe. That was also the case in Dinokana. Even though many Bahurutshe men were in the employ of the Boers in the area, helping with the building of the residential houses or performing other construction work, sometimes even having been convinced of the new building style, they were nonetheless obliged to keep on living in their round huts. It was only when Moiloa II asked the missionaries to build him a rectangular house that further houses in Dinokana were allowed to be built in that style. Missionary Lohann, who had not found deployment in another tribe at that time, helped Thomas Jensen to build the new house for the chief. "In 1866, with the assistance of Brother Lohann … I built a house for Moiloa, approximately 40 × 15 feet."[195] Many Bahurutshe now followed this pattern. They built similar square or rectangular houses for themselves. The old village structure with its round huts has nevertheless been preserved to this day. And both building styles can frequently be seen on the same homestead.

3.1.2.1 Clothing

While passing through Dinokana, Dorothea Schröder had not only noticed the huts. Driven by curiosity to see the missionaries, many Bahurutshe had gathered at the side of the road. One particular young woman caught D. Schröder's eye. This Bahurutshe woman had adorned herself more flamboyantly than the rest of those standing there. D. Schröder writes: "Along came … presumably the king's daughter who was admittedly also wearing only an animal hide but who was richly adorned with all kinds of strings of beads. She also wore brass circlets around her arms and legs."[196] The woman by whom D. Schröder was so fascinated was particularly beautiful to behold. Her adornments alone set her off from the crowd of curious onlookers. D. Schröder classified her as being of noble lineage, deeming her to be a princess. She was probably right. The eye-catching adornment of

[195] Thomas Jensen 1874 p. 21.

[196] In Schütte, p. 157. – "Hier kam … vermutlich die Königstochter, welche freilich auch nu rein Fell umhatte, welche aber sehr geschmückt war mit allerlei Perlenschnüren. Dazu hatte sie Messingringe um Arme und Beine."

this woman leads to the assumption that the Bahurutshe were not a poor tribe.

The chief's wives, as well as their children, were usually not obliged to work in the fields. This was done by the women of the other families. Men and women performed tasks according to their role in the community. The men went hunting. The work in the home and on the fields was assigned to women. When the British-Scottish missionary J. Moffat drove past Mosega in 1835, he saw women working in the fields. He was surprised to see that some of them weren't even wearing a leather loincloth. They were totally naked. "We passed a cornfield in which were about half a dozen women, two of the lustiest were in a state of perfect nudity."[197] Before the European merchants supplied the various tribes with bales of cloth, clothing played a minor role in the lives of the Bahurutshe. In this particular instance the women were amongst themselves. They probably also didn't expect that strangers would be able to observe them on the fields.

After Thomas Jensen had arrived in Dinokana, he noticed a change in the men. They had taken on the Boers' custom of wearing trousers. "Most men wear trousers made of tanned goatskin."[198] The men no longer wore their leather loincloths. The new fashion of wearing "trousers made of tanned goatskin" constituted merely a transition to European clothing, a temporary invention. Cloth began replacing the goatskins. The Christian men were the first to wear trousers made from cloth. The traditional believers followed suit. Amongst the latter it was mainly those men who were sympathetic towards the Christians, who attended the church services and who sat at the back of the church. Was the fact that the Christian men wore European clothing a contributing factor amongst the traditional believers, making them more sympathetic towards Christianity? However that may be, the women continued to wear their traditional clothing. "The majority of men are clothed, whereas the women are frequently still wrapped in animal skins."[199]

The clothes that the chief wore were different to those of his subjects. He no longer appeared in his traditional clothing. His upper body was now also covered. He had adopted the European style to an even greater extent.

[197] In Wallis 1945 p. 69.

[198] Thomas Jensen 04.08.1864 p. 3 – "Die meisten Männer tragen Hosen von gegerbten Ziegenfellen."

[199] Thomas Jensen 04.08.1864 p. 7 – "Die Männer sind fast alle bekleidet, die Frauen aber vielfach nur in Fellen eingehüllt."

Thomas Jensen writes: "He always walks around fully clothed, on workdays like a Boer, on Sundays in an attire of black cloth. If he should perchance be with us while we're eating, he will eat with us, and knows how to conduct himself."[200] As with many other matters, the chief also assumed a leading role with regards to clothing. Why did he wear black clothes on Sundays? On the one hand this was the clothing of the Christians, seeing that they wore these clothes to church. On the other hand, few people had spare clothes during those early days of the onset of civilisation. As a rule they only had one garment.

After cloth could be purchased from European merchants travelling throughout the country, the Bahurutshe changed the way they clothed themselves within a few years. The men were the first to do so, but the women were not far behind. Only the small children now still wore leather loincloths. The wealthy families were the first to opt for full body clothing. The Christians were the first to have done so. While attending the church service the people would not be outdone by one another. As a result, it was merely a question of time before all the Bahurutshe people would be one step closer to civilisation.

3.1.3 Work and nourishment

The Batswana lived in the interior of southern Africa and were a self-sufficient people (practising subsistence agriculture). They lived off the land, from agriculture and stock farming. Schapera writes: "Formerly the Tswana were almost entirely self-supporting. They produced their own food, chiefly by raising crops and breeding livestock."[201] Basic foods were readily available. Grain sorghum *(mabele)* is a specific type of corn. The grains of this cereal are pounded and made into a porridge which is augmented with milk and sugar. To this day grain sorghum porridge is, similarly to the potato in Germany, the daily staple food of the Batswana. The average family will consume this porridge with beef about once a week. On their migrations they only had cattle with them. It was because of the herds of cattle that neighbouring tribes often engaged in war with one another to rob each other's cattle. Even today heads of cattle remain the most coveted

[200] Loco citato. – "Er geht immer gekleidet, des Alltags etwa wie ein Bauer, des Sonntags in schwarzen Tuchkleidern. Trifft es sich, dass er gerade bei uns ist, wenn wir essen, so isst er mit uns, und weiß sich gut zu benehmen."

[201] Schapera 1976 p. 20.

animals. A head of cattle needs to be slaughtered for any larger celebration, and the bridal dowry, too, was negotiated exclusively with cattle. Ferdinand quotes a heroic song on cattle in four verses:

> *"1. O ye herds of bloody encounters, Gods ye are with ever clammy nose.*
> *Burning like scald-hot milk ye are, nay, toxic herbs that singe the heroes' beard.*
> *Goddess of our home you are, cow, breeder of discord amongst tribes.*
> *How many men have perished, because to you.*
>
> *2. You have no cares, you women, but we, the men, we destroy each other,*
> *Kill each other, charging into battle. It is not for nothing*
> *That vultures are already perching on trees, human flesh, they get the scent,*
> *Heroes' flesh, they who fight for their cattle.*
>
> *3. Behold me one more time, mother, when I go to herd the cattle at dawn,*
> *I know not whether I return; the blood of a young warrior*
> *Like me will oft-times stain the grass,*
> *Flowing crimson over the ground.*
>
> *4. Who was it that first called a head of cattle by its name?*
> *Alas, he ought to have named it piercer of a hero's chest, spine-breaker,*
> *Hero slayer he should have called it; constantly it shatters*
> *The backs of many warriors."*[202]

---

[202] Ferdinand Jensen, *Das Heldenlied,* p. 373. – Following these verses Ferdinand Jensen aptly defines the etymological explanation of the term *kgomoladilo* for this heroic song: "Cattle/cow in Setswana is called *kgomo,* an abbreviation of the word *kgomoladilo.* – The verb *go kgomola* = to snatch, gain possession – *dilo* = objects, things. – *Kgomoladilo* would therefore mean: possession = i.e. sign of good luck." If one augments this explanation by the fact that possessing many heads of cattle also demonstrated power and prestige, one is able to more readily understand the risky raids carried out by the Africans in those days. –
"1. O, ihr Herden blut'ger Waffengänge, Götter ihr, mit immer feuchter Nase.
Ach, ihr brennt wie glühendheiße Milch, ja gift'ge Kräuter, die den Bart des Helden sengen.
Rind, du Göttin hier bei uns zu Hause, Zwietrachtsä'rin unter Völkerschaften.
Rind, wie manchem Manne nahmst du schon das Leben.
2. Nichts belästigt euch, ihr Frauen, wir jedoch, die Männer, wir vernichten uns,
Töten uns, indem wir in den Kampf uns stürzen. Nicht umsonst schon hocken die Geier
Auf den Bäumen, Menschenfleisch, das wittern sie,
Fleisch von Helden, die um die Rinder kämpfen.
3. Einmal noch, o Mutter, sieh mich an, wenn ich am Morgen früh die Rinder
Auf die Weide treibe, ich weiß nicht, ob ich dann wiederkehre;
Den wir jungen Recken färben oft mit unserem Blut den Rasen,
Dass es rot dahinströmt über das Gelände.
4. Wer rief wohl das Rind zuerst bei seinem Namen? Ach, er hätt' es lieber
Heldenbrustdurchbohrer heißen sollen, Rückgratbrecher, Heldentöter
Hätte er es nennen sollen; den noch immerfort

This heroic song gives no names. It does say, however, who all these heroes are. They are men. The men who herded the cattle were under threat from raids of neighbouring tribes. In that event they were compelled to defend their cattle and put the assailants to flight. The battle continued until there were casualties (dead or wounded), one opponent had been subdued and the other was able to lead the cattle away. This song does however not imply that the men only proved themselves as heroes in the defensive position. They might also have been the assailants themselves, intending to enrich themselves with the cattle of another tribe. That demanded courage. The men wanted to produce evidence of their strength. More often than not the cattle were merely used as pretence for a bloody struggle. A large herd also meant that one was stronger and more powerful than the others. The cattle therefore gained centre stage, bestowing honour on the victorious and belligerent men.

The Batswana also keep chickens, goats and pigs. They added the latter to their farm stock after having settled down. Chickens, goats and pigs were less valuable than cattle. Nobody fought for them. Therefore they don't feature in heroic songs. Today chicken is served as a second meat dish alongside beef at all celebrations. Goats and pigs are consumed within the family and not offered to guests.

Apart from the Bahurutshe's domesticated animals, agriculture and stock farming for consumption purposes, they also hunted. Thomas Jensen writes: "The people live from agriculture, stock farming and hunting."[203] Zimmermann relates incidents of lions and a hyena lurking outside his house at dusk.[204] Wherever these carnivorous animals were present other quarry abounded. During the 19th century, large herds of buffalo and wildebeest existed on the plains of the Transvaal.[205]

Zerschlägt's den Rücken vieler Mannen."

203 Thomas Jensen 04.08.1864 p. 3. – "Das Volk lebt von Ackerbau, Viehzucht, und Jagd."

204 Zimmermann 1874 p. 10f.

205 A German settler lost his life during a buffalo hunt in the Transvaal: "One day a German by the name of Wolhuter was hunting buffalos. The hunter shot a buffalo, wounding the animal. The animal immediately charged ... The raging animal gored Wolhuter with its horns and trampled him under its hooves. The hill was subsequently named Wolhuterskop" – De Beer, p. 525. [Op 'n dag het 'n Duitser met die naam Wolhuter op die buffels jag gemaak. Die jagter het 'n buffel geskiet, maar die dier gekwes. Die dier het onmiddellik gestorm ... Die verwoede dier het Wolhuter met die horings deurboor en hom verder onder sy pote vertrap. Die kop het toe die naam Wolhuterskop ontvang.] – To this day, the hill at the bottom of which Wolhuter was killed is called Wolhuters Kop.

Because the Europeans hunted with rifles the game was reduced considerably. But it was not only the Europeans who hunted with rifles. The Batswana were clever enough to obtain rifles, too. One person who provided rifles and ammunition to the Bahurutshe, apart from the abovementioned Livingstone, was Viljoen, their Boer neighbour.[206] Viljoen was anxious, also seeing that he lived in close proximity to the Bahurutshe, to establish a good relationship with the Batswana. The Batswana enjoyed the meat of wild animals just as much as the Europeans.

Before rifles were introduced the Batswana hunted with bow and arrow, as well as spears. They not only hunted individual animals but also larger herds or packs. The neighbouring tribe of the Bahurutshe, the Bafokeng, chased the animals into a funnel constructed of heaped-up stones, at one end of which they killed the animals.[207]

Hunting was the reserve of men. Women worked on the fields, weeded and harvested. Thomas Jensen describes the allocation of work for men and women: "The women till the fields but the men also lend a helping hand. The men are lethargic and lazy, but not as much as the Zulus. Their main occupation is to prepare hides to sew karosses,[208] herd the cattle and go hunting."[209] The work to be done was distributed. Apart from their work in the fields, the women also did the housework. This entailed raising the children, sweeping the yard, cooking in the open cooking place, brewing beer and gathering and carrying bush wood on their heads back home. By all outward appearances it seems that the workload was unevenly distributed and that the women bore the brunt of the work.

The men herded the cattle, went hunting, sewed cloaks, blankets and mats to sit or sleep on from the skins of wild animals for their women. They were also obliged, and this is less well-known, to protect their families from all kinds of physical and psychological danger. The father of a family was,

---

It is a singular hill, situated next to the highway between the Hartebeespoort Dam and Rustenburg.

206 Manson 1990 p. 92; 105. On one occasion Viljoen, with the support of the Hermannsburg missionary Schröder in Botswana, managed to provide Chief Setshele with ammunition from public funds: "Viljoen suggested to Pretorius in 1859 that Setshele should be given ammunition ... The Volksraad gave its permission – partly on the recommendation of Schröder – and in April 1859 Viljoen handed Setshele 200 pounds of gunpowder and 400 pounds of lead." Grobler p. 253.

207 Bammann 2010 p. 21f.

208 Karosses are blankets or cloaks made from animal skin.

209 Thomas Jensen 04.08.1864 p. 3.

apart from his clearly discernible tasks, also obliged to function as medicine man for his family. In his capacity as medicine man he had to ward off or cure disease and illness, and to protect his house, homestead and family from evil spirits. These activities were frequently performed secretly.

The Bahurutshe men helped the women in the fields. This appears to have been unusual and may be attributed to the Christian influence of the missionaries. Thomas Jensen's assessment of the men as being "lazy" is measured against European standards. As mentioned above, the Zulus come off even worse in his estimate.

Another task that the men had to perform was blacksmithing, something the Bahurutshe were very adept at. The women required hoes for their work in the field and these field hoes had to be crafted from iron. The men, on the other hand, required spears, arrows and pikes for purposes of defence and hunting, and these were also made of iron. To this day several smelting furnaces are still discernible at Ga-Ditshwene. Seeing that they had mastered the art of blacksmithing, they also utilised this skill in Dinokana.

Gunpowder had meanwhile supplanted the spears. The Boers had come into the Transvaal from the Cape, armed with rifles. They had to defend themselves en route against attacks and wild animals.

The advantages of wheel construction remained surprisingly alien to the Batswana for a considerable time. Whenever they needed wood from the bushes they dragged it home using their harnessed animals. The wheel was only introduced to them much later by the Europeans and Arabs. The Bahurutshe viewed the ox wagons of the Boers as marking a distinct progress for themselves and proceeded to purchase such wagons from the Boers. The blacksmith in Dinokana repaired the wagons. The adornment worn by the princess that caught the eye of D. Schröder while passing through the town had possibly also been forged in one of Dinokana's smithies. Zimmermann praised the handiwork of the Bahurutshe, rating it as being "culturally capable". "The Bahurutsi – as well as other tribes – produce their own iron, they have iron smelters and hammers, albeit in very primitive conditions, but they craft their own assegais, hoes, rings, thick and thin wire, also made of brass, and many other things. Admirable proof at any rate as to how culturally capable these people are."[210] We don't know whether Zimmermann

[210] Zimmermann 1874 p. 8. – "Die Bahurutsi – auch noch andere Völker – fertigen ihr eigenes Eisen, haben Eisenschmelzen und Hämmer, freilich in ganz primitive Zuständen, aber sie fertigen doch Assegais, Hacken, Ringe, groben und feinen Draht, auch von Messing, und manche andere Dinge. Immerhin schöne Beweise, wie kulturfähig diese

actually ever visited a forgery. The itinerant traders also had ornamental objects and craftsmen's tools on offer that could replace those the Bahurutshe already had. It can nonetheless be assumed that Zimmermann found remnants of artisan manufacturing amongst the various families, and that this led to his assessment.

Due to the colonisation by the Boers the land of the Bahurutshe was put under increased pressure but, on the other hand, they gratefully took up the challenge posed by the civilisation that was also brought into the country by the Boers. Instead of tilling the soil with their hoes they now employed a plough. They trained their oxen for this purpose, just as the Boers did. The work in the field was now not only easier, the men now took over this task, to wit, relieving the women of this arduous work. The size of the tilling field could now be increased and the harvest yield doubled. Schapera writes: "In the old days fields were seldom larger than two or three acres, but since the adoption of the plough the usual size has become between five acres and 20."[211] The usual crops were admittedly still being planted: grain sorghum, sugar cane *(ntshe ya sukiri),* African peas *(ditlhodi)*, the leaves of which were eaten like spinach. Wild bush fruit like *mogorogororoane*[212] and *motlhatswa*[213] augmented the diet. Maize and other grains were now added. A great variety of tropical fruit was now planted and vegetables cultivated.

Instead of the traditional skin cloaks, clothing in a variety of colours were now worn. Shoes in the style of the Europeans now also became very popular, seeing that they offered protection against thorns and snake bites. The change in building style has already been mentioned. A round hut was now only constructed on very rare occasions. A great deal had changed in the lives of the Bahurutshe since they had ceased their migrations.

When the Bahurutshe resided on the Pooe Mountain, the stream in the valley below had not only carried a sufficient amount of water but also contained fish that the Bahurutshe utilised as food. Thomas Jensen writes: "Mathebe is a little stream that passes about 5 minutes away below the mission grounds. It holds three types of fish. (. . .) They are: 1. the so-called barbel, a tasty, oily fish, the best we have here. 2. the white- or yellow-fish, also tasty, 3. the third is the fish commonly known in Germany as *Ka-*

Völker sind."

211 Schapera 1976 p. 21.

212 Has the outer appearance of an apple.

213 Looks like a small yellow plum.

rausche."[214] The yield in caught fish declined, however, as the Bahurutshe built canals to irrigate their gardens and fields with the spring water.

In the above quote Thomas Jensen refers to the mission station as "mission grounds". He, too, had utilised the water, had established a garden with all kinds of tropical fruit and had cultivated a large tract of land which he irrigated for himself and his family. "When I arrived here, Moiloa gave me so much (land, HB), that I now have about 14 acres under cultivation."[215] He was a model for many Bahurutshe with his garden and his agricultural practises. They observed him when he planted fruit trees and cultivated the land and did likewise.

Locust plagues no longer exist. In the 19th and 20th century it was a totally different scenario, however, with a particularly vicious plague having occurred in 1894, for instance. When the locusts infested the country for the fourth time they not only destroyed the harvest but also ate the leaves off the trees, stripping them bare so that they could no longer provide shade.[216] Since the locusts passed through in great swarms, they provided shade of a totally different kind, albeit only for a fleeting moment. Thomas Jensen kept an eye on the locusts: "They sometimes come in swarms so dense and large in size that they eclipse the sun."[217] Aside from the enormous damage done by the locusts, a small benefit was nevertheless derived from them. During the cool hours of early morning, when the locusts were still too numb to crawl or fly, the women and children would chase them, gather them, and take home as many as they could. The locusts were roasted and dried and provided meals for many days and weeks to come.

When the locusts had eaten the harvest there was no food that could be stored. If the rain should subsequently stay away or even a succession of arid years ensue, the result was a prolonged period of hard times in nature, and also amongst the Bahurutshe in Dinokana. Such a period of hunger and

---

214 Engl: crucian carp (Carassius carassius). Thomas Jensen 1874 p. 3 – "Mathebe ist ein kleiner Fluss, der etwa 5 Minuten unterhalb des Missionslandes vorbeiläuft. In demselben sind drei Sorten von Fischen. (…) Es sind: 1. der hier sogenannte Barbe, ein wohlschmeckender, fetter Fisch, der beste, den wir hier haben. 2. der Weiß- oder Gelbfisch, auch wohlschmeckend, 3. die dritte Sorte ist die in Deutschland bekannte Karausche."

215 Thomas Jensen 1874 p. 1f. – "Als ich hierher kam, hat Moiloa mir soviel (Land, HB) gegeben, dass ich nun etwa 14 Morgen unter Cultur habe."

216 Id. 1894 p. 5.

217 Thomas Jensen 1874 p. 10. – "Sie kommen bisweilen in Schwärmen so dicht und so groß, dass sie die Sonne verfinstern."

suffering could only be bridged in the second half of the 19th century, after diamonds had been discovered in Kimberley, and gold in Johannesburg.

The discovery of these precious treasures beneath the surface of the earth induced many Bahurutshe men to leave their village to go and work in the mines. The men who had up to that point earned a little money on the farms of the Boers, now took on the hard labour in the mines. In times of drought they sent some of their earnings home, which enabled the extended families to survive. Thomas Jensen welcomes the decision of his parishioners to go and work in the mines. He wrote a letter of recommendation for them, something that was highly appreciated by the mine authorities.

3.1.4 Celebrations and Days of Rest

Throughout the year the Bahurutshe observed various celebrations. All celebrations were initiated by the chief, he had to mandate them. He stipulated the days of festivity and also determined their commencement.

After having been in Dinokana for 10 years, Thomas Jensen had gained an overview of the traditional ritual celebrations. Although all celebrations were religious in origin, he was however unable to discern the kind of religion as he conceived of it. "The people no longer have any religion to speak of, but all their customs are in any event of religious origin."[218]

When Thomas Jensen states that he cannot discern a religion with the Bahurutshe, he draws on the Christian religion by way of comparison. He has been shaped by and firmly believes in Christianity. It is his benchmark in relation to the traditional belief system of the Bahurutshe. It is however impossible to proffer a comparison in this way. Both religions should, for a start, be viewed as being on an equal footing next to one another. The decision as to which religion is the more appropriate one then rests with the individual believer, in the way it proves itself in his everyday life and in his declaration of belief in the religion. The life experiences with the values of one religion also make an impression on the members of another. With Christianity it is always a matter of proclaiming the gospel, the conduct and service of love of a Christian. Thomas Jensen also wanted to be a witness for Jesus Christ. He had false expectations in this regard. He was apparently expecting to find a sacral building, a ritual site and priestly attire with this

[218] Thomas Jensen 1874 p. 69. – "Religion haben die Leute sozusagen gar nicht mehr, aber alle ihre Gebräuche sind jedenfalls religiösen Ursprungs."

African religion. He found none of that. At least he acknowledges a "religious origin" in their customs and traditions. This religious basis can be discerned with all the celebrations. And there were many of those.

All ceremonies commenced with the appearance of the chief. He was not only the secular leader of his tribe. The responsibility to uphold the religious traditions and to officiate as the tribal priest also resided with him. This did indeed look very different from Christianity. The rainmaking ritual, for instance, was something extraordinary. The chief was compelled to attract rain. He was the mediator between the living and the ancestors. It was his privilege to communicate with the ancestors during times of need. These matters formed part of the daily obligations of his office. No special order was in place for this. In the event that an unforeseen situation disrupted tribal harmony, a speedy solution had to be found with the help of the ancestors.

Apart from the numerous, regular celebrations, a number of non-regular feasts were held now and then for the most diverse reasons. Annually recurring festivals included New Year's Day and the Celebration of the New Moon. And every time someone died a burial ceremony was held.

After the Boers and the missionaries had introduced the observance of Sundays, this day was also presently declared by the chief to be a day of rest. In doing so, the traditional believers were included, who still constituted the vast majority of tribe members.

The period of the circumcision school also saw many celebrations, even if no day of rest was decreed in such cases. Almost all other celebrations went hand in hand with a day of rest. If a taboo that had been decreed by the chief should be broken in this regard the culprits were punished severely.

Below we will elaborate on the celebrations, beginning with the Day of Rainmaking. The rain maker required all tribe members to be on his side. Under no circumstances were the ancestors to be offended. On this day of rest, the chief had imposed a taboo on the women. They were forbidden to cook. All fires had to be extinguished in the homesteads. When the first Christians refused to perform this expression of traditional homage, the neighbouring traditional believers came to extinguish the open fire pits of the Christians. Only after all the fire pits had been extinguished a new fire was rekindled in the tribal gathering place, in accordance with an old tradition of the Batswana. This took place as follows: A stick of hardwood was rubbed on an underlay of hardwood. An indentation had been carved into the underlay. The stick was placed into this indentation and rubbed.

When the stick had been rubbed between both hands for a while to generate heat, dry blades of grass were placed next to the rubbing surface. The blades began to smoulder and catch fire. A special medicine was prepared at the same time. Thomas Jensen describes this as follows: "The fire is lit by rubbing two pieces of wood, and medicine is simultaneously used, which is then carried into all the gardens in order to doctor them, as they call it. After this has been done the rainmaking ceremony can commence."[219]

The ritual of the lighting of the fire signified a new beginning. The prepared medicine was subsequently dispersed in all the gardens, and the magical properties of the medicine was supposed to attract the rain. This grand offensive required an utmost concentration of all cosmic powers. This necessitated a strict day of rest.

After the day of rest, work could be resumed in the fields. The eagerly anticipated rain was now a concrete possibility. The seed was sown and would grow. The soil as weeded and a good harvest expected.

Before the harvest could be brought in the New Year was celebrated. The chief decreed the date of celebration. Thomas Jensen writes: "There have to be young crops at their New Year's celebration, especially gourds. They call it *go loma* in their language, i.e. to bite, because either the chief or his son have to take a bite from a gourd."[220] After the chief had publicly bitten into a gourd the day was declared to be a day of rest. The following day the harvest could begin on the fields and in the gardens.

After the congregation at Dinokana had grown, the celebration of Thanksgiving was introduced. This celebration later replaced the New Year's celebration, and the traditional believers subsequently abandoned their New Year's celebration.

In connection with the New Year's celebration, Thomas Jensen once mentioned the observance of the feast of the "new moon" as well as the "feast of the dead".[221] On both these celebrations he only notes that, on the morning of the day in question, a day of rest was proclaimed by the tribal crier from the gathering place. No Mohurutshe was allowed to work in the

---

[219] Thomas Jensen 1874 p. 71. – "Das Feuer wird angezündet durch zwei Hölzer gerieben und Medizin dabei verwendet, die dann in alle Gärten hingebracht wird, um dieselben zu doktoren, wie sie sagen. Nach diesem kann nun das Regenmachen vor sich gehen."

[220] Thomas Jensen 1874 p. 70. – "Bei ihrer Neujahrsfeier müssen junge Früchte vorhanden sein, besonders Kürbisse. Man nennt es in ihrer Sprache *go loma,* d.h. zu beißen, den der Häuptling oder sein Sohn muss an einem Kürbis beißen."

[221] Id., p. 69f.

garden or on the fields on those days. If someone broke this taboo, they were punished.

We can bring our own thoughts into play where both these celebrations are concerned. One can imagine that the moon played an important role with the ancestors of the Bahurutshe, together with other Batswana groups, on their migrations from central Africa towards the south. The moon accompanied and protected them at night. At some point it was awarded mythological reverence, which endured to modern times. One is unable to ascertain from Thomas Jensen's remark as to the frequency of such rest-day declarations for the new moon. One can surmise that it occurred once a month.

The burial ceremony signified the loss of a tribe member. The entire tribe showed its sympathy and participated in the burial ceremony. A day of rest was proclaimed in remembrance of the deceased. The purpose of this day was also to commemorate the ancestors. The medicine man had to launch an inquiry and ascertain whether the deceased had died of natural causes. If that was the case, then everything could proceed normally. Then the ancestors had called him. He would now embark on his journey beyond the earth and reach and be admitted into his ancestral collective after one year. If evil spirits had sent him to his death, however, or a jealous relative had induced a lethal disease, this would elicit a nasty reaction from the ancestors. His journey into the hereafter would be disrupted and his spirit would demand reparation from the living. If the deceased had not died a peaceful death, he would return. That is what was feared by the living. Nobody knew what might happen on the journey into the hereafter. It was for this reason that the medicine man had to provide his analysis with every death that occurred. If a death was reported to the chief he decreed a day of rest as well.[222]

Since the Boers had already acquainted the first Christians with the observance of Sunday as a rest day, they experienced no further difficulties in

---

222 The paralysing effect that a burial ceremony could have on daily activities because of collective tribal stipulations is illustrated by an entry recorded by Schulenburg about the neighbouring Balete tribe: "Every time someone has died a day of rest is declared. One is only too easily able to calculate the disruption this causes with every kind of work, given a settlement of around 6,000 residents." – ['Jedes Mal, wenn jemand gestorben ist, ist ein Ruhetag. Man kann nur zu leicht ausrechnen, wie störend dies bei jeder Arbeit, bei einer Stadt von etwa 6.000 Einwohnern, wirken kann.'] – In Mignon p. 44. – Apparently the observance of the burial ceremony was on the decline in Dinokana. Thomas Jensen makes no special mention of it.

paying heed to the Third Commandment: "Thou shalt observe the Sabbath day". For the Christians this day was Sunday, on which they commemorated the resurrection of their Lord Jesus Christ. Their missionary had taught them as much. The chief had reacted to this, relented and declared Sunday to be another day of rest. The vast majority of traditional believers had no objections.

Zimmermann had adopted a habit he had brought over from Germany, namely to view the Sunday to be of such importance that it should be declared publicly. To this day his idea still finds its imitation on a few outstations. He took a disused plough share and hung it from a tree. He placed an iron rod against the tree trunk. Half an hour before the church service commenced a church elder would busy himself banging against the share with the iron rod. He called the share a bell. Environmental noises, of the kind that we only perceive on a subconscious level these days, did not exist back then. A pronounced silence prevailed everywhere. The sound of the plough share could therefore be heard across the entire settlement. After a while, after the Bahurutshe had grown accustomed to this sound, they named Sundays after the name of the plough share. "They call Sundays *'tsatsi ya tsipi'*, its literal meaning being 'day of the iron', because of the bell that is sounded on Sundays."[223]

The chief was in favour of Sunday rest. He espoused the adherence to the canonical Sabbath day with the same energy as for the traditional days of rest. Zimmermann comments: "If someone went out to work on a Sunday, that person received a beating and his working implements were confiscated; if someone gathered wood or fruit on a Sunday, these were taken away from him, confiscated; if the women went to the stream to fetch water, too late to avoid church people on the way or in the afternoon before the church service was over, he ordered their pots to be destroyed. For the sake of peace and quiet he prohibited dancing- and drinking parties, even during the week, but if they could nonetheless be heard he saw to it that the participants were raided, given a beating and the beer confiscated. It didn't take long before everything was so orderly and quiet, especially on Sundays, that a stranger would have concluded that only pious people resided there. Then that old man of mine (Moiloa II, HB) was so glad that his eyes shone."[224]

---

[223] Zimmermann 1874 p. 14. – "Den Sonntag nennen sie *'tsatsi ya tsipi'* wörtlich 'Tag des Eisens' von der Glocke, die des Sonntags geläutet wird."

[224] Zimmermann 1874 p. 14. – "Wer am Sonntag ausging zu arbeiten, bekam Schläge

The chief ruled over the traditional believers as well as the Christians. All days of rest were instituted by him. This included Sunday rest. The traditional believers were even obliged to down their tools when the small Christian congregation held its service on Wednesdays. The purpose of the Wednesday service was to sanctify the Christians. This custom had been adopted from the revivalist period in Hermannsburg. The absolute obedience displayed by the traditional believers cannot be understood, however, as being solely due to the chief's prohibition. On a daily basis Zimmermann sat alongside the leading traditional believers in the tribal council. His fellowship with these believers and his conduct during the tribal gatherings had in no small part contributed to the fact that the traditional believers responded in obedience, and also accepted the punishments meted out by the chief.

The justification for the decree regarding rest days, both from the Christian understanding as well as that of traditional belief, was essentially the same from the chief's point of view. In Judeo-Christian tradition, resting on the Sabbath is a commandment of the almighty God. On this day humans should extract themselves from their daily toil and understand the church service and holiday as being a means to give thanks for the life bestowed on them by God, and to pray to him in the fellowship of other believers. The decrees of traditional belief were not founded in scripture but had rather arisen from traditions, whose observance and continuation it was the chief's responsibility to ensure. He personified the link between thc tribe and spirit world. It was in this capacity that he decreed days of rest: the spirit powers had ordained a period of rest.

The effect of the accord that existed between Moiloa II and Zimmermann could be felt in the entire tribe. One can presume, however, that Zimmermann had an influence on Moiloa II. Both religions, the Christian as well as the pagan, bcnefited from Zimmermann's influence.

---

und seine Arbeitsinstrumente wurden confisciert; wer Holz oder Früchte am Sonntag einbrachte, dem wurden sie weggenommen, confisciert; gingen die Frauen zum Fluss Wasser holen, zu spat, um Kirchenleuten nicht zu begegnen oder nachmittags ehe der Gottesdienst aus war, so ließ er ihnen die Töpfe zerschlagen. Tanz- und Saufpartien verbot er der Ruhe wegen, selbst für die Wochentage, und sie wurden dennoch gehört, so ließ er sie überfallen, durchhauen und das Bier confiszieren. Es dauerte nicht lange, so war es so ordentlich, und still, besonders des Sonntags, das sein Fremder hätte meinen sollen, da wohnten lauter Fromme. Dann freute sich mein Alter, dass ihm die Augen leuchteten."

When Zimmermann was compelled to leave Dinokana the atmosphere began to change. Thomas Jensen had different priorities from Zimmermann. He did take part in the tribal gatherings, to wit, but the core of his work was to build up the congregation. His influence on the tribe is not as discernible as was the case with Zimmermann. The traditional believers in the tribe began to make their presence felt again with extravagant festivities. Moiloa II lost some of his authority. After a particularly good harvest year, morality sank to a very low level. Thomas Jensen writes: "The heathens are reluctant to leave behind their heathenish ways. (...) In no other year ... have they drunk, danced and exhibited their heathenish nature so much, in no other year have so few (of the traditional believers, HB) come to church."[225] The traditional believers had distanced themselves from the Christian congregation and its teachings. It was not only the absence of traditional believers in the church service that was disappointing to Thomas Jensen, but their excessive and boisterous feasts annoyed him with their loud music and singing. The noise in the evenings and at night became unbearable. What could he do? Nothing! He had to wait patiently for the time of this noise and racket to pass. What was saddening about this time of rowdy celebration was that the observance of the rest days was also subsequently neglected.

The celebrations that accompanied circumcision posed a great difficulty for Thomas Jensen. While Zimmermann also describes the disruptive noise of the circumcision celebrations as being "a nightly spectacle"[226] but otherwise ignored it for the most part, Thomas Jensen had a more sensitive reaction to it. He avails himself of the commonly-used German expression "*heidnisches Spektakel*" (heathenish racket) when he says: "In Germany they may well speak of a *heidnisches Spektakel*, but here we still experience what a heathenish racket actually is."[227] The racket of the traditional believers was apparently unbearable to him. Every time the circumcision ceremonies were carried out the nocturnal racket would carry on for weeks. The circumcision school ceremonies had a specific religious meaning. The circumcision school constituted a form of sacrifice. By burning their fore-

---

225 Thomas Jensen 03.01.1872 p. 1f. – "Die Heiden wollen das heidnische Wesen nicht verlassen. (...) Kein Jahr ... haben sie soviel gesoffen, getanzt und ihr heidnisches Wesen gezeigt, kein Jahr so wenig zur Kirche gekommen."

226 Zimmermann 1874 p. 14. – "nächtliches Spektakel".

227 Thomas Jensen 01.04.1867 p. 3. – "Man spricht in Deutschland wohl vom heidnischen Spektakel, aber hier erfahren wir noch, was heidnischer Spektakel ist."

skins after having been circumcised, the young men symbolically surrendered themselves to the ancestors. The ancestors were under no circumstances allowed to fall asleep during the time of circumcision, and were therefore kept awake by a constant racket. Other celebrations that did not require such a "heathenish racket", like the weddings held within families, or the enthronement ceremony of a new chief, lasted only for a few days were easier to tolerate. Thomas Jensen does not mention them as being noisy.

3.1.5 Taxes and Final Resettlement

It has previously been mentioned that the Boers were of the opinion that they had liberated the Batswana from a land occupation, and that they therefore were the rulers now. All the land belonged to them, and not to the indigenous people. They therefore deemed it justifiable to levy taxes on them as well. This was something the Batswana were completely unfamiliar with. Why should they pay taxes to the Boers if the land belonged to their chief who protected them? But times had changed. The Boers not only imposed taxes on the Batswana, but they also began appropriating more and more land from them for their agricultural purposes.

A number of Boers wanted to seize and occupy Dinokana, and then establish a Boer town close to the water springs. The Bahurutshe should be relocated and resettle somewhere else. When the Bahurutshe got wind of the Boers' plans they were outraged at this audacity. But what could they do to stop the Boers? Not much. Thomas Jensen observes: "The station will probably not remain here for much longer for I can hardly doubt that the tribe will have to relocate next year, and then I have to go with them of course; where to, I don't know yet, maybe into the desert."[228] With the desert Thomas Jensen means the Kgalagadi semi-desert in Botswana. It was however not yet certain whether the relocation would actually take place. But if the Bahurutshe were compelled to leave, he was prepared to go with them. Things had not reached that stage yet. The Bahurutshe, to wit, told him the exact opposite. They said that they were prepared to pay

[228] Thomas Jensen 04. 08. 1864 p. 1. – "Wahrscheinlich wird die Station nicht lange hierbleiben, den ich zweifle fast nicht daran, dass das Volk nächstes Jahr wegziehen muss und dann muss ich natürlich mit, wohin aber weiß ich noch nicht, vielleicht in die Wüste hinein."

the annual tax of 3 pounds sterling[229] per family, but that they did not want to relocate.[230] We don't know whether this position had an influence on Thomas Jensen. He was prepared, in any event and just like Zimmermann before him, to draft a letter, with the Bahurutshe's consent, to the Boer president.

The relocation referred to by Thomas Jensen had already been under discussion during Zimmermann's time. Indeed, Zimmermann had previously had an altercation with the Boers due to the harsh treatment of their labourers. One can imagine that Jensen, too, now pleaded the case for the Bahurutshe in this matter of forced removal with the same amount of fervour. According to Manson, both missionaries made representations to the Boers. "Prominent Marico Boers, particularly Casper Coetzee and his brother-in-law Diederick Coetzee were casting around for a site for a town in the Marico District. Dinokana with its plentiful supply of water was the obvious choice, and for several months plans were afoot to move the Hurutshe to Mabotsa, site of Livingstone's station with the Kgatla, but still within Moiloa's reserve[231] … Zimmermann immediately objected in writing to President Pretorius and negotiated with Viljoen to prevent the proposed removal of the Hurutshe. The following year Jensen resumed the missionary protest … There was a good deal of self-interest behind the missionaries' endeavours."[232] If both missionaries wrote a letter then it was probably true that they also represented the Bahurutshe out of self-interest, as Manson alleges. The protest of the two Hermannsburg missionaries probably contributed to the circumstance that the Boers did not immediately implement their plans.

When the Boers delayed their plans to forcefully relocate the Bahurutshe, something else occurred quite coincidentally. Thomas Jensen had come to the Transvaal on his own. He now received word that his fiancée, Karoline Witte, had arrived in Natal. He immediately started out to go and fetch her. Halfway through his journey, at Mooi River, he happened to come across the Boer President Pretorius. He took this opportunity to convey to

[229] A comparison between the exchange rate of the English pound in 1875, as opposed to modern times: 1 pound = 98 USD = 75 Euros; 1 shilling = 5 USD = 3,80 Euros; 1 pence = 0,40 USD = 0,30 Euros. Cf. http://futureboy.us/fsp/dollar, under 'Historical Currency Conversions', accessed 22. 12. 2011.

[230] Thomas Jensen 29.06.1865 p. 3.

[231] Land reservations of the Bahurutshe, allocated to them by the Boers.

[232] Manson 1990 p. 144.

Pretorius the troubles of the Bahurutshe. During his trip he had actually been thinking of something completely different. Now the surprising opportunity presented itself whereby he could speak to Pretorius about pressing matters relating to the Bahurutshe. During this encounter he also broached the subject of taxes which had, in his estimation, been set far too high for the Bahurutshe.

After Thomas Jensen was back in Dinokana for some time after he had returned from Natal, he received a letter from the President, asking him to relay the message contained in it to the chief. The letter read: "If Moiloa is not in favour of a town then it should not be established, and the taxes are to be reduced to one pound."[233] Not only Thomas Jensen, but the chief and the entire tribe were delighted with this news.

The vast majority of the Bahurutshe still resided on the Pooe Mountain. But when they heard the news that they would no longer be forced to relocate they made preparations for their last move into the valley below. This time it was out of their own volition and in their own interest.

The Bahurutshe relocated one last time before finally settling down. Thomas Jensen reports this event, having been an eyewitness. He was amazed at the speed with which the Bahurutshe were able to abandon their round huts, only to erect new ones at the same time. Within a short period of time the large number of rondavels was demolished and reconstructed in the fertile valley of Dinokana.[234] Missionary Wilhelm Behrens, too, who still resided at Dinokana at that time, marvelled at the massive relocation. "The Bahurutshe have abandoned their old settlement and are building a new one. The old chief Moiloe has now consolidated into a settlement his entire tribe which, up to this point, had resided here and there in small kraals, this new settlement now having attained such a notable size that one can only now see how large the tribe of the Bahurutshe actually is."[235] Behrens' quote bears witness to the fact that now those Bahurutshe, too, who had lived scattered across the area had also resettled in the vicinity of

233 Thomas Jensen 29.06.1865 p. 3; cf. Manson 1990 p. 148. – "Wenn Moiloa das Dorf nicht will, sol les nicht angelegt werden, und die Abgaben sollen auf ein Pfund verringert werden."

234 Thomas Jensen 29.06.1865 p. 4.

235 W. Behrens 01.10.1865 p. 2. – "Die Bahurutse haben ihre alte Stadt verlassen, und bauen eine neue. Nun hat der alte Häuptling Moiloe sein ganzes Volk, was hier und da auf kleinen Kraalen wohnte, zusammengezogen in eine Stadt, sodass die neue Stadt einen besonderen Umfang erreicht, und man nun erst recht sieht, wie groß das Volk der Bahurutse ist."

their chief. They were probably those members of the Bahurutshe tribe who had not taken part in the previous relocation to Taung, as well as those who had had the courage to leave the Pooe Mountain at an earlier stage and, on their own responsibility, to settle in an area close by. Several Bahurutshe constructed their houses only "ten minutes" away from Thomas Jensen's house.[236] For the time being everything was peaceful.

3.1.6 Succession Quarrels

The tribe now lived peacefully for ten years. Everything seemed to run smoothly. Could anything else happen to them, seeing that the Boers left them in peace? Yes, they themselves created new upheaval. One particular quarrel even led to the eventual split of the tribe. Moiloa II had died. Until he passed away the tribe had experienced inner peace. Now a quarrel ensued over the rightful heir to the throne. Moiloa II was at the root of this quarrel, even if this dispute was not carried out while he was still alive. He had appointed his successor. It was not customary to do that; neither do we know what his motivation was. Maybe he had a personal fondness for Mokgatlhe's son Gopane. Moiloa II had learnt a great deal from his uncle Mokgatlhe. They had ruled the tribe together for many years. Moiloa II certainly favoured Mokgatlhe's son, his nephew *Gopane.* The latter was very pleased about this, of course, and he proceeded to gather a number of tribe members around him who supported him. There was another group at the same time, however, who advocated the selection of a successor to be determined according to the relevant regulations. This group had decided upon *Ikalafeng,* a grandson of Moiloa II.[237] Ikalafeng, too, proceeded to gather his adherents around him. The understandable consequence was that there were visible tensions within the tribe that did however not escalate. That in itself was extraordinary. Thomas Jensen possibly also did his part to prevent one side from inflicting violent acts on the other. Each of the two contenders had the support of roughly half the tribe behind them. The Christian congregation was not very large yet, but the majority of parishioners were sympathetic towards Gopane. Only a few Christians supported Ikalafeng.

---

[236] Thomas Jensen 29. 06. 1865 p. 4.

[237] Breutz 1953 p. 98.

When the Boers were involved in a war with Sekhukhune, the chief of the Bapedi, in the eastern Transvaal, the former called on the Bahurutshe to provide them with ancillary warriors. Both contenders to the chieftainship despatched the same number of young men to join the war. Thomas Jensen comments: "Some time ago the government asked the two chiefs for assistance against *Sekokuni,* and so they both sent 107 men with four wagons each; amongst them 14 baptised Christians."[238] Regarding the Christians it should be noted that they requested that their missionary provide them with a church elder, so that he could pray for them during battle. When the congregation was informed of the request of these young men, one church elder volunteered to make himself available to minister to their spiritual needs.

After the war with the Bapedi in the Eastern Transvaal[239] the British annexed the Transvaal for a short period. This annexation dated 1878 provided the adherents of Ikalafeng with an opportunity. They were sympathetic towards the British and were hoping to receive some kind of support from them when they seized power in Dinokana. And that is exactly what happened. Manson writes: "They were successful with the English in 1878 after the annexation, for Sir Theophilus Shepstone directed that MOILOA's grandson Ikalafeng … was to rule Dinokana, whilst GOPANE was to leave."[240] Moiloa II had already died back in 1875. For five years Gopane had ruled his adherents in Dinokana. In 1880 he moved to Maanoane. He settled in the vicinity of the place where Livingstone had resided together with Edwards for three years. That was where Inglis had visited Edwards. It was from Maanoane that he had undertaken his exploratory journeys to the Bahurutshe at Ga-Ditshwene.

After the Boers had escorted Edwards and Inglis from their stations to Potchefstroom, and the Bakgatla were compelled to flee from Maanoane to Botswana because of the Boers, the site had been left vacant and could be resettled. In Thomas Jensen's estimation Maanoane lay only four hours to the west of Dinokana.[241] He regretted this relocation as most of the Christians left with Gopane. Only a hundred members of his congregation stayed with him in Dinokana. Church attendance declined accordingly. This

---

238 Thomas Jensen 02.01.1880 p. 3. – "Vor einiger Zeit hat die Regierung die beiden Häuptlinge um Hilfe gegen Sekokuni gebeten und so haben sie jeder 107 Mann mit vier Wagen geschickt; darunter 14 Getaufte."

239 This province is now called Mpumalanga.

240 Manson 1990 p. 88.

241 Thomas Jensen 02.01.1880 p. 3.

changed again after a couple of months, however. After the split, to wit, the number of traditional believers who attended the services increased again. Thomas Jensen was delighted. "Even the chief, who has never previously come to church, now attends the services."[242] Further good tidings were on the way. Gopane asked for a missionary to be sent to Maanoane. "Thus the good Lord has turned out everything to the best. Praise be to Him."[243]

3.1.7 Ikalafeng's attempted Insurrection in the Reservation

Up to the Anglo-Boer War in 1879, political events in the Transvaal were largely determined by the Boers. The chiefs of Dinokana were awarded only limited powers in ruling their tribes, on a clearly demarcated piece of land that had been assigned to them. They thus resided in a reservation. The first land record, signed by Moiloa II with President Pretorius in Potchefstroom, had gone missing. In another document, which had been drawn up by the government and can be inspected in Ferdinand Jensen's records, the following statement can be found: "He (Moiloa II, HB) went to Potchefstroom and requested the Boers, who had driven Umzilikazi away to allow him to re-occupy their old country. Permission was given him by the President Andreas Pretorius and the Commandant-General Hendrik Potgieter, on the condition that he was to be obedient and faithful, but the land was to be Government land set apart for their use as long as they complied with the condition."[244] Compared to other tribes the Bahurutshe had been allocated a larger piece of land. They had accepted the allocation perforce, but had continuously maintained that the land they had been given was not enough.

The Bahurutshe viewed the land as belonging to the tribe. Therefore it was the prerogative of the chief to divide the land as he saw fit. Each clan had the right to apply for a piece of land. The allocated piece of land did not require any form of payment. After the Boers had occupied the country they applied their European standards for land distribution outside the reservation. The Batswana wielded no influence in this matter. Each Boer had the right to obtain two farms. "The Boers had a right to two farms, generally one being set aside for agriculture."[245] Even if individual members of

[242] Id., 26.01.1880 p. 3. – "Selbst der Häuptling, der sonst nie zur Kirche kam, kommt jetzt auch."

[243] Loco citato, p. 3. – "So hat der liebe Gott alles zum Besten gelenkt. Ihm sei Lob dafür."

[244] Ferdinand Jensen, File B item 63, Document par. 3 p. 2.

[245] Manson 1990 p. 88.

the Batswana people had wanted to obtain a farm outside the reservation, they were not granted permission to do so. Since the Bahurutshe resided in a reservation they were allowed to regulate their internal affairs themselves, but they had no say in all matters pertaining to the outside of the reservation. The Boers had no intentions of initiating trans-regional political discussions between the two ethnic groups. The Boers controlled the Bahurutshe and confined them to their reservation. It was obvious that this oppressive situation could not continue indefinitely.

British settlers had meanwhile also entered the Transvaal. Some of them resided amongst the Boers. The possibility that the Boers and British would come to blows in the Western Transvaal was small. The British accepted their subordinate position with regards to the Boers, and even went on hunting trips together. They even forged friendships, as long as the plains of the Transvaal provided sufficient game to be hunted. Consequently, several marriages occurred between the two nations that were otherwise in competition with one another. Manson writes: "There was no antipathy between English and Boer hunters; in fact, they formed their own 'jagtersgemeenskap', a fruitful alliance of English finance and Boer skills."[246]

After the Boers and the British had started using fire arms for their hunting, it was only a matter of time before the Batswana were also in possession of their first rifles. Some of them received their fire arms from Jan Viljoen, as already mentioned before. Others obtained them from travelling merchants.

Hunting proved to be a flourishing trade. The Europeans needed base camps in the territory of the Batswana for their hunting expeditions and their trade in trophies. They established one base in Zeerust, a Boer town in the vicinity of Dinokana; Zeerust later became a border town into Botswana. Another base was to the west of where the Bahurutshe were situated, via Vryburg and Kanye towards a northerly direction.[247]

All members of the Bahurutshe who owned a rifle began to prosper. They brought the hunted game to Zeerust to be traded, or they sold it to the merchants who came to Dinokana to purchase the slain animals.[248] This did not only signify the dawn of a new era. The Bahurutshe abandoned their subsistence farming, began to participate in the trans-regional public trade

---

246 Manson 1990 p. 124. One marriage took place, for instance, between Westbeech, an Englishman, and Cornelia Gronum, the daughter of a prominent Boer in Mosega.

247 Manson 1990 p. 126.

248 Id., p. 127.

and profited from this new market. Officially the Bahurutshe were prohibited to own a fire arm. During the peak period of this general hunting frenzy, nobody cared about hunting permits. What was bound to happen eventually happened. Because of this large-scale big game hunting the game was virtually wiped out, which left the Batswana much worse off since a large proportion of their natural resources had been depleted, a circumstance towards which they had admittedly also contributed greatly. Where they had previously endeavoured to conserve nature and to consult their ancestors before slaying a wild animal, their religiosity ceased to be of relevance during the great hunting era and the amount of slain animals took on hitherto unknown proportions.

After the time of great trade had come and gone, during which the first Englishmen had obtained land and houses from the Boers, a larger number of Brits now began settling in the Transvaal. This immigration increased the British influence. Apart from the Hermannsburg missionaries, only a handful of Europeans resided in the Bahurutshe reservation by exceptional permission, but the stronger influence wielded by the British had not escaped the notice of the Africans, causing many Batswana to be sympathetic towards them. The British had initially started off on a bad footing with Thomas Jensen. For one thing, they had introduced "brandy". The Boers also drank a moderate amount of alcohol. The British, on the other hand, frequently indulged in large amounts of alcohol. Thomas Jensen laments: "Almost all the British in this country are drunkards."[249] In spite of this crushing judgement that Thomas Jensen passed down on the first British settlers, he reviewed his opinion seven years later. But not only increasing numbers of new British citizens immigrated to South Africa, Britain had also despatched several war ships with a great number of soldiers. Britain had declared the Cape Colony as well as Natal to be under its rule. They were now planning to take the inland provinces of the Boers as well: the Orange Free State and the Transvaal. To conquer them would not come about without military conflict. And so the Boers and the Brits went to war against each other. The Boers had left the Cape in order to live in freedom and found their own republics. Now the British had advanced on them. The Boers went to war with them because they "… want to sacrifice their life for their freedom, as they say."[250]

[249] Thomas Jensen 02.07.1873 p. 3. – "Die Engländer hier im Land sind fast alle Säufer."
[250] Id., 02.01.1880 p. 2. – "… wollen, wie sie sagen, ihr Leben für ihre Freiheit opfern."

The Africans did not have much to do with this war. Neither did it affect the Bahurutshe reservation in any way. The Bahurutshe nonetheless observed the conflict. They hoped for a victory for the British, from whom they expected to be treated better. It was therefore all the more disappointing to them when this first war was concluded in favour of the Boers. Only during the war had the Bahurutshe been spared the hardships placed on them by the Boers. Thomas Jensen writes: "The hopes of the 'natives' have come to nought, they are dissatisfied and don't want to submit themselves to the Boers again."[251] With regards to the Bahurutshe he observes: "… our people here, the Baharutse, have made themselves guilty where the Boers are concerned. They have come to the help of Montsiwa, a Barolong chief. The Boers view this as an act of hostility against them."[252] What had occurred?

Ikalafeng had come to power with the support of the British. He subsequently felt indebted to them. His dislike for the Boers was well-established by now.

A tribe called the Barolong resided in the Mafikeng area. The Barolong were embroiled in internal strife. Montshiwa, their chief, asked Ikalafeng to come to his aid. With the help of Ikalafeng, Montshiwa defeated his adversaries. Emboldened by his part in Montshiwa's victory, Ikalafeng proceeded to take on the Boers. It began with his refusal to pay taxes to the Boer government. Breutz writes: "Ikalafeng felt strong enough to refuse taxes and prepared to engage in a war with the Boers."[253] He was probably aware of the fact that he would not be able to take on the Boers all by himself. He did after all only rule half the tribe. The second half had left for Maanoane with Gopane. He could not hope for any support from them. But the British were still an option. He had hoped that they would move to Dinokana. The British, however, had no interest in defending Dinokana. Right from the start he fought a losing battle. An Austrian natural scientist by the name of Holub, who happened to reside at Dinokana for three months during that time writes: "And so he decided to perform one of the most nonsensical acts of his life, namely to prepare for war against the Boers by erecting a low stone wall without cement around his settlement, despite having been dis-

[251] Id., 08.06.1881 p. 4. – "Die 'Eingeborenen' sind in ihrer Hoffnung getäuscht, sind unzufrieden und wollen nicht wieder unter die Bauern."

[252] Thomas Jensen 08.06.1881 p. 4.

[253] Breutz 1953 p. 146. – "Ikalafeng fühlte sich stark genug die Steuern zu verweigern und bereitete sich auf einen Krieg gegen die Buren vor."

suaded by the missionary Reverend T. Jensen."[254] The tribe was meanwhile armed with the rifles that the Bahurutshe had used for hunting purposes. Armed with rifles and crouching behind the low stone wall, the tribesmen were to ward off the attack of the Boers.

The Boers got wind of Ikalafeng's plans and confronted the virtually defenceless Bahurutshe with a commando of 800 soldiers. In view of the devastatingly superior power of the Boers a fight did not even ensue, the Bahurutshe called for a truce. The Boers took Ikalafeng captive and marched him off. "In 1882 General Piet Joubert arrested the chief … "[255] A heavy penalty was inflicted on the tribe, the burden of which was also placed on Thomas Jensen. The Boers forced the Bahurutshe to work on their fields again and exacted further heavy payments from them. The penalty was specified to be to the amount of 18,000 pounds sterling. Since the Bahurutshe were not able to come up with this sum of money, they were compelled to make the payment with cattle. "The Boers divested them of 6- to 8,000 heads of cattle, as well as 3- to 5,000 sheep and goats."[256] The Boers were aware of the fact that Ikalafeng did not stand a chance against them. The demands of the penalty were therefore even the more outrageous, and constituted more of an act of subjugation. Thomas Jensen's entire herd was formed part of the penalty payment. He did however lodge a protest against this and his herd was subsequently returned to him.[257] The Bahurutshe had been impoverished in one fell swoop, even if they did not suffer the loss of human life. Did the subjugation by the Boers and the removal of his entire herd of more than a hundred head of cattle contribute towards the fact that Thomas Jensen now viewed the British in a slightly more positive light than before, as mentioned above?[258]

After the alleged rebellion of Dinokana of 1882 the political situation between the Boers and the Bahurutshe did not give rise to any further insurrection for the following thirty years. The Bahurutshe accepted their ghetto. But something else had occurred. The Bahurutshe remembered their ances-

[254] Holub p. 128. – "So entschloss er sich zu einer der unsinnigsten Taten seines Lebens, dass er gegen die Buren rüstete, indem er, trotz des Abratens des Missionars Herrn T. Jensen eine niedrige und zementlose Steinmauer um seine Stadt aufführte."

[255] Breutz 1953 p. 146.

[256] Thomas Jensen 02.01.1883 p. 3. – "Es waren 6 bis 8.000 Kopf Hornvieh und 3 bis 5.000 Stück Schafe und Ziegen, die die Bauern ihnen abnahmen."

[257] Loco citato.

[258] Id., 03.01.1882 p. 2.

tors again. Ikalafeng had provided the impetus. In one part of the barricade they had constructed, on the outskirts of the old settlement, they gathered a large number of stones and piled them into a heap. The cairn grew bigger and bigger. To this day the members of the Bahurutshe tribe contribute towards the building of the cairn.

The idea of cairns as commemoration sites for the ancestors has irrational associations. In earlier times cairns were piled up at the spot where a powerful chief had been laid to rest or where a victory had been obtained.[259] In special times of need the tribe made its way to that site to call on the ancestors for help. Every person, too, who walked past a cairn on his journeys did not fail to add another stone. While doing so he remembered his ancestors and asked them for protection and assistance. The Bahurutshe live with their ancestors and the cairn serves to keep them in their thoughts.

The British had meanwhile defeated the Boers in yet another war, lasting from 1899 to 1901. The Boers nevertheless remained dominant in their two provinces.

The various chiefs were hugely agitated when the Europeans made plans to redistribute the entire country of South Africa yet again. The impetus for this did not come from the Boers on this occasion, but rather from the British. In 1910 the Union of South Africa had been founded under British rule. A superordinate policy for all native Africans in South Africa was to be implemented. The land issue was on the table yet again. The Bahurutshe were also affected by this. Hasselhorn writes: "The first task of the white government under Prime Minister Botha was the conception of the basics for a uniform native policy. The Land Act of 1913 denied the African majority important land rights. It prohibited the purchasing of land by Africans, except in specially designated areas, and the leasing of land to Africans outside these areas. In 'white' South Africa the African was merely to be tolerated as a worker without rights."[260] The Europeans had

[259] Examples of cairns as an ancestral commemoration site for a deceased chief have been attested with the tribe of the Bafokeng. Breutz 1953b p. 61 par 158; cf. Bammann 2010 p. 84.

[260] Hasselhorn 1988 p. 104. – "Die erste Aufgabe der weißen Regierung unter Premierminister Botha war die Konzipierung der Grundzüge einer einheitlichen Eigeborenenpolitik. Mit dem Native Land Act von 1913 wurden der afrikanischen Mehrheit wichtige Rechte genommen. Das Gesetz verbot ihr den Kauf von Land außer in besonders abgegrenzten Gebieten sowie die Verpachtung von Land an die Afrikaner außerhalb dieser Gebiete. Im 'weißen' Südafrika sollte der Afrikaner nur noch als rechtloser Arbeiter geduldet werden."

designed new laws without consulting with the Africans in these matters. They were denied citizenship in the entire country. And once again the issue at hand was the distribution of land.

The missionaries of the various mission societies reacted in different ways to this issue. Most of them rejected the new act, some welcomed it.[261] The chiefs would now have to be informed about the new law. Ferdinand Jensen requested of the government to invite him and the chiefs of the Marico District to Mafikeng, where this act and matters of mutual interest were to be discussed. The focus of the discussion was mainly on the land issue and ended with the chiefs rejecting the new land act. "The land held by the natives in the local area, covering about 150,000 acres, will probably be increased by 60,000. In spite of this … there is great discontent in view of the new law and the Marico chiefs have consequently joined the 'South African Native National Congress'."[262] Ferdinand Jensen was only able to understand this move by the chiefs to a certain extent. He was unable to place much trust in the Africans' ability to maintain and champion a unified, common political position over an extended period of time. He was of the opinion that it would not take long for them to be at loggerheads with one another again. "It is hard to say at this point whether this liaison will last, but I don't believe, given the great amount of discord and jealousy amongst our black people, that it will have a great future."[263]

His guarded scepticism would be proven wrong in the long term. Even if he didn't take a definite stance, the following sentence nonetheless demonstrates that he was sympathetic to the Africans' cause and that he put his trust in them. "This process is in any event an indication thereof that the natives are gradually awakening and that they are no longer prepared to put up with everything from the white population."[264]

The political tensions between the Bahurutshe and the European rulers, most notably the Boers, were due to two trouble areas. The Bahurutshe were, for one thing, obliged to make payments to the Boers for things they did not understand. They had been robbed of their freedom, for another

---

261 Elpick p. 353; 366.

262 Ferdinand Jensen 1913 p. 2f. This Congress was founded in 1912. It changed its name in 1923 to the "African National Congress", the ANC.

263 Ferdinand Jensen 1913 p. 3. – "Ob dieses Zusammentreffen von Bestand sein wird, lässt sich jetzt schwer sagen, doch glaube ich nicht, dass es bei der großen Uneinigkeit und Eifersucht unserer Schwarzen untereinander eine große Zukunft haben wird."

264 Loco citato.

thing, by the fact that their land had been assigned to them, something in which they had had no say whatsoever. Neither had this changed when the British took over. An equitable co-responsibility had been denied to them both by the Boers and the British. That would lead to consequences in the future. This discrimination formed part of the policy that had been introduced by the Boers and the British, known as Apartheid, and would continue for another seventy years.[265]

3.2 Knowledge of the Traditional Religion

3.2.1 Rites of Passage

All nations of this earth pay particular attention to rites of passage. They are in line with phases of human transition. As a rule, there exist four prominent stages of human life to which traditional rituals are attached all over the world: birth, puberty, wedding and death. Normally most people pass through all four stages. Each stage signals a transition to the next, more advanced phase of life, calling for physical change. They constitute creative gifts that no human can refuse or escape by their own efforts. They are life's key- and cornerstones. Even if humans are able to bring about many other changes in their lives, they cannot change the stages of life. They are miraculously motivated and animated by benign forces. The control of a human being fails, he or she relies on the higher power that positively influences the new phase of life. Disruptive factors of hostile powers must be warded off, inhibited or contained. All religions have developed mechanisms for these processes that effect the protection of the higher power, by means of a traditional ritual, against possible harm during these transitional phases of life. Family, state and society at large generally welcome what their religion has to offer, since they acknowledge their meaningfulness or at least their usefulness. Corresponding ceremonies are well-established and bestow official status to the rite of passage. This was certainly the case where the

[265] The above-mentioned ANC was supported by the vast majority of Africans. Being a well-organised movement that was prohibited to make any kind of political public appearances, it nonetheless stood up for the rights of the oppressed population for 80 years in many different ways. In its unremitting struggle against segregation and Apartheid, the ANC assumed political power in South Africa after the first democratic elections were held in 1994 for people of all races and origins. The first African president of South Africa was the civil rights activist Nelson Mandela.

Christian churches and the missionaries were concerned. Anybody is able to easily and openly discern the traditions, rites and rituals.

In African tradition it is the medicine man who assumes responsibility for the religious ceremonies. Much of what is done takes place in secret and covertly.

3.2.1.1 Birth

Birth is the first transitional phase. In the old days only women assisted with the birth of a child. The Batswana put a heavily pregnant woman into a room where she remained in seclusion (= gender segregation) for three months after she had given birth. Only women who were experienced in childbirth assisted her during the birth process and cared for her afterwards. The woman was not allowed to leave the room. Men were forbidden to enter. Even her husband was not allowed to visit her during this time of seclusion. The birth itself received no particular attention, neither by the family nor in public. The new-born was only acknowledged as a human if it had survived the first months of its life. The birth process was fraught with too many dangers. Illness or evil spirits could have brought death to the child. Gollbach writes: "The Tswana do not consider a new-born child, lesea, to be a person as yet. (…) They know that a new-born lives a borderline existence between the world of the ancestors and that of the living."[266] If a child dies during infancy the Batswana say that the ancestors have taken it back. In doing so, they bear the vigour of the tribe in mind that may not be allowed to dwindle. The life force of the weak child has returned to its origin. This life force can be utilised within the ancestral collective for other vitally important things, or bestowed during another birth.

Setiloane assigns the return of an infant to its ancestors to their benevolence: "The reason why children are more susceptible to attack by *'badimo'* is because they are a gift of *'badimo'* – withholding them or withdrawing

[266] Gollbach p. 72. – "Die Tswana betrachten ein neugeborenes Kind, lesea, noch nicht als Person. (…) Sie wissen, das sein Neugeborenes in einem Grenzbereich lebt zwischen der Welt der Ahnen und der der Lebenden." – There has been made frequent mention of the ancestors in this book. J. Mbiti introduced the term "the living dead" instead of "the ancestors" into the mission-theological debate, a term more readily understood in the context of the traditional religions of Africa. J. Mbithi, p. 179. From a religious-historical point of view, the term "the living dead" is of significance. It is rarely applied in theology, however.

them (by death) … they are weak and are easily affected by rapture in relationship with the unseen."[267] After reading the first half of this quote one could draw the conclusion that the ancestors are jealous, and this conclusion is in fact sometimes drawn by missionaries when the latter view them in a negative light. The second part of the quote however disproves this superficial attitude. One must rather assume that the Batswana commonly believe the prevailing sentiment of the ancestors to be concern. If an infant is very weak, the ancestors seize it before it can be infected by evil spirits. As a general rule, a child was only considered to be a human once it was able to scream loudly. This usually happened around the time of the appearance of its first teeth.

The Batswana placed quite a number of taboos on childbirth. A wooden beam was placed in front of the entrance of the hut where the woman stayed in her confinement. This beam indicated to everybody that nobody was allowed to enter. Her own husband, as mentioned above, only saw his wife and child after three months. Then it was carried outside and shown to everyone. Neighbours and close relatives then came along to welcome the baby.

During those three months of seclusion, only one man was granted access to the hut: the medicine man of the family. He came early in the morning before sunrise so that the neighbours could not see him. After he had performed his protective procedure he disappeared just as unnoticed as he had arrived. Sometimes even the medicine man was not able to save a child, during a miscarriage for instance. Schapera comments: "It was essential that the foetus of the miscarriage or abortion should be buried inside the woman's hut or in some other shady spot. If it was buried out in the open, it will spoil the country and make it dry, so that no rain will come."[268]

Thomas Jensen was not superstitious, nor did he want to enforce the superstitions pertaining to infants. This might explain his disinterest in the Bahurutshe mother and child. Naturally he as missionary also had no access to women in their confinement.

One particular incident especially scared him off. The Bahurutshe adhered to the superstition that infants and small children had to be killed if something unnatural occurred during birth or early childhood. He writes about a petty chief who killed his own child: "… just because the teeth

[267] Setiloane p. 264, cf. footnote 23.

[268] Schapera 1971 p. 97.

appeared at the top of the mouth first."[269] According to Bahurutshe belief, it would have brought misery to the family if the petty chief had not killed his child. He kept this incident in mind and mentioned it even many years later[270]

Thomas Jensen was not able to understand this radical, superstition-based method of selection where infants were concerned. Neither did he exhibit much interest at all in the Bahurutshe's traditional ways of a mother and her child. It is possible that he was unable to relate to this subject matter in an appropriate way because his wife had experienced a stillbirth during the period when the above instance occurred. The birth of his child took seventy hours and ended in tragedy "... because there was no medical help nearby."[271]

3.2.1.2 Initiation

Every growing child passes through puberty. During those years a child's body matures into adulthood. It is the onset of the second phase of the rites of passage.

Amongst the Batswana puberty constituted the only time in a child's life that it received some kind of education from the community. This education was bound up with the ritual of circumcision. This ritual descended from ancient times and had been adopted by previous generations. Circumcision was regarded as being an integral part of society and was executed every time one of the chief's sons had reached the age of puberty. For these youngsters, circumcision was the highlight of a ten- to twelve-week-long training- and learning period, which took place outside the settlement. The circumcision itself was performed during the first week already. A couple of rest- and healing days followed. The remaining weeks served to introduce the initiates to the entire spectrum of their social responsibilities.

There are three aspects worth emphasising that were of significance to the initiates during the circumcision school period. Being led towards the status of adulthood comprised the acceptance of one's own life which is inextricably linked to customs and practises, as well as the obligatory responsibility to support these customs and practises in both family and

[269] Thomas Jensen 29.12.1865 p. 8. – "... nur weil die Zähne oben im Munde zuerst zum Vorschein kamen."

[270] In Thönike p. 19.

[271] Thomas Jensen 28.06.1866 p. 4. – "... weil keine ärztliche Hilfe in der Nähe war."

After concluding their initiation ritual, the young girls of the community are publicly presented

community. This also meant, by way of example, the obligation to start one's own family. It was considered to be taboo to have sexual intercourse before the start of the initiation school. If someone was caught in the act before having been circumcised, he was killed. After having absolved the initiation school the initiates were free to find themselves a partner and fall in love. Another sphere of responsibility was the traditional belief system with all its rituals and taboos, the adherence of which was demanded by the ancestors on a personal- as well as tribal level. A third aspect was also not to be scoffed at. It concerned obedience. For tribal society to survive required absolute obedience. The young people had to subordinate themselves to all their leaders, the older people of their family as well as the chief; they furthermore had to honour their obligations towards the ancestors.

The initiation school guaranteed an intact tribal social structure. A tribe could only be successful if the strict stipulations of the leading men and women of the initiation school were adhered to and implemented. The chief himself had little to do with the initiation school. The community of traditional believers made their own arrangements in this regard. He was however included in all preparations and in all processes during the course of circumcision.

After circumcision the youngsters adorn their bodies and proudly walk about the village in small groups with their peers

The initiation schools for boys and girls were in separate locations. The boys' school *(bogwera)* took place on a mountain. The girls' school *(bojale)* was placed preferably close to a waterhole on level ground. Both schools were conducted in winter. The girls' school was organisationally linked to the boys' school. While the boys had to undergo the procedure of circumcision there is no evidence to show that the girls were also circumcised.

The chief gave the sign for the initiation school to commence. First the tribe was informed. The tribesmen discussed the adolescent members of their tribe in clandestine meetings. Then the families whose children were involved were informed. The matter was hardly ever discussed in public. Whoever had been informed about particulars concerning this matter remained silent. The names of the initiates were then called out during tribal assemblies. The initiates themselves were not informed until the day they left for the school. They received no preparation. They required no clothing, no suitcase or any other paraphernalia. They were only allowed to take a woollen blanket.

News of the initiation school often only reached Thomas Jensen after it had already started. The initiates (boys) began by spending roughly one week with the chief in the central area of the village. Not much took place there. The initiates were divided into smaller groups of six to eight boys, each group consisting of boys from the same clan. The purpose of the first week was that the boys could get used to one another and to live together in close quarters. Their custodians beat them often and hard. Thomas Jensen writes: "For one week they are beaten severely with a stick every morning. (...) While the initiates are beaten everybody sings and dances, making a most awful racket." The beatings involved an act of obedience, which entailed that the boy was not allowed to cry. Whoever began crying or even screaming while he was beaten had failed the first test. If a boy cried on several occasions he was sent home, which was seen as a humiliation for the entire family.

The entire village was present during this obedience training, and everyone sang as loudly as they could, thereby stifling the screaming of the initiates. The loud singing of the community never stopped. They sang for days and nights on end. Even when the initiates had already been led away to the mountain, the village community continued singing loudly for the entire duration of the initiation school.

According to J. Comaroff, the stick that was used to beat the boys also had a different meaning. Comaroff points out that the stick can also be understood to symbolise masculinity.

Only men who have previously suffered beatings on their own bodies are allowed to carry out beatings. Only men who have passed through the circumcision school have the right to wield a stick. If a boy wants to be a man he has to demonstrate that he can take a beating. Comaroff articulates it as follows: "... those associated with the postliminal stage revealed the switch to be the palpable symbol of emerging manhood."[272]

The singing and dancing of the sympathising community was not only due to the joy they experienced or because they wanted to drown out the loud wails of the boys. The unspoken, implied, specific nature of this behaviour was that the initiation school could not commence or be concluded without the blessing of the ancestors. The loud noise, the singing and dancing – all that was designed to prevent the ancestors from falling asleep. Setiloane explains why this loud noise is of such importance in Batswana society. "However, '*badimo ba rata modumo*' (ancestors like company). They are pleased when kin are gathered together for feasting and drinking. Therefore, rituals addressed to them are always social in character ... they may be celebrated at different social levels ... They may be 'occasional' rites – birth, death, rainmaking. Or they may be daily or annual events."[273]

[272] Comaroff p. 92.

[273] Setiloane p. 66; Matumo translates *modumo* with 'sounds, noise, rumour'. Matumo, Setswana/English Dictionary p. 247.

Setiloane throws some light on the actual significance of the noise that is not only made at the time of the initiation school but at all social gatherings. By translating '*badimo ba rata modumo'* with 'ancestors like company' he supplies a further explanation. The literal translation is 'ancestors like noise'. Seeing that this noise cannot be generated by one person alone but always arises from a group of people, he cites the metaphorical, less offensive version of the adage: "ancestors like company." His explanation is not incorrect but downplays the actual translation of this saying.

The boys of the village community were presented to the chief for a whole week. During this week they had suffered beatings, had found their place in the group and had proven themselves on their path towards the circumcision mountain. Early in the morning, when the village was still asleep, the custodians took the boys to their new destination. Absolute silence was maintained during the journey. Nobody was allowed to utter a word. Their leaving should not be disturbed in any way. The site on the mountain where the small groups settled had been demarcated with twigs, similar to a rondavel, but open at the top. When the searing sun reached its zenith or a thunderstorm erupted, the boys had no shelter. Circumcision took place during the first days on the mountain. An experienced medicine man performed the procedure. The foreskin was removed from the penis and thrown into a fire that served as sacrificial site for the ancestors. Then a time of healing ensued. The boys slept on the bare ground. Apart from the woollen blanket they had no other clothing. At night they used the woollen blanket to sleep on, and during the day to cover themselves. The custodians kept watch over them.

Each small peer group had its own custodian. The boys were inducted into the traditional rituals and customs by a number of adults, which also included a lesson in conduct towards women. The custodians constantly wielded a stick, using it as an educational tool. In the evenings the boys sang. The texts of the songs contained encrypted words. Comanoff writes: "The days in the circumcision lodge were deployed in continuous and carefully structured activity. Much time was spent on rote instruction through the medium of song and dance: *Dipina tsa molao* (songs of law) provided the semantic frame: at the level of explicit reference, they dealt with some normative basis of the social order and with the principles that underpin authority."[274] If it had only been social disciplinary measures the boys were

[274] Comaroff p. 93f.

subjected to, the procedures that took place in the seclusion of the mountain would not have to be kept secret. However, what happened on the mountain was much more, and of much greater significance.

The circumcision could not be performed in the presence of women. As such it signified an essential aspect of an authoritarian male-dominated society, the adherence of which was imperative. This seclusion also afforded the necessary discretion, since the men were sworn to secrecy about the proceedings. Everything that occurred on the mountain was forbidden to reach the outside world. The encrypted songs formed a part of this, with sometimes only the choir master being privy to their meaning. The singing could be heard in the village. It was a pleasant, beautiful kind of singing, nothing like the racket emanating from the village.[275] When the boys began to sing on the mountain the noise in the village subsided.

After the circumcision operations had been performed and the wounds had healed, the boys were sent out to hunt during the day. They had no weapons and had to prove that they possessed enough skill in catching small game like hares, rabbits and antelopes with their bare hands. This hunt was meant to symbolise their ability to provide meat for their own family one day.

Food in the form of grain sorghum porridge was brought to them daily by married women. They placed their pots in a specific spot, the boundaries of which had been demarcated by piled-up stones. The stones had been marked with a minus on one side and a plus on the other.[276] The minus

[275] Two texts of circumcision songs had been entrusted to Ferdinand Jensen. He recorded them and kept them concealed. 60 years after his death his literary legacy was submitted to the archives of UNISA. This legacy contains one song for girls and one for boys. They were subsequently translated with the assistance of Nono Monageng.The song of the girls (*bojale*): *Ga nke ke lala le mogami a nkga ditshoang a ke reke lonaka go tlala motishana pee* = 'I cannot sleep with a milker who smells of kraal dung, I would rather buy a horn that can fill my pot." (Expression of pride: I am a woman who doesn't just settle for any man.)The song of the boys *(bogwera)*: *Noto Morolong, bathudi bomang boo Rasekganyane, go tla ba kganya ka Kgopha ya Tswai, Tswai ke ye ope, key a o nyangle ene k emo ye, ke tlosa letshipho kgoloane e sale le mong le mong masale* = (An attempt at translation) "Noto Morolong (name of a person), where are the master smiths of the Rasekganyane family, will they be as persuasive as a snake in the open field, the field is nowhere, I go from here to there, I am speaking about a serious matter, where are they?" An attempt at an explanation: It is the smith that is being addressed. The men are in need of shields and spears. The tradition of iron forgery is not allowed to go extinct.

[276] These symbols could be seen in 1978 in Motswedi, denoting border posts on the circumcision mountain.

symbol was directed at the women. The food was fetched by the custodians after the women had left. An encounter was strictly forbidden. Taboo stipulated that all men who were involved in the circumcision school were forbidden to have sexual intercourse during this time. An encounter between men and women was therefore to be avoided at all cost.

It sometimes happened that the healing process did not advance as expected, and the wound became infected. A boy might also occasionally hurt himself while hunting. In such cases the medicine man's expertise was required. It nevertheless occurred occasionally that one or two of the boys died because of these infections, other illnesses or because of an accident. After the conclusion of the circumcision school the woollen blankets of these boys were secretly placed in front of the entrance of their parents' houses. No personal explanation was given for a boy who died on the circumcision mountain. The woollen blanket provided all the explanation that was needed, and no further investigations took place. The taboo mentality of the Bahurutshe prevented the bereaved family members to make further enquiries. The chief was informed of the boys who had died. He, too, had no obligation to notify the parents of their son's death.

Towards the end of the circumcision school, the chief came onto the mountain to speak to the boys. He congratulated them that they were now able to join the ranks of the tribesmen, and participate in the tribal gatherings. He provided the peer group with a name *(mophato),*[277] with which every newly-initiated boy identified himself from then on. If the chieftain should subsequently call out this name from his tribal seat, each one of these boys knew that this call was meant for him. With this group name the boys were obliged to do the chief's bidding in his fields, while hunting, as well as rendering their obedience as a unit during warfare.[278]

During Thomas Jensen's tenure it happened time and again that boys who had been baptised or had signed up for baptismal instruction would suddenly and without explanation stay away from church services or baptismal classes. These boys had, more often than not and without their consent, been taken from their beds by relatives of traditional belief and presented to the chief. There they were forced to get in line with the other initiates. Thomas Jensen reports that they were "... abducted by heathen

[277] W. Behrens also calls the place of circumcision *mophato.* He called the peer group 'Kompanie'. 1874 p. 86f. Breutz translates the term *mophato* with 'Regiment'. 1953b p. 150.

[278] Schapera 1976 p. 38f.

relatives during the night ... "[279] This angered the missionary. He had discussions about these incidents with his parishioners on Sundays. Moiloa II had enforced a strict separation in this regard. Ikalafeng, too, had promoted the separation of circumcision school and church membership. All this had changed under the current chief, Israel.

One day, four boys failed to attend the church service. The size of the congregation was manageable. It was immediately apparent when four youngsters at once failed to turn up. Ferdinand Jensen lodged a complaint with Israel, who had no intentions of maintaining the authority of his predecessors. He could also not conceive of these four youngsters to have to run around naked on the mountain, seeing that they had always worn clothes in the congregation. But worse things were to come. These youngsters had not been abducted. They had entered the circumcision school with their peers of traditional belief out of their own free will. Neither Ferdinand Jensen nor the congregation were able to do anything since the chief was not on their side. "The only punishment we can carry out is exclusion from the congregation, but the apostates don't care much about that, on the contrary, they say openly and freely that they will in any event be readmitted sooner or later, if they should wish it."[280]

For Ferdinand Jensen circumcision lay at the core of the traditional belief system. He called it the "cornerstone of heathendom".[281] For Africans, circumcision lay at the heart of traditional life. It was an act of submission and obligation to one's ancestral spirits. The sacrifice of the foreskin was a reflection of sexual procreation. Offering it to the ancestors symbolised the surrendering and offering up of one's entire being to the ancestors. This belief cannot be reconciled with the Christian faith. In the Christian faith the focus and central point is and remains one's personal belief in Jesus Christ. For Christians, a comparable sacrifice to the one offered up by traditional believers has become obsolete. The circumcision school was a thorn in the side of the missionaries, not only because of the grave theological differences, but also because of the intolerable concomitant circumstances.

One day Thomas Jensen had entered into a conversation with his infor-

---

279 Thomas Jensen 05.07.1878 p. 2.

280 Ferdinand Jensen 07.07.1905 p. 2f. – "Die einzige Strafe, die wir vornehmen können, ist Ausschluss aus der Gemeinde und danach fragen die Abfälligen wenig, ja sprechen es offen und frei aus, dass sie doch kurz oder lang wieder aufgenommen werden, wenn sie es wünschen."

281 Id. 1912 p. 2. – "Grundpfeiler des Heidentums".

mants about the circumcision school. He asked them about its origins and they gave him the following reply: "In ancient times there lived a man who not only hated his wife, but all women. But when his wife turned this over in her mind as to how she could remedy it, the thought occurred to her to circumcise him. But when the man had recovered again he told his king (chief, HB) about it, who ordained that all young men should be circumcised henceforth. He considered it to be a disgrace, however, that such a thing should originate from a woman, who was consequently killed so that she was unable to speak ill of anyone, and it remained a secret amongst men. Women may, under threat of death, not have knowledge of any of this."[282] It remains unclear as to how much folklore or truth is contained within this tale.[283]

3.2.1.3 Wedding

Amongst the Bahurutshe the wedding was not only an event on a specific date, but rather a process that was protracted over a number of years. Several meetings between the two families in question occurred in temporal sequence. A wedding was not simply a matter of two young people having fallen in love and proclaiming their commitment publicly. A wedding signified the merging of two extended families. The young couple was, for the time being at least, of lesser importance. The man's clan started proceedings by despatching a delegation to the clan of the woman, informing them that they wanted to discuss a marriage. Then both sides revealed the names of the two young people. During this first encounter, and after the message had been accepted, the guests were offered beer. Lestrade writes that, all in all, three such meetings took place.[284]

---

[282] Thomas Jensen 29.12. 1865 p. 6. – "In uralter Zeit ist ein Mann gewesen, der seine Frau, wie überhaupt alle Frauen, hasste. Als seine Frau aber darüber hin und her dachte, wie dem abzuhelfen wäre, kam sie auf den Gedanken, dass sie ihn beschneiden müsste. Als der Mann aber wieder gesund war, erzählte er es seinem König, der von da an befahl, dass alle Jünglinge beschnitten werden sollten. Er hielt es aber für eine Schande, dass solches von einer Frau herrührte, darum wurde die Frau getötet, damit sie nichts nachsagen konnte, und so blieb es als ein Geheimnis unter den Männern, die Frauen dürfen bei Todesstrafe nichts davon wissen."

[283] For more information on the circumcision school, cf. Schapera: 'Bogwera-Kgatla Initiation'; Purnell pp 24–29 (Nelson Mandela's circumcision).

[284] Lestrade p. 938f. In the German town of Hermannsburg during the 19th century, the practise of three meetings taking place before a wedding also still existed, albeit in a

During the second encounter the amount of cattle was discussed that the future husband's family was obliged to present to the family of the bride by way of a dowry. If both families belonged to the social middle class, two or three heads of cattle would suffice. This is borne out by an old wedding song sung by the suitor, the contents of which means, freely translated: "Mother/aunt, kindly open the door. I am here with good news. There are two heads of cattle, maybe even three. A wedding is in the offing."[285] If the family was well-off or if, in later times, a woman had had an education, the dowry was increased to around ten heads of cattle and, in the case of a chief's family, that amount was doubled once more. The bridegroom attended the third meeting and was introduced to his parents-in-law. He had, for his part, prepared himself for this encounter and presented his parents-in-law with a personal gift of a calf or a goat.

When the agreed-upon heads of cattle were led to the bride's homestead, her uncle (*malome*) had a specific task to perform. He had to inspect the cattle. If they were too thin or too small, negotiations were resumed once again. If all heads of cattle had been presented and the inspection yielded a positive result, the bride could start making preparations to relocate. If a defect was detected, she stayed put. Since the bride's family took care to ensure that their daughter was treated with respect, all agreements had to be adhered to. This could sometimes take one or even two years. After the successful conclusion of the second negotiation the groom was allowed to have sexual intercourse with his bride. A child was subsequently sometimes born before the last heads of cattle had been handed over. If the bridegroom's family was, for whatever reason, unable to honour the reached agreement during the final meeting, the child remained with the bride's family. She herself was taken to her husband's family, however.

The practise of dowry is upheld to this day. Europeans often refer to the dowry as bride price.[286] The correct translation is however dowry. The terms bride price or wife-purchasing are derogatory terms, the use of which

---

shorter period of time. The first encounter was called *Besehen* = taking a look. The bride's parents took their daughter to the homestead of the future parents-in-law. The engagement was agreed upon six weeks later. During the third visit the marriage could be sealed as *Tausag*. Von der Ohe, in Gercke p. 93.

285 *Mangoane mpulele, ke neeloa ke pula, fa di le pedi, fa di le tharo, di nyala mosadi.*

286 The following authors use the term 'bride price' for *bogadi:* Sundermeier p. 87f; Hasselhorn 1988 p. 22; Fiedler p. 29,57; Voges p. 249. Others who clearly espouse the usage of the term "dowry" are Ferdinand Jensen 1931 p. 4; Gollbach p. 92; Mignon p. 141f.

attests to a rather superficial knowledge of that particular foreign culture. British missionaries erroneously described the practise of *bogadi* as 'undisguised wife-purchase' and forbade their Christian families to engage in it: "The early missionaries regarded the giving of *bogadi* as undisguised wife-purchase, and forbade Church members to practise it."[287] Following Schapera's quote and speaking generally about the Hermannsburg missionaries, Voges also states: "The bride price, which was given to the bride's family by way of thanks and served as legal security for the wife, was branded as being wife-purchasing and forbidden for Christians."[288] Hasselhorn illustrates, however, that a generalisation of the prohibition on the dowry is not possible as far as the Hermannsburg missionaries are concerned, but rather that this decision was taken at a specific point in time by just one congregation in Natal, for instance: "By taking a strong line with regards to the station ordinance, the mission administration believed that it could thereby avoid a kind of Christianity that was merely superficial in nature. This led to resistance from the Hermannsburg congregation in 1882, when the payment of a dowry was disallowed."[289] One is unable to clearly discern which translation Hasselhorn actually favours. The same applies to Sundermeier. They both use both terms. For instance, Sundermeier states that the bride cannot be purchased, but then proceeds to use the terms bride price, bride price system, child price and bride price debts several times.[290]

The African understanding of this concept is that a woman is not purchased. The dowry is of other significance: First and foremost, it is deemed to be an expression of thanks, which is reflected in the gifts. The negotiated cattle cannot be bought with money. In rural areas they are quite simply essential to sustaining life per se. If the cattle died out, the life of humans was also in peril. A wedding provided all participating parties with the promise: life goes on.

Consequently, the cattle served as the connecting link of life between two families. The union of the bridal couple simultaneously created a bond

287 Schapera 1939 p. 84f.

288 Voges p. 249. – "Der Brautpreis, der als Dank für die Brautfamilie und Rechtssicherheit für die Frau galt, wurde als Frauenkauf abgestempelt und für Christen verboten."

289 Hasselhorn 1981 p. 92. – "Durch die energische Handhabung der Stationsordnung glaubte die Mission, die Gefahr eines bloß äußerlichen Christentums vermeiden zu können. Dies führte in der Gemeinde Hermannsburg 1882 zu Widerstand, als die Zahlung der Brautgabe verboten wurde."

290 Cf. Sundermeier p. 87f.

of friendship between two extended families. One family would look after, protect and assist the other family in times of need. The Africans held this perspective in high esteem. Ferdinand Jensen is of the opinion that the dowry was given for the future children of the couple and not primarily for the woman. "Therefore one cannot speak of a wife-purchase amongst the Bahurutshe, since the wife doesn't become the property of the husband but continues to live at her parents' house up to the birth of her first child, where she remains under the protection and authority of her clan. Thus the husband is also unable to sell her on to someone else."[291]

The wedding was a mutual endeavour between the two extended families, who had become acquainted with one another in the years during which the dowry was negotiated. The wedding also highlighted another important aspect. The young couple bore children, as many as possible. The status of a family was increased if it had a great number of children to show. Children were of great significance to parents. They constituted their insurance. They provided for their parents in their old age. Who else would do it? There were no life insurance companies and old-age homes. Children had to look after their ageing parents and, when they died, bury them in accordance with the traditional rituals and customs. No person was allowed to die in anonymity and bereft of all good spirits. That would bring disaster upon the families concerned.

Weddings did not only take place because two people had learnt to know and love one another. Many unions were arranged by the parents. If the parents were friends with another family, it happened quite frequently that they closed a marriage deal on behalf of their children. The children were forced to oblige. It was not uncommon for the children of two families to be betrothed to one another even before they were born. Both Jensen missionaries tell of incidents where the parents had decided on a marriage over their children's heads. Thomas Jensen writes in 1874: "Matrimony amongst the Bahurutshe finds itself in dire circumstances, one can hardly call it a marriage, it is really nothing but adultery in most instances. The betrothal is brought about by the parents, in most cases when those to be

[291] Ferdinand Jensen 1931 p. 4. – "Man kann darum nicht von einem Frauenkauf bei den Bahurutshe sprechen, da die Ehefrau nicht in das Eigentum des Mannes übergeht, sondern auch vielmehr nach der Eheschließung bis zur Geburt des ersten Kindes im Elternhaus und unter Schutz und Gewalt ihrer Sippe bleibt. Darum kann sie der Ehemann auch nicht weiter verkaufen."

betrothed are still children."[292] Thomas Jensen finds it impossible to condone such traditional forms of marriage amongst the Bahurutshe. He judges them from his Christian point of view. He objects to two aspects: he first mentions the betrothal. Children are betrothed to one another while they are still too young to know what marriage actually entails. Later they are compelled to submit to this arranged marriage, irrespective of any mutual affection they might have or even develop for one another. Following this first aspect, Jensen comes to the second conclusion that these spouses will have a relationship with another person whom they actually love. He therefore draws the conclusion that most married people are adulterers.

In 1931, more than half a century later, Ferdinand Jensen writes: "Thus it happened that the girls were betrothed to someone straight after birth, some parents entered into a contract by which the unborn children were betrothed to one another. This betrothal is called *Peelelo,* from *go beelela,* to save, put aside. It simultaneously constituted a marriage that was binding on both sides."[293] Upon comparing these two quotes by father and son, is becomes apparent that father Jensen was in a confrontational frame of mind. He is faced with the reality of the situation and takes his position in accordance with the commandment of the Decalogue "Thou shalt not commit adultery". His son Ferdinand Jensen tries to understand and explain with the meaning of the betrothal term as to how it originally came about that the patriarchs provided for the future in this way. A fair amount of self-interest undoubtedly played a role, too. The parents' considerations were however also informed by the desire to lead their clans into the future and to reside in good neighbourliness with their best friends. In the old days, when the collective was geared towards a closed society, unions of this kind posed the possibility to preserve one's own clan.

[292] Thomas Jensen 1874 p. 76. – "Mit der Ehe unter den Bahurutshe steht es sehr schlecht, man kann es eigentlich keine Ehe nennen, sondern in den meisten Fällen ist es lauter Ehebruch. Die Verlobung wird von den Eltern zuwege gebracht, meistens wenn die zu Verlobenden noch Kinder sind."

[293] Ferdinand Jensen 1931 p. 4. – "So kam es, dass die Mädchen gleich nach der Geburt verlobt wurden, manche Eltern machten einen Kontrakt, demzufolge die ungeborenen Kinder einander versprochen wurden. Die Verlobung heißt *Peelelo*, von *go beelela,* aufbewahren, zur Seite stellen. Sie war gleichzeitig Eheschließung und auf beiden Seiten bindend."

3.2.1.4 Death and Burial

The Bahurutshe buried their dead immediately after death had occurred. Why did they do this? There are several reasons for this. One reason lay in the climatic conditions. The sun burnt down from the sky. With very few exceptions, almost every day of the year was hot. Under such conditions an odour of putrefaction could soon be expected to emanate from the corpse. There were no mortuaries and cooling facilities. The deceased had to be buried the same day. The situation in the village was manageable and news of the death of a person was proclaimed by the tribal crier and carried into each house within minutes.

Another reason had to do with the superstitious belief of the Bahurutshe. In their view there was always a sinister cause for death, nobody died of natural causes. Death always occurred as a result of some calamity. Certain suspicions cropped up repeatedly. Death could have occurred due to a hunting accident or because of disease. The question remained at the back of people's minds, however, as to the root cause behind these occurrences. Who or what had caused someone to die? Evil spirits, or discontented ancestors whose conduct humans were unable to grasp? Or had death been caused by people with evil intent in the neighbourhood, who had clandestinely banished their adversary from the living with magic potions of sorcery? People were gripped by uncertainty, which instilled great fear in them. That was why the medicine man was so important. He was summoned immediately after someone had died to clarify the cause of death. After his analysis the community could either immediately proceed to bury the deceased, or it was postponed. If hostile forces were the cause of death, he had to use his skills to reconcile them via the realm of sorcery. After that the deceased was released for burial.

Various rituals had been put in place for the burial. One ritual was concerned with the idea that the deceased should leave this earth in a similar way as he had entered it. The infant in embryonic posture had grown into an upright adult. The dying person needed to be restored to his original posture and therefore had to be buried in an embryonic position. His soul *(seriti)* should continue its wanderings into the other world in a humble posture. There, upon arrival, the ancestral forces would straighten it up again. This ritual contained another reason why burial had to be undertaken speedily after death had occurred. The burial in an embryonic position could only take place as long as the body was still flexible and rigor mortis had not yet set in.

The rituals that were prescribed for the burial had to proceed smoothly so that the spirit could come to rest. Until such time that the body was buried, a wake was held so that the body was surrounded by humans until its interment. Cleansing provisions had to be observed and abstinence adhered to. The soul was in a state of upheaval, a period during which it was deemed to be especially vulnerable to the influence of evil spirits seeking a portal in order to do it some harm. The medicine man inspected the house. The risk of misfortune could lurk anywhere. He scattered protective medicine all over the house and yard. It was compulsory and in the personal interest of each relative to attend the funeral ceremony. If someone was absent, suspicion would be cast on that person being responsible for the evil that had led to the demise of the deceased.

Even after burial the oppressive situation showed no sign of abating. The traditional belief that the soul had to continue on its wanderings after death instilled just as much fear into the living as the uncertainty with regards to the destructive powers before death. The wanderings to the ancestral collective lasted one year. There was no guarantee as to the successful conclusion of those wanderings. There were many temptations for the soul of the deceased along the way. If the wandering was not clearly indicated the soul could go astray and take a wrong turn. Other spirits were also on the same wandering, some of them evil, who could try to lead the good souls astray. The evil spirits could harm the soul. Then the wandering would be interrupted or even halted completely. This was also the function of the medicine man, to remove all uncertainty in this respect. If there was any indication that the soul could come to harm, the entire family was summoned and the medicine man proceeded to remediate the damage before their eyes. It was an extremely sensitive area. Too much was at stake.

If people are buried a few hours after they have died there is hardly a way to establish whether a state of apparent death had occurred, for whatever reason. So it might definitely have happened in such exceptional circumstances that a person was buried alive. The Bahurutshe did not have a medical practitioner, to wit, who could determine and certify that a person had indeed died.

Matlhanka was almost buried alive. Thomas Jensen estimated his age to be around eighteen or twenty years. He worked on one of the Boers' farms; a diseased cow was being slaughtered there on one occasion. Matlhanka ate from the meat of this animal, immediately fell ill and lost consciousness.

His parents were informed, who requested that he be brought to Dinokana. Seeing that he exhibited no signs of life at all, his family declared him to be dead. His grave was dug and his family made preparations for the burial. While they were still busy Matlhanka unexpectedly regained consciousness. Thomas Jensen comments: "The heathens here have the custom to bury the corpses straight away, just after they have passed away."[294]

Thomas Jensen describes the death of his chief, Moiloa II, in great detail. The chief's funeral was attended by a great number of people of all races. His influence had spread far and wide.

Most of the mourners were Bahurutshe. Moiloa II had been the first chief of Dinokana. He was not baptised but nevertheless had had an amiable relationship with Thomas Jensen. Jeffreys/Jensen write: "Moiloa, who had become a great ally of the Boers, died on the 6th July 1875, much lamented by Blacks and Whites."[295] Shortly before he died he summoned Thomas Jensen and told him how he would like his funeral to be. Several of the traditional rituals were to be omitted. When Thomas Jensen asked him what he meant by that, Moiloa II replied that he did not want to be buried while he still gave his last gasps, but rather after he had really died. He didn't want to his body to be bound into an embryonic position with ropes. He furthermore wished to be laid into a coffin, according to European custom. Thomas Jensen was to see to it that his wishes were carried out. And so it happened. Thomas Jensen consulted with the tribal elders who subsequently conformed to the wishes expressed by Moiloa II. They procured a coffin and, since they wanted to be sure that he had actually died, they did not bury him on the day of his death but at a later date. Thomas Jensen reports and explains: "I had to promise him that I would see to it that he would be laid into a coffin. He was afraid of being tied up and buried in the style of the Batswana. They tie up the body, usually even before it has breathed its last breath, into a sitting position; the grave is immediately dug and, even before the body is cold, it is placed into the grave and buried."[296]

294 Thomas Jensen 30.09.1866 p. 2. – "Bei den Heiden ist es hier nämlich Gebrauch, die Leichen gleich zu begraben, wenn sie eben abgeschieden sind."

295 Jeffreys/Jensen p. 178.

296 Thomas Jensen 19.07. 1875 p. 4. – "Ich musste ihm das Versprechen geben, dass ich dafür sorgen wollte, dass er in einen Sarg gelegt würde. Er war bange für das Zusammenbinden und Begraben nach Weise der Betschuanen. Sie nämlich binden, gewöhnlich noch bevor der Odem völlig ausgegangen ist, den Leichnam zusammen, dass er eine sitzende Stellung hat; zu gleicher Zeit wird das Grab gemacht, und noch bevor die

On the day of the funeral the Bahurutshe bade farewell to their chief; the long line of the large number of mourners moved past the open coffin. Thomas Jensen had introduced this German manner of bidding farewell to the Africans. The Africans gladly accepted what constituted a new form of a funeral ritual. While the large crowd of Africans and Europeans moved past the open coffin, a grave was being dug not far from the coffin, in the middle of the large cattle kraal of the tribe. According to the custom of traditional belief the kraal was to be his burial site. The Bahurutshe believe that the deceased have to be supplied with nourishment even after death. The cattle kraal would supply them with ample amounts of meat at all times. Once provision had been safeguarded in this way, it ensured that the spirit would, in its capacity as ancestor, stay with the tribe to protect it and remain approachable during times of need.

It was traditional custom that, during a funeral, one's grief was expressed by means of loud lamentations. The wailing was done by the women. The men mourned in silence. The women's loud wailing also served to awaken the attention of the ancestors. The ancestors played a ubiquitous role, in life, in death, and even after death. No celebration could succeed without commemorating and invoking the ancestors. Moiloa II had planned ahead in this respect as well. He had told the tribe that he did not wish to have any heathenish wailing at his funeral.[297] Therefore only a few women struck up the lament this time. They were reprimanded by the tribal councillors and consequently ceased their loud wailing. It astounded the people that were present that the otherwise obligatory loud wailing was absent from this funeral. The previously mentioned Bahurutshe pronoun, categorised by Ferdinand Jensen in his collection as No. 88, applies in this case: *"Lentswe la kgosi le agelwa lesaka* = the word of the chief holds the tribe/community of the tribe together." He had issued a great number of orders during his rule, most of which had been adhered to. This held true at this funeral too, when the tribe was asked to honour his last wishes.

Speculations may be made as to what had induced the chief to do away with the traditional rituals. Was he convinced that they impeded the development of a civilised way of life at Dinokana? Or did he feel that he couldn't expect of the numerous Europeans that were present at his funeral to put up with the loud wailing? Was he afraid to die? Was he afraid of

Leiche kalt ist, wird sie hineingesetzt und begraben."

[297] Thomas Jensen 19.07. 1875 p. 4.

being treated like a prisoner who is placed in his grave while still barely conscious, only to die under the ground? Was it due to his Christian conviction that he no longer attached much importance to the traditional customs in the face of the new “Lord over life and death”? Maybe it was a mixture of all of the above which induced him to find new ways.

4 Harmony and Disharmony amongst the Bahurutshe

The Bahurutshe's existence was constantly threatened by two factors. On the one hand they found themselves in constant peril from the cosmic powers that caused unforeseen and unpredictably disastrous catastrophes to befall them, leading to devastating consequences within the tribe. The Bahurutshe deemed themselves to be helplessly at the mercy of the spirit world. If the spirits became querulous the Bahurutshe feared for their lives. The well-being of and peace within the tribe were in jeopardy.

On the other hand, they were aware that catastrophes not only emanated from above, but that they themselves could be the cause of these. Their own mistakes might bring on a disastrous turn of events. When rituals were not being observed and taboos broken, these transgressions had to be atoned for with an offering. If these transgressions were to be concealed or downplayed, the spirits would not fail to react. Retribution was sure to follow.

Any unresolved conflicts within the community also resulted in misfortune, disaster and punishment. Harmony was the ideal situation to be aspired to, something that was hampered on a daily basis by natural disasters as well as interpersonal transgressions.

4.1 Natural Disasters

It occurred on a regular basis that the spring rains did not arrive at the right time. Sometimes the rain fell too early, causing the seed to sprout and then wither if no further rain came. It also happened that the cosmic powers withheld the longed-for rain from the Bahurutshe for two consecutive years. In that case nothing was harvested in those two years. During periods of drought life was hard indeed.

But it could also happen that, during a thunderstorm, the rain would pelt down so hard onto the fields that the newly-sprouted seeds were exposed, only to wither in the hot sun that beat down again shortly afterwards. Each year the Bahurutshe were keenly aware of their dependency on an appropriate rainfall. Periods of rain and drought occurred on a regular basis. The periods of drought were harder to endure.[298]

Since ancient times spells of drought proved to be periods of great hardship. Seeing that this was so, the tribal forbears had found a way to combat these periods of hardship with rain-making. Their medicine men had mastered the art of attracting rain by magical means. Sometimes they were successful, at other times less so. Usually all earthly power resided with the chief. Therefore he was in charge of the rain-making process, he could however also delegate this duty. The task was then assigned to one of the most talented medicine men of his tribe. Whoever could conjure up some rain received a special title. He was the *moroka* = rainmaker. During the years of no rain the Bahurutshe regularly called on their rainmaker to deploy his supernatural powers for the benefit of the tribe.

The Christians at Dinokana began following a different path. Instead of attracting the rain by magical means they preferred to pray. Their conduct also differed from that of the rainmaker insofar as the latter performed his task in secret, while they prayed openly. This sent a challenge to the traditional believers. These different forms expressing the quest for rain soon created tensions between the two groups. If the rainmaker was unable to achieve any success with his skills the blame was laid on the Christians. They were said to have been the cause for the rainmaker's impotence in this regard, since they had had failed to attend the traditional gatherings and scorned the old rituals.

1883 proved to be one of those years without rain. The rainmaker had applied his craft to conjure up clouds in the blue sky and send rain to the fields and gardens. He met with no success. Chief Ikalafeng then took command. Since the church had been built on tribal land, he decreed that the entire tribe, Christians as well as traditional believers, should assemble in church on the Sunday before Christmas, and pray for rain. The church was filled beyond capacity. Many had to stand outside due to a lack of seating inside. A couple of thousand people had heeded the call of the chief. Thomas Jensen writes: "Then we prayed for rain and the Lord heard our prayer; …

298 Missionaries who had resided with the Bahurutshe for their entire lives observed the irregular rainfall patterns for many years. They came to the conclusion that the rain patterns formed a cycle of 5–7 years. Each cycle peaked at some point, and then subsided again.

that afternoon we had a fair amount of rain. (. . .) It has however not rained since then."[299]

Could it now be expected that, after the church prayers had been answered, the traditional believers had been persuaded by the public prayer of the Christians to their God, and would abandon their rainmaking practises? Had the heathenish magic proved itself to be powerless? The traditional believers had suffered a defeat, to be sure, but they were not convinced by this once-off occurrence. For the time being the differing views remained between Christians and traditional believers concerning the prayer for rain. Ikalafeng had ordered the rogation service for rain, to wit, but did nevertheless not espouse the Christian cause to such an extent that he placed a prohibition on rainmaking practises. Even so, the Christian message did have an influence on the Bahurutshe, and civilisation increasingly found its way into Dinokana.[300]

Then a period of drought ensued that lasted longer than all previous droughts in living memory. For six years the rainfall had been less than adequate. The traditional believers repeatedly utilised their customary means of making rain, and the Christians prayed. Both sides failed. Only a few drops fell now and again. But the rain drops fell on sandy, arid ground without penetrating the soil, as they evaporated in the heat of the sun in minutes.

---

[299] Thomas Jensen 02.01.1884 p. 3f. – "Wir beteten dann auch um Regen und der Herr hörte das Gebet; . . . den des Nachmittags fiel ein schöner Regen. (. . .) Seitdem hat es aber nicht wieder geregnet."

[300] Setshele, the chief of the Bakwena, had taken a different decision in this regard. He was a conscientious Christian. "As chief Sechele was also high priest with the duty of conducting the rites whose object was inducing rain to fall . . . to the bewilderment of the Bakwena. Sechele now refused to act as rainmaker." Smith p. 156. When Setshele refused to continue in his duty as rainmaker, his brother *Kgoselentse,* who had not converted to Christianity, took over the business of rainmaking. The Hermannsburg missionary Chr. Backeberg, who was stationed at Dithejane during that time, writes: "Rainmaking posed one of the greatest obstacles . . . One of the chief rainmakers was Setshele's brother Kgoselinzi . . . He appeared emaciated, had smeared his face with black paint and had the look of a proper sorcerer about him. Since there was still no rain the people began to have doubts in their rainmaking abilities. . . . On Wednesday we prayed to God (Kgoselentse was amongst them, HB) . . . The following day Kgoselinzi came to us, enquiring in scornful tones as to when the rain was coming? . . . On Friday dark clouds began to cover the sky and on Saturday it rained exceedingly hard all day long . . . On Sunday we all gave thanks to the Lord . . . Kgoselinzi was also in church . . . The following day he came back to us and confessed . . . Since that time Setshele's people have ceased all rainmaking activity." In *Hermannsburger Missionsblatt* 1860 p. 3f.

During this time of waiting for the cosmic powers to do their work, the rain was a constant topic of conversation.

Ferdinand Jensen sought to engage in a discussion with the traditional believers. He wanted to know from them during which periods of drought they had been the most successful in conjuring up rain. He received two different answers. One oral tradition relates the following: "Ancient popular belief knows of two places where the rainmaking ritual yielded positive results. Close to our little town of Zeerust there is a rocky slope that was indicated to me as being the previous abode of the Bahurutshe-god *Tobega.*[301] During times of drought the chief and his people would undertake a pilgrimage to this spot, taking a sacrificial black bull with them, *go kopa pula* (to pray for rain), a loud voice then emanated from the rock, saying: Hurry back home, I am sending a great rain. I have accepted the bull, but I am returning it to you, go and slaughter it in my honour."[302] Jensen's informants told him that the rain started to fall the very same day. Why did a black bull have to be sacrificed? According to the Batswana's magical belief a black

---

301 The demigod Tobega has a long tradition, according to H. Lange. "A Mohurutshe by the name of Tobega was attacked and killed by a wild buffalo while out hunting. On its way to the great God, his spirit was detained by another spirit named Mogalagatsela. The latter commanded him to return to earth and henceforth be the guardian spirit of his tribe." Lange, in *Die Vögel…* p. 190. Another version, pertaining to a disproportionately large footprint that can be seen on a rock outside Dinokana, is related by the medicine man Kabelo: "The creator God *Lowe* (about whom very little is known amongst the Bahrutshe besides his name, HB) dispatched his assistant *Matsieng* to inspect the recently created earth. Matsieng put his foot onto the rock, which turned out to be nothing but muddy ground. Matsieng had wings. He flew to the other end of the earth, where the same thing happened. Then he rose and flew back to where he came from." – The story of the demigod Matsieng was related on site by Josia Matsie for the first time in 1979, and again in 20.7.2011. It is possible that this orally transmitted story is tied up with a family tradition. The demigods of the Bahurutshe deserve to be further explored. And the deity *Modimo,* too, has only been touched on briefly in this book, regarding his significance in the cultural worldview of the Bahurutshe. For further reading on *Modimo,* reference is made to his attributes in Setiloane pp. 77–86, Bammann 2014 p. 213–219.

302 Ferdinand Jensen 1931 p. 1f. – "Der alte Volksglaube erzählt von zwei Stellen, bei denen man mit Erfolg um Regen gebeten hatte. Nicht weit von unserem Nachbarstädtchen Zeerust gibt es einen Felsenabhang, der als die frühere Wohnung des Bahurutshe-Gottes *Tobega* gezeigt wird. Hierhin pilgerte in regenlosen Jahren der Häuptling mit seinem Volk, als Opfer einen schwarzen Stier vor sich hertreibend, *go kopa pula* (um Regen zu bitten) eine laute Stimme habe dann aus dem Felsen heraus gesprochen: Eilt nach Hause zurück, ich schicke einen großen Regen. Den Stier habe ich angenommen, aber ich gebe ihn euch zurück, schlachtet ihn mir zu ehren."

bull could, seeing that it resembled dark clouds in colour, be more able to trigger the rainfall. Schapera's sources are consistent in this regard: "All informants concur that it had to be a black ox, seeing that rain clouds are black."[303]

The Bahurutshe's second attempt took place at a different site. They resided at Ga-Ditshwene at that time. The countryside was undulating with rocky mountains. The water of a spring on one of the mountains fell into a ravine that was roughly 40 meters deep. The Bahurutshe called this area the "holy mountain Tsoenyane". The rocky ravine with its waterfall had been dedicated to *Ramathakga,* Tobega's assistant.[304] Ramathakga himself was not able to provide the Bahurutshe with rain, seeing that he was only Tobega's assistant. Normal people were forbidden to come near this site. This privilege was only reserved for the *moroka.* On one occasion, when another drought had made itself felt once again, the *moroka* was asked to conjure up rain. He went to Ramathakga's mystical ravine, scooped out water, dug up the bulb of a water lily and concocted a potion with it. A voice was said to have sounded from the dark depths of the ravine, assuring the *moroka* that rain would fall. According to tradition, the rain in Ga-Ditshwene was said to have been conjured up in this way on one occasion.

It was not necessary for the rainmaker to exercise his duties each and every year. The whole matter also always required a great deal of effort and dedication. Some people began to have doubts. For a number of reasons, a certain indifference had settled in. For a while the Bahurutshe neglected their demigods. Consequently, these deities were left alone and therefore became angry. The consequence of that was that the demigods of the Bahurutshe never facilitated rain again. They had moved away and were no longer present in their old sacred places.

But even after the demigods had taken action due to the Bahurutshe's neglect, there was nonetheless no cessation of rainmaking. The rainmaker now no longer needed an intermediate station for his work. He now established direct contact to the ancestors. Ferdinand Jensen draws a comparison between the skills of the rainmaker *(moroka)* and those of the medicine man *(ngaka)*: "Since the majority of the natives are still gripped by the fear of sorcery and really believe in the magical power of certain plants and herbs, it is very easy for the medicine men to dupe them."[305] In fact, rainmaker and

303 Schapera 1971 p. 101.

304 Ferdinand Jensen 1931 p. 2. The author visited this isolated and hidden ravine in 2011.

305 Loco citato. – "Da der größte Teil der Eingeborenen immer noch im Banne der Za-

medicine man were often one and the same person. The person who could conjure up rain acted as medicine man during other times of the year.

About the deity Tobega it was said that it had revealed itself under another name as well, that of "*moroa mogalaatsela*".[306] Under this name the deity had only pledged to hear and facilitate the pleas of the Bahurutshe under certain conditions. These stipulated that the people reject sorcery, murder, theft, adultery, and that they promise to live in peace with other tribes. Ferdinand Jensen comments: "Ever since the Bahurutshe no longer comply with Tobega's demands, he has abandoned them and no longer speaks to their chiefs."[307] Seeing that this report dates from later times, it may be assumed that Christian content played a role in its transmission. During the pioneer days of mission work, the traditional believers didn't want to show any weakness by relinquishing their religious traditions. They were sympathetic towards Christian values, considered them to be good and right, and assimilated them into their African religion.

4.2 Cattle Epidemic

The Bahurutshe were dependent on organic natural processes. They lived in and with nature, formed part of it. If nature's equilibrium was disrupted, they were inevitably faced with a problem. There might have existed technically advanced resources in Cape Town, but that city was very far away. The large cities of Johannesburg and Pretoria were not in existence back then. A couple of Boers might have resided there, and the first British people arrived at a later date. Life in the big cities and the accompanying rural exodus were only to come later. The Dinokana of the 19th century was essentially rural in nature. In times of hardship the Bahurutshe used up their reserves in order to survive. The medicine man was their constant source of hope and help. He was supposed to know everything, do everything and cure everything. He was after all the ancestral medium.

But he, too, had his limits. We have already seen this with the rain man. Would he be able to help if a devastating virus were to start spreading?

uberfurcht steht und wirklich an die Zauberkraft gewisser Pflanzen und Kräuter glaubt, haben die Medizinmänner leichtes Spiel sie zu betrügen."

306 Translated: Son of the owner of a pathway.

307 Ferdinand Jensen, File G item 176 'The Bahurutshe' p. 1f. – "Seitdem die Bahurutshe diesem Verlangen Tobegas nicht mehr nachkommen, hat er sie verlassen und spricht nicht mehr mit ihren Häuptlingen."

Would he be able to help if a plague were to afflict one family after the other? It was obvious: He held no sway over the cosmic powers in such events.

The Bahurutshe's wealth was tied up in the large number of cattle they possessed. These animals were ubiquitous. Heads of cattle were harnessed as draught animals, and for feast days they were used to drag wood from the bush into the settlement. Oxen were harnessed to plough the fields. As previously mentioned, a feast was unthinkable without the consumption of cattle meat. Cattle just formed an integral part of village- and homestead life. They were milked in the mornings, were subsequently driven into the bush by the herd boys, returned in the evenings and spent the night in the kraal close to the entrance of the hut. It was inconceivable to imagine that there would be no cattle one day, even if losses occurred occasionally.

In 1896 a nationwide epidemic broke out. The largest proportion of cattle became ill and no help was in sight. What preventive measures could be taken to protect the rest of the herd? The medicine man knew nothing of vaccinations. The cattle died of the rinderpest, a disease that had hit the entire region. If no relief was forthcoming the people could also die. Matlakana, who had consumed diseased cattle meat, was evidence of that.

The Boers lived in close proximity of the Bahurutshe. Their cattle had also succumbed to the rinderpest. This disease had become such a great threat that the Boers decreed that all heads of cattle that were still alive should be slaughtered to prevent further contagion. Hunger and poverty ensued. Within a short period of time the wealthy Bahurutshe tribe had suddenly become bitterly poor. The cattle not only constituted their wealth but also their livelihood as such. It was a very difficult time for the Bahurutshe, and also for the Jensens.

Thomas Jensen had no other life insurance besides his heads of cattle. Since he had to adapt to hard times just as much as the Bahurutshe, he had reared quite a number of cattle over the years. When the rinderpest broke out he had over a hundred cows, calves and oxen. At the onset of this plague he had taken precautionary measures and separated the herd. Two thirds perished, and a third survived. After the Boers had issued their country-wide decree they also came to him and killed the surviving cattle. "The assets which we have accumulated over the past 32 years really only consisted of cattle, and these were taken from us in just one day, as it were. (...) It is a good thing that we didn't set our hearts on it, otherwise it would have been a grievous situation. Now we were wholeheartedly able to say with Job: The Lord gave and the Lord has taken away; may the name of the Lord be praised."[308]

While the rinderpest swept the country, more people than usual attended the church services. More than a hundred churchgoers attended the daily devotion services, "… an indication that a yearning exists for the Word of God."[309] Similar situations exist all over the world. When people are faced with great hardship they increasingly seek the presence of God and more people enter into a place of worship than during normal times.

4.3 Transgression of Tribal Laws

Natural catastrophes and epidemics brought with them great dangers. They emanated from another world, from above, from outside. Humankind somehow always behaved iniquitously, even if this iniquity could not be clearly defined.

Transgressions could be more easily discerned, however, if they arose from one's own ranks, from below. It was usually a case of individual people having carelessly done something, or neglected in doing something, thereby violating tribal laws and rites. Sometimes they were just annoyed about something and behaved inappropriately, thereby making themselves guilty.

In addition, there were clandestine acts of retaliation, brought about by sorcerous abuses. The community was seen as a whole. Everybody belonged to the same tribe. They lived together in family clans. Living in this collective meant living in a closed community, informed by numerous obligations and precepts. All family members formed part of a hierarchical system. No-one was able to extract him- or herself from that to go individual ways. The lower social groups were represented by their proxies in the next higher social entity. The leaders in each group, usually men of good standing, had proven themselves over a protracted period of time within their social entity and were responsible for maintaining law and order. Nobody

[308] Thomas Jensen July 1896 p. 3f. – "Unser Vermögen, das wir in 32 Jahren gesammelt haben, bestand ja nur in Vieh und das ist ja sozusagen alles an einem Tag genommen. (…) Es ist gut, dass wir unser Herz nicht daran gehängt hatten, sonst wäre es schlimm gewesen. Nun konnten wir von ganzem Herzen mit Hiob sagen: Der Herr hat es gegeben, der Herr hat es genommen, der Name des Herrn sei gelobt."

[309] Loco citato. – "… ein Zeichen dafür, dass ein Verlangen nach Gottes Wort vorhanden ist."

was elected into such a position. Strangers and newcomers were excluded anyway. They were obliged to accept a subordinate role to their leaders. The latter's responsibilities were however not limited to maintaining peace and order. They also had to be well acquainted with their traditional belief system, for example. This position of leadership was normally held by the oldest man in the clan, except if there were very compelling reasons not to do so. He had the most life experience and the dealings with the ancestors had been conferred to him. He also assumed the function of a family priest, even though he was never ceremoniously inducted into this position. It was his great responsibility to protect and safeguard his family's quality of life in all things. If transgressions and breaches of regulations occurred under his jurisdiction, he had to react and take measures.

The chief had to preside over all tribal matters at the highest level, representing it to the outside world.[310] The tribe identified itself with its chief, and his reputation reflected that of the tribe. All petty chiefs were of assistance to him. They met with him on a daily basis during the tribal gatherings. The petty chiefs brought up the topics to be discussed. The chief sat in silence. At the end of the debate he summarised what had been said, arriving at a decision that was universally binding. If he rose to speak during judicial hearings, he declared a verdict. His verdicts could not be retracted.

All cases that the petty chiefs were unable to deal with themselves were brought before the chief, as well as all transgressions of rules and laws pertaining to interpersonal relationships. These also included cases of sorcery. In the event that an incident of sorcery or a poisoning were being openly discussed within the tribe, these occurrences were taken exclusively before the tribal council. The culprits were severely punished by the chief. Many problems existed in the closed community of the tribe that did not occur, or at least not to that extent, in a more open society. The chief had quite an appreciable workload.[311] Minor misdemeanours were atoned for by beatings. For slightly more serious violations the cattle of the culprit were seized. The chief imposed the death penalty for serious offences. The right to sentence members of his tribe to death had been given to the chief by the demigods and ancestors of the Bahurutshe.[312] He acted in accordance with

310 On all the various functions of a chief, cf. Gollbach 1992 pp. 63–66.

311 Breutz 1953 p. 8 provides an overview of the annual ordinances and decrees issued by the Bahurutshe chief Gopane of Maanoane. On the judicial hearings of the Batswana, cf. Schapera 1976 p. 56f.

312 Bammann 1990 p. 88f.

their wishes since he was, by virtue of holding the highest rank within the tribe, thought to be closest to them.

4.4 Diseases

After Thomas Jensen had taken over the little congregation in 1864, the Bahurutshe initially exhibited a guarded attitude towards him. This soon changed, however, as he began to attend to the sick people in Dinokana. In his first half-year report he submits the schedule of a normal day: "During the morning I teach in school, and after school I go and visit the sick of whom there are usually a great number in summer as that is a rather unhealthy time of the year."[313] School lessons took place within a manageable framework, which provided him with the latitude to make extensive house calls. During these visits the traditional believers also took an interest in him. It was not customary in African society to pay house visits. The head of the family had to ensure the wellbeing of his dependants, and this also entailed that no member of another clan was allowed to cross the threshold of his homestead. Thomas Jensen visited the family units of the Bahurutshe and, while doing so, came across all kinds of diseases and illnesses. He carried homeopathic remedies with him and dispensed these to the sick.[314]

He specifically mentions two illnesses that occurred extensively in Dinokana. The first one was influenza (the flu), which caused a great number of deaths. The medicine men, who could cure and heal in other cases, apparently did not have the right remedies at hand for this febrile viral infection.

The second disease was smallpox, also viral in nature and highly infectious at that. When this epidemic broke out in 1884, many tribespeople succumbed to it.[315] Thomas Jensen was aware of the dangers of this disease and took precautions. The homeopathic remedies at his disposal would however not suffice. He was able to obtain vaccine via connections to certain friends. He vaccinated Christians as well as traditional believers. The lives of many people were saved due to these protective inoculations. In his congregation, which had already grown in 1884, only one man and a child died, both of whom had refused to be vaccinated. Many traditional

313 Thomas Jensen 04.08.1864 p. 8. – "Des Vormittags halte ich Schule und nach der Schule besuche ich die Kranken, die es im Sommer gewöhnlich viele gibt, da es dann ziemlich ungesund ist."

314 Thomas Jensen 1874 p. 46.

315 Id., 02.01.1885 p. 2f.

believers died. They had sought a cure from their medicine men and had not allowed the missionary to inoculate them.

Thomas Jensen had offered to vaccinate all the Bahurutshe. This all-embracing offer emphasises the fact that Jensen's concern was not only for the salvation of souls. During times of distress he offered his help by providing a social, charitable and medicinal service to all people.

5 Mission Work in Dinokana

5.1 The first Christians

5.1.1 Local Converts and those from other Tribes

In 1849 Louis Harms had founded the Hermannsburg Mission Society in Hermannsburg, Germany. His first students had to undergo a four-year training course to prepare them for missionary theological work. In those days this was deemed to be adequate training, no university degree was required. With his missionizing method, Louis Harms adhered to Biblical principles. Jesus had sent his disciples into the world in small groups of fellowship, sending them out two by two (Mk 6.7). Many of his disciples had remained unmarried. Harms himself was not married either, neither were his first missionaries. Colonists were dispatched together with the missionaries. They, too, remained single. The colonists were practical people who brought artisanal skills into the mission work.[316] Combining their efforts, the missionary and colonist had the task of establishing Christian congregations in Africa. The joint sending of missionaries and artisans was also done for financial reasons. Harms didn't have the funds to pay for the upkeep of the families. His mission society depended on donations. The rural population in and around Hermannsburg was poor. The missionaries were obliged to be self-sufficient in Africa. Initially they received no salary, and later only a very small one. On all the mission stations they acquired a piece of land in order to provide for their own needs. In 1870 the colonists were released from the services of the mission society by Theodor Harms, Louis Harms' successor, receiving as compensation ten heads of cattle each.[317] The missionaries remained in the service of the mission society.

One can also observe the coexistence and mission work of missionaries and colonists in Dinokana. As previously mentioned there was also a

[316] A colonist named Meier, who had relocated from Dithejane to Dinokana together with Zimmermann, is neither mentioned in Zimmermann's chronicles, nor in Thomas Jensen's reports. It may be assumed that he worked with Zimmermann in Dinokana for a while and, when his skills were no longer needed there, that Meier took his leave from the services of the mission society.

[317] The consequences of the separation of missionaries and colonists were particularly felt in Hermannsburg/Natal, cf. Schroeder p. 73.

colonist amongst each of the first two groups of missionaries who were sent to Botswana. The third group was unaccompanied by a colonist. If we are to understand the approach of Louis Harms correctly, a small congregation consisting of non-local members was already in existence in Dinokana. It was the task of the missionaries to bring the local population into the congregation.

Zimmermann and Thomas Jensen lived together in Dinokana for another three months. Zimmermann prepared for his departure and handed over the small congregation he had founded to Thomas Jensen.

Members of other tribes had come to settle in Dinokana as well. They had relocated from the areas around Mafikeng and Kuruman. One of the families who came from Kuruman had already been baptised by the British missionaries. The head of this family was the previously mentioned Sehuneloa. Zimmermann writes: "Apart from the previously mentioned black quasi-teacher and his family, who have moved from Kuruman to come and live with the Bahurutsi, I didn't come across any other baptised Christians in Linokana."[318] Sehuneloa spoke Dutch, as the Boer language was called in those days. Zimmermann had become acquainted with Low German in Hermannsburg, and was thus able to understand the Boer language. Sehuneloa and Zimmermann communicated with one another in Dutch as well as Setswana. During Zimmermann's early days Sehuneloa proved to be of great help to him. Since he was already baptised, Zimmermann deployed him in the school he had established in Dinokana. They worked together successfully for four years. The congregation had grown during this time.

When Thomas Jensen took over the congregation he began with 42 baptised members. During the time of collaboration between Zimmermann and Sehuneloa, baptised Christians from other tribes had also come to settle at Dinokana. Not all of these 42 Christians had been baptised by Zimmermann. He was however able to already perform baptisms in the first year. One can assume that the candidates for baptism came into the congregation via Sehuneloa, since he was one of those people who had relocated to Dinokana himself. On 27 November 1859 Zimmermann baptised the first six adult men in Dinokana. The first and last names of the new members of the Dinokana congregation were: *Sebeti Molepisi, Mamba Ra-*

---

318 Zimmermann 1874 p. 13. – "Außer dem erwähnten schwarzen Quasi-Lehrer und dessen Familie, die von Kuruman zu den Bahurutsi gezogen waren, fand ich auf Linokana keine Getauften vor."

masibi, Maishuanyani Mongali, Tsalikane Molefi, Moruntsi Moroane and *Khabinyani Molapisi.*[319]

Thomas Jensen made other demands on the members of his congregation than Zimmermann. After he had acquainted himself with the parishioners, he summarises: "The congregation that I found here consists of 38 souls, except for two married couples who have been excluded due to adultery, and whom I have not yet been able to admit.[320] Of these, 10 have been baptised in Kuruman, one in Dithejane, and one in Griquastad. Of those that have been baptised by Zimmermann there are 10 adults, the rest are children. There are 19 adults, the others are all children younger than 19 years of age. On the whole I found the congregation to be very ignorant, not all of them were able to recite the 10 Commandments and the Lord's Prayer by heart, not one of them could recite the three Articles of Faith, not even the old school teacher."[321] Half of the baptised parishioners were adults, the other half consisted of their children. Thomas Jensen criticises their inadequate knowledge of Christian instruction. His criticism was not so much aimed at the parishioners but rather at their two teachers, Zimmermann and Sehuneloa. He made higher demands on his parishioners.

5.1.2 The Problem of Polygamy, as illustrated by the Example of *Tsetlana*

The commandment "Thou shalt not commit adultery" was accorded a high degree of significance by the pioneer missionaries. Many Africans struggled to adhere to this commandment, causing them to fall from grace. The trespassers of this commandment were excluded from partaking in Holy Communion. If they had assumed some kind of official function within

---

319 The first baptismal registry of Dinokana was consulted by the author on 14. 04. 2001.

320 Usually any excommunicated member was readmitted after a period of probation. The number 42 comprises 38 parishioners 'beyond reproach', as well as the two excluded couples.

321 Thomas Jensen 04. 08. 1864 p. 1 – "Die Gemeinde, die ich hier vorfand, besteht aus 38 Seelen, außer zwei Ehepaaren, die wegen Ehebruchs ausgeschlossen sind und die ich noch nicht habe aufnehmen können. Davon sind 10 in Kuruman, einer in Dithejane und einer in Griquastadt getauft. Von den anderen, die hier von Zimmermann getauft sind, sind 10 Erwachsene, die anderen Kinder. Die Erwachsenen der Gemeinde sind 19, die anderen Kinder unter 19 Jahren. Im Ganzen fand ich die Gemeinde sehr unwissend, nicht alle konnten die 10 Gebote und das Vaterunser auswendig, auch kein einziger die drei Glaubensartikel, auch nicht der alte Schullehrer."

the congregation, they were suspended. These measures were however not meant to apply for ever. If parishioners saw the error of their ways, and a period of probation had passed, they were rehabilitated by the congregation to attend the church services as fully entitled parishioners.

Polygamy also fell into the category of adultery, albeit not on the same level. It was implicitly equated with adultery. The missionaries had no proper response to polygamy. It was completely normal in Africa and had hitherto not been drawn into question. Christian principles called for the exclusive practise of monogamy, however. Polygamists who wished to be baptised had to dismiss all but one of their wives. How difficult this proved to be in practise is illustrated by the example of Tsetlana.

Tsetlana led a polygamous life with two wives. He was sympathetic towards the Christian faith, wanted to go to school, learn and be baptised. To be baptised one had to attend school, to be sure, but the first was not the obligatory result of the latter. Tsetlana had decided to take Christian instruction in order to be baptised. He knew that he could only receive baptism if he sent one of his wives back to her parents. That proved to be difficult. He was nevertheless determined to go down that path and sent his second wife back to his father-in-law. Tsetlana went to school, was baptised and became an active member of the congregation.

Not long after Tsetlana had been baptised, his remaining wife fell ill. A son that they shared subsequently also fell ill and died. Thomas Jensen writes: "After having been baptised he had to live through a serious ordeal. (…) Many people believe that both have been poisoned by the parents of his second wife who really hated him after he had abandoned their daughter. This is a strong possibility, as this kind of thing takes place frequently amongst the heathens."[322] Conjectural indications pointed towards poisoning. But no-one was able to prove it. The father-in-law was understandably disappointed and upset. All those drawn-out wedding negotiations had not failed because of a quarrel or a disagreement between the two families, but rather because of the church's rejection of polygamy. His reprisal was however not aimed at the church but rather at one of its members, his son-in-law. Thomas Jensen was not able to do anything as there were nothing but suspicions to go on. Tsetlana, who was convinced that his father-in-law

[322] Thomas Jensen 1874 p. 40. – "Nach der Taufe hat er eine schwere Prüfung durchmachen müssen. (…) Vielfach glaubt man, dass beide von den Eltern seiner zweiten Frau, die ihn sehr hassten seitdem er ihre Tochter verlassen hatte, vergiftet waren. Das ist auch leicht möglich, den so etwas kommt häufig unter den Heiden vor."

had instigated the plot to poison his family members, could himself have sought the services of a medicine man of his choice, thereby repaying in kind for the iniquity that was done to him. But he didn't.

It should be noted, and this is borne out by other incidents of this kind, that Tsetlana was not attacked directly. His first wife and his child were the ones who were punished. This sheds an important light on the structure of the social order. This conduct, utilising esoteric evil forces, eventually also brings about the ruin of Tsetlana, the actual adversary. It just takes longer. The family must know and be made to feel the guilt that the head of the family has incurred.

The consequences of this subtle form of revenge were not long in coming. News of the illness of his wife and the death of her son had of course reached the ears of the family of this wife. Her father was a respected petty chief in the village. He aligned himself with the suspicions doing the rounds in the village and cast the blame on Tsetlana. He singled out the baptism of his son-in-law as the real cause for the retaliatory measures undertaken by the father of the second wife who had been sent back to her parents. Both fathers-in-law were traditional believers. In order to avert even more disaster, the father of the first wife now took his daughter back to her family.

Tsetlana was one of the foreigners who had settled with the tribe, and the Bahurutshe had expressed their trust in him by allowing him to marry two of their women. After he had converted to Christianity and chose to live in monogamy, the two fathers of the bride, being adherents of traditional belief, joined forces and rid him of both his wives by different means. In the end Tsetlana was all alone.

At one point Tsetlana could no longer stand to live alone in Dinokana. He went to a Boer and worked on his farm. But he never entirely gave up his affiliation with the congregation. Being baptised had apparently effected a real change in him, giving new focal points to his life. He eventually came back and settled in the vicinity of the mission station. When his first wife heard that he had come back she left her father and moved back in with him. They both became loyal members of the congregation. There were no further acts of reprisal from the traditional believers. We hear from Tsetlana again a little later.

5.2 The Work of the two Jensen Missionaries

5.2.1 Rites of Passage within the Church and Mission

The result of the apostles receiving Christ's gospel and taking it to the world was that Christian congregations were established. These congregations eventually formed the Church, whose function it is to safeguard and provide a framework for the Christian faith. Throughout life, a Christian is in need of support- and holding points that serve to guide, strengthen and reassure the believer, and to repeatedly re-entrust him or her to God's blessing. Apart from the sacraments of Baptism and Eucharist, there exist three additional, integral offers by the Church to give support and counsel throughout a Christian's life: the confirmation, the wedding blessing, and the Christian burial. With baptism these offers from the Church are aligned with the natural progression of a person's life. The transition from one stage of life to the next are accompanied by severe changes of a physical as well as psychological nature. Throughout one's life the Church gives its support to these transitional phases. In order to do so, it has created rituals.

The Hermannsburg missionaries took over this offering of church rituals, utilising them as an open door for their mission work amongst the Bahurutshe in Dinokana.

5.2.1.1 Baptism

Baptism plays a crucial role in all Christian churches. Baptism is not merely a sacrament of the church. It also signifies the commencement of church membership. The Lutheran churches baptise adults as well as children. According to Lutheran doctrine baptism constitutes an act of grace by God. If the baptised person embraces this grace and engages with it effectively throughout his or her life, it will lead him/her beyond this life into the eternal glory of the triune God.

Martin Luther preceded his substantiation for baptism with Matth. 28,19 and Mk 16,16: "In these words you must note, in the first place, that here stand God's commandment and institution (...) So also I can boast that Baptism is no human trifle, but instituted by God Himself, moreover, that it is most solemnly and strictly commanded that we must be baptized or we cannot be saved ... "[323] Louis Harms' writings are in a similar vein.

[323] Martin Luther Large Catechism – Holy Baptism (bookofconcord.org, accessed 04.08.2015).

He emphasised baptism as being a precondition for eternal life.[324] Taking baptism as basis, he formulated the Order of Salvation (*ordo salutis* = series of conceptual steps towards salvation) as meaning to follow the Will of God.[325]

During the revival period in Hermannsburg, infant baptism was taken very seriously. Parents brought their newly-born infants to be baptised in church on the first Sunday after their birth. Following in this tradition, and in view of the theological relevance of God's protection, the missionaries placed special emphasis on baptism. After realising how greatly the Bahurutshe feared evil spirits during the birth process, they modified their theological explanation to baptism. The concept of grace continued to be important, but now emphasis was being placed on the promise of a new power. The belief in the forgiveness of all sin in baptism creates a new person, protecting him or her against all onslaughts of evil. The prayer for the child or person to be baptised and his or her surrender to the "Lord over all power" had such an empowering effect on the first Christians that they now also took their babies to be baptised directly after birth. The father could see his baby immediately. It no longer remained hidden from him for three months. The closest relatives took it to be baptised in the name of Jesus Christ. This constituted a liberation from the spellbinding, terrifying powers of traditional belief.

During the early days of mission work, however, more adults than children initially received baptism. The adults were illiterate. Therefore they should first learn to read and write. Christian instruction took place simultaneously during these lessons. It became apparent in these lessons who would change over to baptism classes. The missionary would have liked to see all his pupils to receive baptism. But the decision to be baptised lay with the individual pupil.

In the first year the Bahurutshe distanced themselves from Thomas Jensen. Not a single traditional believer sought to be baptised. School lessons continued unabated, but not one pupil changed over to baptism classes. There were probably various reasons for this. For one thing Thomas Jensen was still a stranger to the Bahurutshe. All information about him was conveyed to them by the teacher who had been appointed by Zimmermann, Sehuneloa, who was not necessarily well-disposed towards Thomas Jensen.

---

324 L. Harms 1886 p. 191ff, 243f, 339f, 363f.

325 Heinrich pp. 223–225.

Sehuneloa had grown accustomed to Zimmermann. But a friendship with Thomas Jensen did somehow not come about. Another reason may be found in the fact that the Bahurutshe had, generally speaking, become distrustful of missionaries. Every single attempt by the Paris missionaries, the Americans and the British missionary Inglis, as well as that of Paul the evangelist to gain a foothold amongst the Bahurutshe, had failed. And, on top of that, the first Hermannsburg missionary to have become well acquainted with them had been recalled by his mission administration.

During his second year as missionary in Dinokana, six pupils enrolled for baptism classes. There was however not one Mohurutshe amongst them. They were all individuals who had settled in Dinokana from other tribes. Four of them received baptism. They retained their Setswana names, a practise that Jensen took over from Zimmermann, something that was not common elsewhere in the mission. The missionaries in Dinokana constituted an exception in this regard, which should retrospectively be viewed in a positive light. The baptism candidates' names were: *Mohetoane, Ramakoka, Molebane* and *Tsetlana.* Thomas Jensen comments: "They kept their Setswana names on being baptised as is the custom here anyway, and to which I could not object, since it so happened that none of them had a name with bad meaning."[326] When Thomas Jensen states that all of those baptised had good indigenous names and also makes mention of "names with bad meaning", there must be a reason. And indeed there was. The Bahurutshe were superstitious. When they had had bad experiences with evil spirits they gave their children "bad" names. They believed that bad names would deter evil spirits. Spirits shun public places. If a spirit was given a name, a mockery would be made of it and it would retreat.[327]

In the same report of 1866 in which Thomas Jensen writes of baptism, he mentions that he was busy building a new church and that the baptised Christians were to settle around the church once it was completed. In order to accomplish this, he had entered into negotiations with Moiloa II, who

[326] Thomas Jensen 28.06.1866 p. 1. – "Bei der Taufe behielten sie, wie es hier überhaupt Gebrauch ist, ihre Setswananamen, wogegen ich nichts haben konnte, da sie gerade keine Namen von schlechter Bedeutung hatten."

[327] Similar examples can be found in the traditional European belief in spirits. Old churches are adorned with hideous faces on their outside walls. Evil spirits were given a face to act as a deterrent. They were disgraced. These public images were seen as being simultaneously conducive in overcoming the belief in spirits. In Africa the deterring of spirits was linked to a bad name.

had welcomed the building of a church and had assigned him a piece of land close to the mission station. Jensen writes: "I have now finally brought matters to a stage where all baptised Christians should reside in the vicinity of the church."[328] The construction of the church dragged on for several months. He combined his church-building endeavours with an additional benefit. If the baptised Christians settled around the church, it would make it easier for him to enlist their services in building the church, as they would be close by. He also reasoned that the baptised Christians would then be able to attend classes on a regular basis and that their children would find it easier to resist the temptations posed by the children of traditional believers.

Tsetlana was one of the first to be baptised. The news of a settlement close to the church might have appealed to him as well, inducing him to leave his work with the Boers and return to Dinokana in the hope of rekindling his relationship with his wife. He was amongst the first to secure a site close to the church. One needs to remember, however, that Tsetlana was one of those who had come to Dinokana from another tribe. If it was predominantly foreigners who started settling around the church, but Thomas Jensen's objective was that "all baptised Christians should reside in the vicinity of the church", one should think that this would create tensions between the local people and those from elsewhere. But this seems to not have been the case.

During the course of the years that followed, Thomas Jensen regularly baptised small groups of people. In 1885, twenty-five years after he had begun his work at Dinokana, he baptised eighteen adults and twenty children. The number of baptised Christians increased with each year, remaining nonetheless relatively low. In comparing his small group of converts with the great number of traditional believers he was of the opinion that there should have been much more by now who wished to be baptised. On those occasions when this thought depressed him, he reminded himself of the comforting Word of God according to which victory over heathendom would ultimately be obtained. "It is admittedly not a large number but, even so, one step closer towards victory over heathendom, a sign that the Word of God is not professed in vain but rather achieves that for which it is given."[329]

---

[328] Thomas Jensen 28.06.1866 p. 3. – "Denn ich habe es jetzt endlich so weit gebracht, dass alle Getauften in der Nähe der Kirche wohnen sollen."

[329] Idem 02. 01. 1885 p. 1 – "Es ist zwar keine große Zahl, doch immerhin ein Schritt weiter zum Sieg über das Heidentum, ein Zeichen, dass das Wort Gottes nicht umsonst gepredigt wird, sondern ausrichtet, wozu es gegeben ist."

One reason why no large-scale baptisms took place could be found in the practise of polygamy. The men could not be baptised because they did not want to be separated from their wives and children, and the wives stood by their husbands. The number of polygamous marriages in Dinokana was once revealed some years later. The Boer government conducted a national census in 1921. Ferdinand Jensen was asked to oversee this in Dinokana. He produced the following result: Dinokana had 5,223 inhabitants, of whom 1,487 were baptised and 3,736 were traditional believers. During the census special mention was made of 485 heads of families: 421 were in a monogamous relationship, while 64 led a polygamous life. Of those men living in polygamy, 55 had two wives, 8 had three, and 1 man had five wives.[330]

The man with five wives went by the name of *Merogo*. One of his wives belonged to the Lutheran congregation. She had lost her husband, who had been a son of Merogo's. After her husband's death she had no-one to look after her. It was customary amongst the Bahurutshe for the father of the deceased husband to be able to marry his daughter-in-law, and that is what Merogo did. Maybe his Christian daughter-in-law made a particularly positive impression on him, but, be that as it may, Merogo held the Christian faith in high esteem and proceeded to found his own church. In order to do this, he invited a Baptist preacher to Dinokana. Every evening this preacher held his orations in Merogo's front yard. These public sermons did not go unnoticed amongst the village people. They came and sat on the bare ground and listened. The preacher also introduced them to the speaking of tongues during which he entered into a state of ecstasy. Merogo's daughter-in-law and other Christians who had been baptised by Thomas Jensen were amongst those in the audience. After a couple of such evenings the preacher began baptising people and administering the Eucharist to them. The Bahurutshe were enamoured by his conduct and accepted his baptism offer. This new religious persuasion enjoyed a speedy flourishing period, but after the preacher had moved on the interest of the Bahurutshe waned just as speedily.

Merogo had failed to attract any members for his church. The re-baptised Christians returned to the Lutheran church. The brief flourishing of another faith had nonetheless aggrieved Ferdinand Jensen. He expressed his sentiments as follows: "No inquiry was made after an individual's life, no church fees exacted. (. . .) But by God's grace the matter has died down

330 F. Jensen 09. 01. 1922 p. 2f.

much faster. (...) The Christians quickly became convinced that a church that baptises the most brazen sinners without instruction and proof of conversion, even pronouncing them to be good, cannot be the right church."[331]

It becomes apparent in Ferdinand Jensen's quote what the Hermannsburg missionaries of that time expected as prerequisite for baptism. An adult baptism could not be obtained by cheap pardon. The sinner had to provide proof of his or her conversion. He or she had to receive Christian instruction prior to baptism, and it was during this process of spiritual counsel that it became apparent if he or she was serious in cherishing their baptism and in subsequently proving their faith within the congregation. His parishioners, too, were convinced of the validity of this approach.

On one occasion the baptism of two men came about in a rather unusual way. A number of outstations under Ferdinand Jensen's ministry had been established during the early 20th century. One of these outstations was *Mokgola.* On one occasion, while he was on his way to this outstation, he saddled down to have some breakfast. He had a long way to go, and that without a car. While he laid out his spread *Dihutsoe*, who lived close by, joined him. Ferdinand Jensen shared his breakfast with him. Dihutsoe was an old man and told him that he had been a cow herd with Zimmermann for four years. He had had three wives, two of whom were already dead. Now he still lived with his remaining wife. He told Jensen that he had made an agreement with his friend *Kgampi,* with whom he had attended circumcision school. "These two old men had made a pledge to each other to ask for Holy Baptism together, and that neither of them should take this step without having notified the other one first."[332] Dihutsoe had taken the decision to be baptised but Kgampi was not ready yet. Ferdinand Jensen cites Dihutsoe as follows: "I have lived up to my promise and have informed my friend of my decision to be baptised, however he has let me come to you alone, but his hour will come too."[333] Kgampi fell ill and subsequently also wanted to

---

[331] F. Jensen 1921 p. 6 – "Nach dem Leben des Einzelnen wurde nicht gefragt, auch kein Kirchengeld verlangt. (...) Aber durch Gottes Gnade ist die Sache viel schneller still geworden. (...) Die Christen kamen schnell zu der Überzeugung, dass das die rechte Kirche nicht sein könne, die ohne Unterricht und ihre Beweise einer Umkehr die frechsten Sünder tauft und sie gar für gut erklärt."

[332] Id., 1924 p. 6 – "Die beiden alten Leute hatten sich gegenseitig das Versprechen gegeben, zusammen um die Heilige Taufe zu bitten, und dass keiner diesen Schritt tun solle, ohne den anderen benachrichtigt zu haben."

[333] Loco citato. – "Ich bin meinem Versprechen nachgekommen, und habe meinem Freunde den Entschluss mitgeteilt, mich taufen zu lassen, aber er hat mich allein zu dir gehen

be baptised. Both men had decided to become Christians long ago. But as they had led a polygamous life they had hitherto been prevented from receiving baptism. Since their wives had died the obstacles towards baptism had been removed.[334]

One can view the lifelong, binding companionship of Dihutsoe and Kgampi as being rudimentary to the old Setswana tradition. Both had attended the same circumcision school, during which the initiates were obliged to stand together as a group and to support one another in all circumstances. They were aware that this pledge was binding into old age. Their commitment to one another ultimately led them to be baptised together.

5.2.1.2 Confirmation

In the Lutheran church confirmation serves to validate infant baptism. It is bound neither to a sacrament nor to adult baptism. Longer tuition units impart to adolescents a basic biblical knowledge and teach them how to conduct themselves as responsible Christians in church and society. During confirmation these young people affirm their Christian maturity. The church has created a ritual to accompany the confirmation ceremony, which comes into effect during a special worship service.

In the early years of their work, the pioneer missionaries placed a varying degree of value on confirmation. This is reflected with F. Zimmermann and Thomas Jensen. Zimmermann deemed the baptism instruction that the adult baptism candidates received to be adequate. They were subsequently introduced to the sacrament of Holy Communion, making confirmation superfluous. Christian instruction ceased with baptism. Thomas Jensen took a different stance. He wanted to introduce the confirmation ceremony to adults. He reckoned that baptismal instruction units only dealt with aspects that were designed to lead to baptism. To lead a responsible life as a Christian however comprised a further instruction in biblical stories as well as

---

lassen, aber auch seine Stunde wird kommen."

[334] Another circumstantial requirement becomes apparent. Dihutswe and Kgampi had made a lifelong pledge to one another dating back to the circumcision school. In the old days the initiates were asked to take a pledge to support one another in good as well as bad days. Throughout their lives these two men had taken this binding obligation seriously. Schapera comments: "Members of the same regiment not only work and (if men) fight together, they are also intimate companions and equals (*balekane, bankane,* mates) and have strong solidarity as a group." Schapera 1976 p. 39.

being able to recite the "Small Catechism of Martin Luther". In his view the confirmation ceremony was a church ritual that could be compared to the circumcision ritual of traditional believers. Right from the start he wanted to institute the confirmation ceremony. He was not successful, however, as the people failed to understand why Zimmermann had deemed this ceremony to be expendable, while he, Jensen, now deemed it a necessity. He first had to compel the necessary respect for his stance. "There are several who should be confirmed but it is difficult to lead them to an understanding as to why they should be confirmed, since no confirmation was ever held here, seeing that Zimmermann doesn't hold it in high regard, as he has told me himself."[335]

It didn't take long before the Bahurutshe came to trust Thomas Jensen as well. Nevertheless, it still took a number of years before the initially stipulated age for confirmation was lowered from between sixteen to twenty years down to fourteen years. It was only after the first confirmation ceremonies had taken place that the Bahurutshe took a liking to them. An increasing number of parents sent their children to confirmation classes. More and more parents approved, since Thomas Jensen presented his classes in greater detail and the children subsequently also became more educated and open-minded by attending these classes.

Ferdinand Jensen introduced an innovation to his confirmation candidates. Having first obtained the consent of the chief, the period of confirmation did neither end with a ceremony in church nor with a family celebration at home, but rather with a collective family celebration of all the candidates. This was more in line with the socio-cultural, unifying tribal thinking of the Batswana. This ceremony required a great amount of work with the families. It took place outside the village on the banks of a river, some distance further down from the spring, under shady acacia trees. The Bahurutshe call this place *kwa sekhutlong,* the place where the conclusion of learning is celebrated.[336] These community celebrations were held on a regular basis and became part of a widespread tradition. It was introduced to other Bahurutshe settlements and is viewed as being unique to the Bahurutshe. The debate, however, as to whether adults should attend confirmation classes

[335] Thomas Jensen 04.08. 1864 p. 6. – "Einige sind da, die konfirmiert werden müssten, aber es ist schwer, sie dazu zu bewegen, warum sie konfirmiert werden müssen, denn es ist hier noch keine Konfirmation gewesen, da Zimmermann von derselben wenig hält, wie er mir selber gesagt hat."

[336] Schlag 2002 p. 28.

after their baptism and be subsequently confirmed as well, was still carried on amongst missionaries and parishioners well into the 20th century.

5.2.1.3 The Problem of Marriage

According to European Christian law, marriage constitutes the union of two persons, a man and a woman, and cannot be extended to anyone else. In Africa the situation is an entirely different one. As was the case with the forefathers of Israel (Gen. 16,1–3, Gen. 26,34 and 1 Kings 11,3, for instance), the patriarchal system was in place, with several wives to one husband. The number of wives was first and foremost a question of maintenance. The husband has several children with each wife. They all needed to be fed and cared for. The first woman a man married was awarded a superior position over all subsequent wives. His parents selected her for him. Schapera comments: "The parents of a man normally choose his first wife for him; the others he chooses himself."[337] The first son of the first wife was the patriarchal heir. The youngest son of each wife was obliged to be of service to his mother. As a reward he inherited her household upon her death. Any other children that the wives may have had found their inconspicuous place within the clan collective. The patriarchal system was already embedded in the language. A man married a woman = *o nyala mosadi,* while a woman was married by a man = *o nyalwa ke monna.*

Thomas Jensen was unsympathetic towards a polygamous form of marriage. He firmly believed that a Christian marriage could only be made up of two partners and that husband and wife should live an ethically virtuous life according to God's commandments. He advised this code of conduct to his parishioners and to all men of traditional belief who wanted to become Christians. God's precepts implied an imperative which, according to Jensen's understanding thereof, led to the consequential dismissal of all secondary wives. An example of this has been described above with the story of Tsetlana, who had dismissed his second wife "because he knew that it had to be like that."[338] Problems arose in many such cases, as was the case with Tsetlana, when the Christian husbands returned their secondary wives to their respective clans. In only a few cases were the Christian principles adopted. If an amicable arrangement had been brokered, the husbands

337 Schapera 1976 p. 41.

338 Thomas Jensen 28.06.1866 p. 1 – "... hatte gehen lassen, weil er wusste, dass es so sein musste."

cared for the wives they had returned up until such time that they had found a new husband.

Another problem pertaining to Christian marriages cropped up in the congregation. How should a single woman of the congregation conduct herself if a man of traditional belief proposed marriage? A woman who had been dismissed as her husband's secondary wife came to Thomas Jensen, asking for advice. This case gave Thomas Jensen food for thought. He had no answer but advised her to suggest to her suitor that he enrol for baptism classes. If he were prepared to be baptised she could marry him.[339] It is not known whether this woman from his congregation subsequently married her suitor. The case was not pursued any further.

A few years later more problems arose in the congregation. The Christian men made themselves guilty of deserting their wives for various reasons. *Maseng,* one of the first Christians to have been baptised by Thomas Jensen, left his wife after only a few years of marriage because she was infertile.[340] *Maeshuanyana* left his wife because he was constantly arguing with her. The conduct of both men was not in keeping with their marriage vows. They fell in love with women of traditional belief and were subsequently expelled from the congregation.

Maseng stayed away from the church services but Maeshuanyana continued to attend the services on a regular basis. Maeshuanyane's case began to turn into an awkward situation. Thomas Jensen writes: "… he was one of the oldest members of our congregation and, since he is very talented, the two Brothers Lohann and Tönsing had, in the beginning and seeing that they were not yet proficient in the language, employed him at Limao as preacher and teacher. He was employed as school teacher here, too."[341] When Thomas Jensen speaks of Maeshuanyana as being one of the "oldest members" of his congregation who had been employed by the missionaries Lohann and Tönsing, the place where that took place was Dithejane/Botswana, alias Limao. After the Hermannsburg missionaries had been compelled to abandon their mission endeavours in that area, Maeshuanyana had followed them to Dinokana. It is unfortunately also not

339 Thomas Jensen 01. 04. 1867 p. 1.

340 Id. 02.01.1875 p. 1.

341 Id. – "… . denn er war einer von den ältesten Gemeindegliedern, und da er gut begabt ist, hatten die beiden Brüder Lohann und Tönsing ihn im Anfange, als sie die Sprache noch nicht konnten, in Limao als Prediger und Schullehrer gebraucht. Auch hier ist er Schullehrer gewesen."

documented how this story turned out in the end. Such incidents do however shine a light on the kind of problems with which the young Christian congregation was confronted. In the baptismal register of 1859 Zimmermann lists Maeshuanyana as one of his first baptised Christians. Exactly how Limao fits into this picture remains a mystery.

Marriage ceremonies were conducted with prayer and blessing in church. Since a prerequisite for marriage was that the couple had to be baptised, it frequently happened that an adult baptism was immediately followed by a marriage ceremony. That was the case on Pentecost in 1885. Twenty-four young adults were baptised during the morning service. Another church service was held in the afternoon, during which nine young couples were married. Their weddings were all performed on the same day. Some of the brides and grooms had received baptism that very morning.[342]

5.2.1.4 Death and Eternity

Death as rite of passage[343] already distinguishes itself from other such rites by the mere fact that the innovative and active changes that occur during the three previously described rites are, in this instance, neither visible nor can they be understood on a rational level. Death is based on a notion. Humans rely on and trust their belief. They don't know what happens on the other side. For Christians and pagans alike death does not signify the end of one's life but rather a transition into the hereafter. They do however define their convictions in this regard rather differently.

Thomas Jensen believed in eternal life after death, shared with all other converted and baptised Christians, and brought about by the death and resurrection of Jesus Christ. The traditional believers saw things very differently, of course. They had no knowledge of a personal saviour who could take away their iniquity and vanquish evil. They believed that they had to carry the burden of guilt themselves. The daily fear that their fellow humans posed a danger to them and that evil spirits and sorcery would rob them of their life force extended beyond death.[344] After death a person's spirit embarked on a period of wandering.[345] As has been mentioned above, the Batswana feared this wandering. Malevolent forces or wicked humans

342 Id. 22.07.1885 p. 2f.

343 Cf. Gollbach pp. 103–144.

344 Id. p. 104; Häselbarth p. 29.

345 Gollbach p. 127.

could prevent its progress to the detriment of the soul. At the end of this wandering the Batswana hoped to be admitted into the ancestral collective of their forbears. Thomas Jensen had little interest in the traditional believers' concept of an afterlife. He had come there to bring them the Good News and sought to achieve their conversion through baptism, with its promise of a fellowship with Christ both in this world and the next. He invited the traditional believers to join him in this new fellowship in Christ.

In 1873 six children succumbed to pneumonia. That was a terrible blow for the affected families and a bitter loss to the small Christian congregation. Thomas Jensen commented: "Our consolation in this is that they are all saved, seeing that they were all still in the grace of baptism."[346] The young children lived in the grace of baptism while the faith of the adults, grounded in the grace of baptism, was put to the test. Eternal life after death was the reward for the belief in Jesus Christ. Loyalty to the Christian congregation provided the assurance for this future promise. Christians and traditional believers were pilgrims on separate paths, and it was the Christians' obligation to discern the difference in everyday life.

Chief Ikalafeng died of a serious illness. The medicine men of the village had been unable to help him. In those days there was a European physician in Zeerust already, who had promised to rid him of the "spirochaeta pallida"-virus within three months. Instead the disease took a turn for the worse. Thomas Jensen writes: "He was so weak that he could no longer be driven [to the doctor] but had to be carried there by his people, and for quite a distance at that. This happened at night since he didn't want to be seen."[347] The chief could no longer be cured and died on 24 June 1894 in Zeerust. A large number of people attended his funeral, which was of a completely different nature to that of Moiloa II, however. He was buried in the large cattle kraal, according to Bahurutshe tradition. Thomas Jensen was absent as he was unable to attend the funeral.

After Thomas Jensen had returned from his journey he heard the sad news of the chief's death. His parishioners had attended the funeral, amongst them the school master of the congregation. During the funeral proceedings he was asked to say a prayer. He refused to do so in front

346 Thomas Jensen 02.07.1873 p. 1. – "Unser Trost dabei ist, dass sie alle selig sind, weil sie noch alle in der Taufgnade waren."

347 Id. 05.07.1894 p. 2 – "Er war so schwach, dass er nicht mehr hingefahren werden konnte, so dass die Leute ihn hintragen mussten und das den langen Weg. Das geschah in der Nacht, denn er wollte nicht gesehen werden."

of the mourners: "Why should I pray; we Christians only say prayers at Christian funerals, not at those of heathens. He lived as a heathen, died as a heathen and is buried as a heathen, therefore I cannot pray."[348] That was a courageous thing to say in public. Why was the school master asked to pray at the graveside of the chief? There might have been various possible reasons.

There were many differences between the prayers of Christians and those of traditional belief. For one, the prayer times differed. Also, the prayers of traditional believers were always accompanied by an offering, and traditional believers never prayed in public or together with others. They prayed secretly, covertly, and didn't want to be seen doing so. Neither did they pray at gravesides. What they did do was to strike up lamentations at the graveside that were screamed out as an expression of grief, something that even the Africans themselves experienced as being emotionally stressful. Traditional believers only became introspective after the emotions of the event had subsided. They left everything else pertaining to the funeral ritual in the hands of the medicine man. Why was the school master asked to say a prayer even as the medicine man was busy cleansing the area of the shadow of death and keeping evil spirits away from the mourners at the same time? The school master was well aware of the traditional way of burial but no longer believed in it. Many Europeans attended Ikalafeng's funeral. Was the idea that he should impart an impression that would accommodate these mourners? Whatever the reason may have been to prompt the school master to say a public prayer, a Christian prayer would most certainly not have done any harm.

The leading men in the tribe were well aware that the Christians prayed publicly and that their prayers consoled the mourners at the graveside, filling their troubled hearts with peace and conciliation. The refusal by the school master to say a prayer was not to give expression to an awkward situation. He refused to pray because he had distanced himself from the traditional believers and did not want to encourage any kind of intermingling to take place between Christianity and the traditional belief system. For him the refusal constituted a profession of his Christian faith.

[348] Loco citato p. 3. – "Was soll ich da beten; wir Christen beten nur bei christlichen Begräbnissen, aber nicht bei heidnischen. Er hat als Heide gelebt, ist als Heide gestorben und wird als Heide begraben, da kann ich nicht beten."

5.3 The Congregation

5.3.1 The Sermon

The sermon forms an essential part in building up a congregation. With its exposition of an Old- or New Testament text, the sermon usually lies at the heart of the Protestant church service. The form that the exposition takes is meant to provide an impetus towards conversion or else serve to strengthen the faith of the believer. Sermons are able to break established structures, and give expression to expectations regarding the conduct of parishioners in various life situations.

On their property in Dinokana the first Hermannsburg missionaries laid out a front yard. They were familiar with laying out such an area, as it was something that was done back home in the Lüneburg Heath as well.[349] The front yard serves to welcome guests that one does not immediately want to admit to one's house. All African families had established such a yard in front of their huts. The missionaries utilised their front yard in Dinokana to hold their morning- and evening devotions, accompanied by a short sermon. A small group of Christians regularly attended these devotions, as well as a number of interested traditional believers.

The front yard was large enough to hold the fairly small group that attended these proclamations of the Word. The *lekgotla* – the chief's gathering place – was a different scenario altogether, though, where Zimmermann held his first sermons. He had a large audience. In the *lekgotla* "... things were done in true heathenish style. At the same time great numbers of listeners nonetheless attended the church services, which had to be held in the chief's kraal for a year as there existed no church building as yet. (...) On a few occasions there were thousands of people."[350] Zimmermann calls the gatherings in the *lekgotla* church services. These services were however not conducted with the singing of hymns and an adjusted liturgy, but consisted of only a sermon and prayer. Christian hymns and a proper liturgy were not yet in existence. Everything was new to the traditional believers. They had come to listen. The sermon provided a good means of introduction to the gospel.

---

349 Thomas Jensen 1874 p. 20.

350 Zimmermann 1874 p. 13 – "... ging es echt heidnisch zu. Dennoch kamen zugleich Scharen Zuhörer in die Gottesdienste, die ein Jahr lang in des Häuptlings Krale abgehalten werden mussten, weil wir noch kein Kirchlein hatten. (...) Einzelne Male kamen Tausende."

Because Zimmermann was welcomed in Dinokana, the chief had heeded his request to invite his tribespeople to the church services. A large number of his subjects had turned up. One might take one's cue once again from the adage: *Lentsoe la kgosi le ageloa lesaka* = When the chief calls, everyone feels spoken to. Zimmermann initially held his sermons in Dutch with Sehuneloa acting as interpreter. The chief always attended the services. He had grasped the content of Zimmermann's sermons and commented on them in his own words: "Harsh words never covert anyone, only God's Word can do that. Whoever seizes this Word will come and surrender to it."[351] We may have an idea which biblical text Zimmermann might have used for his sermon. It may have been 1. Thess. 2,13, where it reads: "And we also thank God continually because, when you received the word of God, which you heard from us, you accepted it not as a human word, but as it actually is, the word of God, which is indeed at work in you who believe." In his report Zimmermann adds to what the chief had said: "A very true word, revealing a deep understanding, and yet he remained a heathen."[352] With the term "heathen" Zimmermann does not refer to Moiloa II's faith but rather to his status of remaining an unbaptised Christian.

After the gospel had been proclaimed in the *lekgotla* for a while, a change occurred. It was by no means all traditional believers who approved of the missionary, taking issue with the fact that they were obliged to listen to him every Sunday, and Zimmermann wanted to integrate his sermon into an extended church service. This motivated him to build a church in the settlement. All the traditional believers were also invited to attend the church service, but now it was no longer obligatory for them to do so as it was not the chief who invited them. It would probably have been more advantageous to his Christianisation efforts if he had used the unique opportunity of the chief's invitation for a while longer in order to propound the message of the gospel in greater detail to the traditional believers in the *lekgotla*. In terms of the proclamation of the gospel the retreat into a church building seems to be rather counterproductive.

Preparing his first sermons took up a considerable amount of time. "Initially the preparation for the sermon kept us occupied for a full 14 days. We

---

[351] Loco citato. – "Harte Worte gewinnen niemand, Gottes Wort kanns allein. Wer dieses Wort ergreift, der wird kommen und sich dem Wort ergeben."

[352] Loco citato. – "Ein sehr wahres Wort, das sehr viel Erkenntnis verriet, und doch ist er ein Heide geblieben."

used to read them to one another."[353] The "we" refers to him and Sehuneloa. Sehuneloa was full of praise. Zimmermann was pleased, as each word of praise meant that he had made progress in his understanding of the language. Later he viewed these sermons in a different light, however: "We carried our written sermons to church very solemnly and ceremoniously, reading them out with equal solemnity and heart-felt sighs to God above, imploring him to bless the sermons; and were of the opinion that the lives and salvation of our audience depended on them … when we subsequently read our sermons at a later stage we could sometimes not stop laughing."[354]

Thomas Jensen no longer preached in the *lekgotla* as Zimmermann had done for a year. He held his sermons in the church that Zimmermann had built. Since Zimmermann had not named the church, Thomas Jensen now gave it one. Seeing that the central message of Jesus Christ was of great importance to him, he named it "*Christus Kirche*" (Church of Christ).[355] In his afternoon services, and in contrast to Zimmermann, he did not adhere to the conventional sequence of sermons.

Thomas Jensen realised that the Bahurutshe followed the authoritarian orders of their chief, accepted commands and prohibitions and adhered to a patriarchal system within their families. This realisation prompted him to select Old Testament texts for his sermons. He possibly had discussions in this regard with the missionaries Behrens and Lohann, who still resided with him at that time. His auxiliary teacher, Moremi, had also been drawn into this discussion. He writes: "We all agreed that it would be better to sermonize on stories of the Old Testament."[356]

Thomas Jensen left the first sermons to his teacher Moremi. He knew that he would not be able to make himself be understood properly. Both sermons to be held each Sunday were prepared by him, together with Moremi. This had the advantage that he was better able to relate to Moremi's sermons. "We take great pleasure in his sermons, which we are now almost

353 Zimmermann 1874 p. 5 – "In der ersten Zeit hatte man vollauf 14 Tage an der Predigt zu tun. Wir lasen sie uns gegenseitig vor."

354 Loco citato. – "Wir trugen unsere geschriebenen Predigten sehr ernst und feierlich zur Kirche und lasen sie ebenso ab mit ernstlichem Seufzen zu Gott, dass er seinen Segen auf die Predigten legen wolle; und meinten, Leben und Seligkeit unserer Zuhörer hinge von ihnen ab … als wir später unsere Predigten durchlasen, fanden wir des Lachens bisweilen kein Ende."

355 Thomas Jensen 30.09.1866 p. 6.

356 Id., 04.08.1864 p. 7 – "Wir meinten einstimmig, es wäre besser, über alttestamentliche Geschichten zu predigen."

able to understand word for word. I ask him to come to me on Saturdays, and then go through both the texts for his sermons with him. As he has quite a considerable knowledge of the Bible and a good memory to boot, he is able to adhere fairly closely to what I told him. I leave the practical application to him for the most part, since he is more adept in this regard and has a greater knowledge of tribal conditions."[357] Little by little he grew into the language, until he reached the stage where he could hold his own sermons during the church service.

5.3.2 The Church Service

In the Lutheran Church the church service lies at the heart of one's spiritual life. There are different types of church services. The main service takes place on Sunday mornings. The reason for this service is the Third Commandment: "Thou shalt sanctify the holy day". The baptised Christians gather for the service to pray, sing, and praise in fellowship, they expect to be given spiritual sustenance for their salvation and seek encouragement for the daily trials of life. As mentioned above, the sermon forms the central focus of the main service. It is framed by liturgical texts derived from prayers and hymns.

During the revival period in Hermannsburg, Louis Harms offered several church services during the week. The increased number of services were a proposition towards believers to lead a sanctified life and to renounce worldly temptations more and more every day.

Thomas Jensen, a Dane by birth, had become a child of the revivalist movement while studying in Hermannsburg. He introduced the Hermannsburg church services to Dinokana as well. He started each day with a devotion, after which the people went to perform their daily work. An hour of singing was put aside in the evenings, a church service was held on Wednesdays, and two services on Sundays. Even though there were two services, Thomas Jensen still held a devotion on Sunday mornings as well. This devotion was meant to serve as preparation for the main service. He

[357] Loco citato. – "Wir können uns über seine Predigten freuen, die wir doch nun fast wörtlich verstehen. Des sonnabends lasse ich ihn zu mir kommen und nehme dann die beiden Texte mit ihm durch, über die er predigen soll und da er ziemlich Bibelkenntnisse und dazu ein gutes Gedächtnis hat, so kann er sich ziemlich daran halten, was ich ihm gesagt habe. Die Nutzanwendung lasse ich ihn zum Teil selbst machen, denn er weiß sie besser zu machen, da er die Verhältnisse des Volkes besser kennt."

expounded the various epistle readings to his parishioners, as they were subsequently only read out in the service. In the beginning Jensen inserted "a little hour of reading and spelling" before each Sunday service for all those who were eager to learn. The service on Sunday mornings had the following liturgical order: "Then I announce the hymn we want to sing and read it out loud. After the hymn has been sung I proceed (during morning services) to read the entire chapter in which the Sunday epistle appears. Then we sing some more, then the preacher rises as the last verse is being sung, and, after having said a prayer, starts his sermon on the gospel text for that Sunday. After the sermon there is another prayer and hymn and then, if we don't celebrate Holy Communion, I pronounce the blessing and the service is at an end."[358]

Zimmermann had held his first services in Dinokana. Initially on the tribal gathering place and later in the church. Most of the traditional believers who attended his services sat on the ground, especially the women. The Africans were not familiar with chairs and benches. Some of the men brought their own stools from their homes. Anybody could sit anywhere. Thomas Jensen changed all that. He was in favour of orderly conduct and began introducing it. To start with he placed the men on one side of the church and the women on the other. He also separated the Christians from the traditional believers. Since he was already able to hold his church services with a small congregation, the Christians were allowed to sit in front while the traditional believers were relegated to the back.[359]

The church services were also brought in line with the annual church festivals. Christmas was to be a special celebration. The congregation still numbered only a few Christians. So Karoline Jensen, after her arrival in Dinokana in 1865, was able to invite them into their house on Christmas Eve. In those early years it was still possible to host a Christmas Eve service in their house. Thomas Jensen conducted the service with singing, praying and a sermon. Afterwards Karoline Jensen distributed Christmas presents. Each guest received a small loaf of home-made bread and some coffee.

---

358 Thomas Jensen 04.08.1864 p. 6. – "Dann sage ich, welchen Gesang wir singen wollen und lese denselben vor. Wenn der Gesang gesungen ist, lese ich (des Vormittags) das ganze Kapitel vor, in welchem die Sonntagsepistel geschrieben ist. Danach wird wieder gesungen und beim letzten Vers steht der Prediger auf, nachdem er gebetet hat, predigt er dann über das Sonntagsevangelium. Nach der Predigt ist wieder Gebet und Gesang und wenn kein Abendmahl ist, dann Segen und der Gottesdienst ist aus."

359 Id., 20.06.1868 p. 2.

This Christmas ritual was repeated over the next four years. The growth of the congregation subsequently broke the mould of such a family-based celebration. In 1870 the Christmas Eve service took place in the church for the first time and was celebrated in the late afternoon.[360] There was a particular reason that made it possible to celebrate Christmas in more popular style, namely the availability of a new Setswana hymnal which contained the traditionally German Christmas hymns "*All praise to Thee, eternal God/Gelobet seist du Jesus Christ*", "*Come, your hearts and voices raising/Kommt und lasst uns Christum ehren*" and *"From Heav'n above to earth I come/Vom Himmel hoch da komm ich her"*.

Another European Christmas tradition was introduced to the African church: the Christmas tree.[361] Thomas Jensen introduced this tradition to the people in Dinokana. In doing so, he didn't use a fir tree, which didn't grow in Dinokana anyway, neither did he use a thorn tree that was ubiquitous in the area, but rather a fruit tree from his garden. After the sermon, which Jensen held on Mt. 1, 18–24, the candles were lit on the Christmas tree, as was customary in his home town. "It was a branch from a peach tree." In his home he had "… a green pomegranate tree bearing blossoms and fruit" as his Christmas tree.

In the years that followed, Ferdinand Jensen brought new ideas to Dinokana from his studies abroad in Hermannsburg. After he had completed his studies he came back to Dinokana on a permanent basis and celebrated Christmas in 1903 with a very special African novelty. He had previously assembled two different groups in his congregation. Brass instruments had been acquired for one of these groups of young men. Ferdinand Jensen had established a trombone choir with them, and, for the first time, the Christmas service was accompanied by brass instruments. The second group formed the church choir. Both groups became an integral part of the work done by the congregation. Ferdinand Jensen conducted both choirs. The work done with the brass instruments did however lose some of its impetus in later years.

The Bahurutshe like to sing, and thus choral singing steadily increased in popularity in Dinokana. It didn't take long before the congregation had a number of choirs in all age groups.

Ever since the Lutheran Church has introduced church-based choir

360 Id., 21. 12. 1870 p. 3.

361 Ibid.

competitions in the late 20th century, the parish choirs of Dinokana have taken home a large amount of trophies.[362]

5.3.3 The Church

When the phrase "sending out" is used in mission terms, it is usually Gen. 12,1 that is quoted as being the first divine mission: "The LORD had said to Abram, 'Go from your country, your people and your father's household to the land I will show you'." After the missionaries had arrived in a foreign land they followed Abram's second example: "… he built an altar there to the LORD" (Gen. 12,7f.).

The mission work of the Hermannsburg missionaries was done according to this principle. Immediately after their arrival they began to hold school classes, to proclaim the Word and, shortly after that, to build the first primitive Bethel, a house of worship. Abram built his altar out in the open. The missionaries, too, built an altar and put a roof over it. They called the building a church.

School lessons were, for the time being, the first priority of the Hermannsburg missionaries. School was usually held in the shade of a large tree. Their teaching activity inevitably led to the necessity to get to grips with the indigenous language. As soon as they were a little proficient in the language they held their first church service. There was no church building as yet. It then was a matter of obtaining the chief's authorisation to hold the church gatherings on the village gathering place. After the first church had subsequently been erected, the building was universally used, with the school lessons also being held in the church. The pupils were now sheltered from the wind and rain. The building was utilised as school during the week, and on Sundays the church service was conducted within its walls.

For about a year Zimmermann had conducted his first services on the chief's gathering place in the middle of the settlement. Then he requested the chief to give him a piece of land for a church. The tribe had not relocated at that time. He was allocated a site at the foot of the Pooe Mountain, roughly a kilometre away from the mission station. The building took on the shape of a very large rondavel to fit in with the style of the round huts in the settlement. He dispensed with an altar for the time being, something that set him apart from other missionaries.

362 For additional remarks on the choirs and on the church service, see Appendix 8.6.

When Thomas Jensen took over the congregation he initially utilised the church building for both school and church services. It didn't take long for him to decide to construct a new church building. There were a number of reasons for this. To begin with, the daily trip on foot to the old church was becoming a strain for him. He also wanted to separate the baptised Christians from the society of traditional believers and resettle them near the church, as we have seen in the case of Tsetlana. Thirdly, the old church was in dire need of improvement. He writes: "The (old, HB) church is in a bad way, it is a pole structure, the walls of which are about to collapse. It has neither an altar nor a pulpit. It is so big that probably around 300 people would have room in it. It will be necessary to build an even larger one, as soon as I know whether I will remain here or not. We are also in need of a church bell and Communion vessels."[363] A bell and Communion vessels were despatched from Germany at a later stage. If Thomas Jensen still held out the possibility that he would have to relocate with the tribe, this uncertainty was removed when the Bahurutshe moved down the mountain into the valley. After this relocation there was no reason to postpone the building of a church any longer. A new church was envisioned, with an altar and a pulpit. There was another important reason for a new church to be built as a matter of urgency. The children no longer attended the school classes in the old church. "The children use the long way they have to walk as an excuse not to come anymore. Since the relocation of the settlement the church, which is indeed also used as school room, is now quite far away."[364]

The new church site that the chief had made available to him was in an open field, "five minutes" away from the mission station. The tribe and the mission society supplied the necessary materials. The chief sent workers to help. Thomas Jensen and Lohann, who was still spending some time in Dinokana, took care of the handicraft. They had neither building plans nor experienced bricklayers, thatchers or building engineers at their disposal. The building costs were kept at a minimum, seeing that the church was

[363] Thomas Jensen 04.08.1864 p. 3 – "Die Kirche ist sehr schlecht, es ist ein Pfahlhaus, wovon die Mauern zum Theil einfallen wollen. Es ist weder Altar noch Kanzel drin. Sie ist so groß, dass wohl etwa 300 Leute hineingehen. Es wird nötig sein, eine größere zu bauen, wenn ich erst weiß, ob ich hier bleibe oder nicht. Eine Glocke und Abendmahlsgeräte sind hier Bedürfnisse."

[364] Id., 29.12.1865 p. 3 – "Dass die Kinder nicht mehr kommen, entschuldigen sie mit dem weiten Weg. Denn seitdem die Stadt verlegt worden ist, ist die Kirche, die ja als Schulhaus gebraucht wird, ziemlich weit entfernt."

built with locally sourced materials and by the local people of their own accord: "Moiloa ordered the bricks to be made and the thatch grass to be cut, furthermore providing people to help us. It is for this reason that the building will only cost us our labour, and a little bit for glass and fittings and locks for windows and doors."[365] He specified the church's perimeters to be 60 by 19 feet. It could hold roughly 600 people.[366] The church was consecrated on 9 September 1866.[367]

Almost twenty-three years later, on 2 February 1899, lightning struck the building out of a virtually cloudless sky; the building caught fire and was completely destroyed in the blaze.

After Moiloa II had died, Ikalafeng ruled the Bahurutshe. Thomas Jensen went to the chief to ask for advice. Thomas Jensen gives the following account of his discussion with Ikalafeng: "He said that the old church had been built by his grandfather, and now God had indicated to him that he should build a new one. He said the church was not only for the Christians but for the heathens as well, who should learn in it and become Christians too, and therefore the entire tribe should help to build the church."[368]

Meanwhile, money had begun circulating as a method of payment, alongside the customary barter trade. In order to facilitate the construction of the new church, the Bahurutshe began collecting money. Other individuals who assisted with donations were the British missionary Hepburn who was a good friend of Thomas Jensen's, as well as Ikalafeng, Thomas Jensen and other friends.

The church was completed after a two-and-a-half-year construction period. During this time of construction, a traveller, a Morolong, had stayed at Dinokana in Sept./Oct. 1890. He had looked at the church construction and subsequently told his tribesmen back home about it: "Mr *Lekota*, son of Montshiwa, left Mafikeng … He entered the area of the Hurutshe *merafe,* and … found Kgosi Ikalafeng (at Dinokana) building a house of teaching

---

[365] Id., 28. 06. 1866 p. 4. – "Moiloa hat die Steine machen und das Deckgras dazu schneiden lassen, dazu gibt er auch Leute, die uns helfen. Darum wird das Gebäude uns nur unsere Arbeiten kosten und eine Kleinigkeit für Glas und Beschlag und Schlösser für Fenster und Türen."

[366] Thomas Jensen 1874 p. 21f.

[367] Id., 30. 09. 1866 p. 5.

[368] Id., 21. 05. 1899 p. 2. – "Die alte Kirche wäre von seinem Großvater gebaut und nun hätte ihm Gott gezeigt, dass er eine neue bauen sollte. Die Kirche wäre nicht nur für Christen da, sondern auch für die Heiden, die sollten drin lernen, Christen zu werden, so müsste auch das ganze Volk helfen, die Kirche zu bauen."

The Dinokana church of 1891, as it can still be seen to this day.

for God. The house was very, very big and was very beautiful. He says it is almost more beautiful than that of the Barolong at Mafikeng, but he says that this one is better and cannot be surpassed."[369]

The old church was called "*Christuskirche*" (Church of Christ). The new church was to retain this name. The consecration was celebrated on 24 June 1891. A huge celebration was planned for this occasion.

The celebrating of a Mission Festival, based on the Mission Festival held in Hermannsburg/Germany, had meantime been introduced in the congregations of the Hermannsburg missionaries. In 1891 the Mission Festival of all the congregations in the region was planned to coincide with the consecration of the new church at Dinokana. The Hermannsburg missionaries who were stationed in other Batswana tribes had all come to Dinokana to attend the consecration. A missionary conference of the Marico District that lasted for several days followed the consecration of the new church.[370]

[369] Moshwele in Mgadla/Volz p. 241.

[370] Thomas Jensen 29. 06. 1891 p. 1; 6.

A large number of people had congregated to celebrate the consecration, amongst them many traditional believers. Thomas Jensen told the assembled crowd what sets a church, being a place of worship, apart from other buildings: "Christ must be proclaimed in it, he must reside in it through his Word. Nothing but the pure gospel should be preached from this pulpit. This baptismal font must serve to administer the Sacrament of Holy Baptism as ordained by Christ. May thousands upon thousands be reborn here of water and the Spirit. This altar must be a place of prayer, for it is through prayer that we bring our offerings to the Lord, but it must be more than that, it must be the Lord's Table from which the Holy Eucharist is administered according to Christ's command. And I must use the holy vessels on the altar to minister the body and blood of Christ in and with the bread and wine, as ordained by Christ for the forgiveness of sins. In the name of God, Son and Holy Spirit. Amen."[371]

Was he also mindful in his remarks of the lightning bolt that had destroyed the old church? Or did he make a conscious decision to not mention it at all, since he didn't know what to make of this virtual bolt from the blue? A single cloud had formed over the church, had emitted the bolt of lightning and then dissipated without a drop of rain. The traditional believers had mocked the Christians: "Why does your God let his house burn down?"[372]

That same year, lightning struck twice more. A woman was killed by a stroke of lightning in the settlement, and on the mission station it destroyed two big eucalyptus trees. However, after the consecration of the new church, when lightning struck yet again, this time destroying the cross on the church tower, Thomas Jensen did indeed become a little unsettled: "It is strange

[371] Loco citato p. 10f – "Denn Christus soll darin verkündet werden und durch sein Wort darin wohnen. Diese Kanzel soll dazu dienen, dass das Evangelium von derselben rein und lauter verkündigt werden soll. Dieser Taufstein soll nun dazu da sein, das Sakrament der Heiligen Taufe, nach Christi Befehl dabei zu verwalten. Mögen Tausende und aber Tausende an demselben durch Wasser und Geist wiedergeboren werden. Dieser Altar soll eine Stätte des Gebets sein, denn durch unsere Gebete wollen wir dem Herrn unsere Opfer darbringen, aber er soll noch mehr sein, er soll ein Tisch des Herrn sein, von welchem das Heilige Abendmahl nach dem Befehl Christi ausgeteilt werden soll. Und die heiligen Geräte sollen mir darauf dienen, dass mit denselben der Leib Christi und sein Blut in und mit dem Brot und Wein dargereicht werden soll auf Christi Befehl zur Vergebung der Sünden. Das walte Gott, Sohn und Heiliger Geist. Amen."

[372] Id., 05. 02. 1889 p. 2 – "Warum lässt Euer Gott sein Haus verbrennen?"

how often lightning strikes here, around our house and the church."[373] He did nonetheless not probe the cause and effect of these lightning strikes any further.

Why were the lightning bolts targeted so directly at the church? Were there powers at play who had attracted and directed the bolts? Were these powerful assaults directed at him personally? At his congregation? Had they been brought about by the camp of traditional believers to serve as a warning and to undermine Christianity?

Why didn't he have the courage to take this matter up with the tribal elders, lodging a complaint against persons unknown? He does not write about his reasons to withdraw and remain silent on this matter. But maybe it was better that way. The people talked about these incidents, but that was about it: No opposing groups emerged because of this. To this day, the newly built church stands at the same place.

5.3.4 The School

Sermons were held in church; lessons were given in school. The sermon and school lesson were two mediums by which the Word of God was to be proclaimed to the traditional believers. The traditional believers came to school to learn, and the sermon drew them towards wanting to hear the gospel. School lessons and the sermon had the same objective in mind: they were geared towards baptism, especially during the early years of mission work.

The sermon formed an essential part of the church service. It served both to strengthen the Christian faith of the parishioners and as an invitation for adult traditional believers to turn to the Christian faith. School lessons were based exclusively on Christian literature. This included the reading of Bible stories, singing from a hymnal and reciting Dr Martin Luther's Small Catechism. This foundation in Christian instruction constituted the preliminary stage of baptism classes.

The Hermannsburg missionaries were not the first to employ Christian literature as learning material in Dinokana. Some members of the Bahurutshe tribe had encountered missionaries of other mission societies in outlying areas and had attended their classes. They had taken their readers back

373 Thomas Jensen 12. 01. 1892 p. 2 – "Es ist merkwürdig, wie oft der Blitz hier einschlägt, bei unserm Haus und bei der Kirche."

home. These people were already able to read and write a little. The Hermannsburg missionaries in Dinokana now offered them continual school lessons based on the European model. The Bahurutshe found it difficult to embrace what was a new method to them. It would take quite a number of years before they had grown accustomed to the new school system. It was only in the long-term that the Bahurutshe were able to grow accustomed to attending school as such, and to the system and permanence of this institution.

Zimmermann had begun with his first school lessons soon after his arrival. He was able to do this so speedily, since he appointed Sehuneloa who had already been baptised in Kuruman. Every person that was baptised could read and write. But Zimmermann's demands on a teacher were higher than the qualifications that Sehuneloa could show. He calls him a "sort-of-teacher". He nevertheless handed over the reins of the school to him as he was keen to start immediately. "Apart from the previously mentioned sort-of-teacher and his family, who had relocated from Kuruman to the Bahurutshe, I found no baptised Christians at Linokana."[374] Sehuneloa needed to be remunerated for the work he did. He was paid, not with natural produce or livestock, but with money.

Zimmermann had paid Sehuneloa one British pound, which was too much in Thomas Jensen's opinion. This high remuneration was probably one of the reasons why Zimmermann was able to hold onto Sehuneloa for such a long time. Thomas Jensen also criticises the fact that Zimmermann had, during the four years of his tenure, hardly given any lessons himself. Zimmermann had constructed the two buildings – the relatively large missionary house as well as the church. In addition to this the matter of work within the congregation was close to his heart. He held church services and took over the baptismal classes. He furthermore deemed it necessary to regularly attend the tribal gatherings. He wanted to establish a good relationship with the Bahurutshe, to immerse himself into their culture and language. The good relations he had with the Bahurutshe were doubtless also one of the reasons why the Boers brought an action against him on numerous occasions. These procedures had also taken up a not inconsiderable amount of his time. All these time-consuming obligations may have

374 Zimmermann 1874 p. 13 – "Außer dem erwähnten Quasi-Lehrer und dessen Familie, die von Kuruman zu den Bahurutsi gezogen waren, fand ich auf Linokana keine Getauften vor."

prompted him to place the school lessons into the hands of Sehuneloa. Zimmermann's extensive engagement was however appreciably acknowledged by the Bahurutshe.

Initially Thomas Jensen was less successful than Zimmermann had been. This was mainly due to his personality. If one would assign the characteristics of introversion and extroversion to the two missionaries, then Zimmermann tended towards extroversion, while Thomas Jensen's conduct could be described as being more introverted in nature. This is already discernible in the fact that Thomas Jensen placed his emphasis on developing the congregation from within. From an early stage he began participating in the school lessons, putting an additional emphasis on confirmation. With his participation in the school the frictions between him and Sehuneloa became clearly visible. Sehuneloa had difficulties in submitting to Thomas Jensen, who eventually dismissed him from his post.

Sehuneloa could not accept his dismissal. He felt aggrieved. His daughter had married an Englishman who had somehow found himself in Dinokana. The two of them joined forces against Jensen.[375] They were however unable to assert themselves with their criticism in Dinokana. Had they been local people things might have turned out differently. So it happened that Sehuneloa and his son-in-law left Dinokana for good.[376]

At that time when tensions between Thomas Jensen and Sehuneloa became apparent, Moremi had made his appearance at Dinokana. Thomas Jensen welcomed his arrival. He is mentioned in Schröder's reports.[377] Mgadla/Volz write about him: "Moremi was baptised by the Hermannsburg missionaries in Botswana. He was the first HMS convert at *Dithubaruba*."[378] When the Hermannsburg missionaries were compelled to abandon their work in Botswana at the instigation of Hardeland, Moremi assumed the leadership of the congregation. He has been mentioned above.

Under Moremi's leadership, harmful influences were allowed to take effect in the congregation. The adherence to the Commandments was no longer taken seriously. He was obviously not able to keep order. *Mogodi*

---

375 Thomas Jensen 1874 p. 32f.

376 According to Volz, Sehuneloa left Dinokana for Botswana. He took over the work from Paul, who had been active in Dinokana before the arrival of the Hermannsburg missionaries: "He ended up taking Paul's place at Moshupa." Volz p. 217.

377 In Schütte p. 173.

378 Mgadla/Volz p. 217. Dithubaruba is called Dithejane by the Hermannsburg missionaries.

writes: "We see a lot of heathenism in the village of Moremi, and the work of God is much despised. It is especially looked down upon those people who were once believers."[379] The situation in Dithejane had become too much for Moremi. He did however not want to part with the Hermannsburg missionaries, left the congregation at Dithejane and came to Dinokana. Thomas Jensen accommodated him and employed him in his school as the substitute teacher for Sehuneloa.

Sehuneloa had initially put his stamp on the school. Moremi had now taken his place. Both had come to Dinokana from elsewhere. No mention is made as to how attractive the lessons they gave were. Zimmermann's half-yearly reports are no longer in existence, and Thomas Jensen's thoughts in his reports probably turned more towards himself and the mission society that had sent him. He wanted to demonstrate his own work performance. The local teachers were therefore of secondary importance to him. Even so, he does provide some information about his daily school routine of the first year, as well as the number of pupils. "The school, which I hold every day for two to three hours, excluding Saturdays, is fairly well attended. I very often have 20–30 adults and between 50–100 children. There are usually quite a number of nursemaids amongst them, who each carry a small child on their back. (…) The school starts with prayer and singing, then I read a Bible story to them and question them thoroughly about it afterwards."[380]

Thc relatively large range in numbers is an indication thereof that the pupils did not all attend every day. They came when they felt like it. School in those days was very far away from being compulsory. Neither should one entertain the notion that all pupils appeared punctually at the beginning of each lesson. The concept of time did not feature amongst the Bahurutshe in those days. The lesson commenced when a handful of pupils had shown up. Anyone else joined in by and by. It is therefore understandable that Thomas Jensen started off with prayer, singing and a Bible story. That was followed by school lessons. The pupils had to engage with mathematical exercises. "Then everyone goes to his or her chart … and learns. Then I recite to

379 Mgadla/Volz p. 65.

380 Thomas Jensen 04.08.1864 p. 7 – "Die Schule, die ich alle Tage zwei bis drei Stunden halte, ausgenommen sonnabends, wird ziemlich (gut, HB) besucht. Häufig habe ich 20–30 Erwachsene und von 50–100 Kinder. Gewöhnlich sind darunter viele Kindermädchen, die dann jedes ein kleines Kind auf dem Rücken haben. (…) Die Schule fängt mit Gebet und Gesang an, dann lese ich eine biblische Geschichte vor und frage sie wieder durch."

them the Creed or the Ten Commandments or the Lord's Prayer or Bible verses, until they know them by heart."[381] The simplicity of it all becomes apparent. The first pupils had neither an educational background nor role models from whom they could learn something. It is therefore understandable when Thomas Jensen brought the deposit of faith and his knowledge thereof into school lessons by the method of memorisation. The daily lesson then ended with prayer and singing again.

During the first five years of his service the Bahurutshe exhibited a great eagerness to learn. The Hermannsburg Mission Society had meanwhile printed school books containing simple exercises. On one occasion, when previously ordered reading primers from Germany failed to arrive, a person from a British mission station procured some school books for them. This further bore witness to the Bahurutshe's fervour. The printed word made a huge impression on them, especially since they were able to acquire these little booklets themselves. Thomas Jensen was astonished: "To learn to read has become such a fashionable thing to do that almost every young kaffir[382] carries a book with him wherever he goes."[383] The eagerness exhibited by some pupils had contributed to a steady rise in the number of pupils. Some of them had understood right from the beginning that, by getting educated, they were advancing their knowledge, thereby rising in the esteem of their peers and amongst those who had recognised the importance of a school education for a promising future.

The first lessons had taken place under a shady tree. Then both missionaries had subsequently held school in their churches. The plan was now to construct a school building, the first of its kind in the Transvaal. Thomas Jensen didn't build it on tribal land but rather close to his house, on mission property. "Finally, after two years, in 1871, I managed to build a school of 40x15 feet as well. I have erected the school a few paces from my house, across the churchyard."[384] From 1871 onwards, school was therefore

---

381 Loco citato – "Danach geht jeder zu seiner Tabelle ... und lernt. Darauf sage ich ihnen den Glauben (Glaubensbekenntnis, HB), oder die Zehn Gebote oder das Vaterunser oder Bibelsprüche vor, bis sie sie auswendig wissen."

382 The term 'kaffir' is Arabic in its origin and means 'unbeliever, infidel'. This term had no negative connotations in the 19th century. It was only awarded a deeply negative denotation during the years of the Apartheid regime. It came to mean something like "stupid black person", and is no longer in public use.

383 Id., 1874 p. 23 – "Das Lesenlernen ist hier so zur Mode geworden, dass fast jeder junge Kaffer ein Buch bei sich hat wo er geht und steht."

384 Id., 1874 p. 23 – "Endlich vor zwei Jahren in 1871 hatte ich noch eine Schule gebaut von

no longer held in the church but rather in a building constructed specifically for that purpose. The one-room structure was made of clay, with a small window providing a small amount of light. During lessons the door stood wide open, brightening the school room more than the small window was able to. The door was only closed in the event of rain or a storm. The lessons were frequently still held outside when the weather was fine. This first school building in the Transvaal was still in operation up until the 70s of the 20th century. It was only when a pre-school facility was to be erected during that time that this old building was demolished.

The Bahurutshe's eagerness to learn was remarkable, to be sure, it did however initially not last very long. After the school had been built, attendance of lessons dwindled. "When I arrived here the school was overcrowded with adults and children from the heathens but their zeal was short-lived. Things quickly abated and now it is only the children of the baptised Christians, the baptismal candidates and a few adults from the congregation who feel like learning more."[385] Conditions at the school continued to fluctuate.

Other Hermannsburg missionaries had also built schools elsewhere in the Transvaal. When the number of pupils steadily rose, the Hermannsburg Mission Society reflected on the possibility of a seminary for indigenous teachers, and built such a seminary in 1874 in Bethanie. After ten years it was relocated to Beerseba. The congregations sent their stalwart church elders to the teachers' seminary. After they had finished their training they returned to the parish schools, which were not necessarily those they had left behind. Thus a teacher from Phalane was sent to Dinokana. Thomas Jensen comments on his qualities: "I can only say good things about the school. It is doing much better than previously. (...) For a couple of months now, we have a teacher from the seminary. Josef ... is hardworking. He teaches well. The children come to school diligently and are making good progress."[386]

40x15 Fuß. Die Schule habe ich einige Schritte vom Hause, dem Kirchhof gegenüber gebaut."

385 Loco citato p. 59 – "Als ich hier (her, HB) kam, war die Schule überfüllt mit Erwachsenen und Kindern aus den Heiden, das war aber nur kurze Zeit, solange das Strohfeuer brannte. Das ließ bald nach und jetzt kommen nur noch die Kinder der Getauften, die Taufkandidaten und einige Erwachsene aus der Gemeinde, die Lust haben weiter zu lernen."

386 Thomas Jensen 02.01.1891 p. 5f – "Von der Schule kann ich nur Erfreuliches berichten. Es geht mit derselben viel besser als früher. (...) Jetzt aber haben wir seit ein paar

The first school in the Transvaal, built in 1871 by missionary Thomas Jensen in Dinokana

Soon all the Hermannsburg missionaries had opened a school on their mission stations. Other mission societies also established schools where they were missionizing. This fact was also known to the people at Dinokana and thus it came about that the local children also attended the schools of missionaries elsewhere.

Meanwhile a political change of great significance had occurred. Twice the Boers and British had gone to war with one another. The British influence could also be felt at Dinokana. Young people were keen to learn in English schools. After the Second Anglo-Boer War several Bahurutshe wanted to enrol in English schools that were far away from Dinokana. When the chief learnt that young people from his tribe had actually gone to the school of the Scottish Mission in Lovedale on the Indian Ocean,[387] he was very disgruntled.

Not long after the Second Anglo-Boer War, Ferdinand Jensen was sta-

Monaten einen Lehrer aus dem Seminar. ... Josef ... ist tüchtig. Er unterrichtet gut. Die Kinder kommen fleißig zur Schule und kommen gut weiter."

387 This school for Xhosa children had already been established by the Scottish missionaries back in 1841. Hodgson p. 80.

tioned at Dinokana on a permanent basis. Thomas Jensen immediately handed over the responsibility of the school to his son. After their victory over the Boers, the British had exerted their influence on the schools. A school inspector paid regular visits to the mission schools of the two Hermannsburg missionaries. When the school inspector visited the parish school at Dinokana in 1903, he proposed that a bigger school be built. The medium of instruction at the new school was to be English. The chief and the two missionaries at Dinokana agreed to the proposal. In doing so, they had contemplated two advantages. They were of the opinion, for one, that parents would then no longer send their children to other schools and would stay in Dinokana. For another, the financial outlay for the school had shown an upward year-on-year trend. Soon they would no longer be able to support the school. By enlarging the building and changing the medium of instruction to English they hoped for financial support from the government. Thomas Jensen writes: "The British government is certainly also doing something for the education of the natives, which was not the case with the previous government."[388] The chief and his tribe took the initiative and immediately committed themselves to the building of a bigger school. It only took a few months to erect the new school, measuring sixty by forty feet.[389] Ferdinand Jensen was appointed as the head master. The hoped-for increase in the number of pupils did indeed come about.

Ferdinand Jensen's next step was to apply at the Hermannsburg Mission Society for a secondary school to be built at the vast settlement that was Dinokana.[390] His application was unfortunately not successful. The amount of finances required for a secondary school were beyond the capabilities of the Hermannsburg mission.

The new school was under the control of the Hermannsburg mission for several years until it was taken over by the government.

5.3.5 Outstations

The Jensens' main area of operation was in Dinokana. The settlement grew and Thomas Jensen was fully occupied with his work in the main congregation. But there were also a number of families who had moved somewhere

[388] Thomas Jensen 19.06.1903 p. 2 – "Die englische Regierung tut ja auch für den Unterricht der Eingeborenen etwas, was bei dem alten Gouvernment nicht der Fall war."

[389] Id., 04.01.1904 p. 2.

[390] Hasselhorn 1988 p. 117.

else. Tensions within the community and a propensity to migrate had led to the circumstance that some families from Dinokana had settled in Zeerust and Jacobsdal. In Zeerust, a European town about twenty kilometres to the east of Dinokana, these Bahurutshe had moved into an already existent settlement. Other families had settled with the Boers in Jacobsdal, which lies roughly ten kilometres to the south of Dinokana. The self-contained tribal society was nonetheless still intact. Those who had moved out retained contact with their relatives in Dinokana. This encouraged them, at least in the beginning, to undertake the long journey back to Dinokana to attend the church services as well as the baptismal- and confirmation classes in the main congregation. In the long-term, and given the quite considerable distance, this was not a good solution, however. As the number of parishioners residing in Zeerust and Jacobsdal grew, the Christians requested of Thomas Jensen to perform his services at their places of residence.

Thomas Jensen did not like that idea very much. He was reluctant to move outside his customary ways in Dinokana. Instead, he allowed them to organise themselves. "They have built a little house for themselves in Zeerust, which they use as church and school. In each settlement they have, with our permission, elected people from their midst who hold church services and Sunday school as best they can. If someone desires to be baptised, they must first come here and attend baptism classes for a while. – Thus we have made these temporary arrangements, we will have to wait and see how this develops."[391] This continued for five years.

When Ferdinand Jensen was given a permanent post at Dinokana he took over the work on the outstations. They were now admittedly better ministered to, but not exactly as the subsidiary congregation at Zeerust, for example, would have wished it. The Hermannsburg missionaries were rurally orientated, which meant that Ferdinand Jensen initially tended only to the rural congregation at Jacobsdal and not to an equal extent to the township in the much larger Zeerust. He opened a school at Jacobsdal and appointed a teacher by the name of Johannes. On Zeerust he comments: "In Zeerust … there are so many church communities at work that it is

[391] Thomas Jensen 07.01.1898 p. 2 – "In Zeerust haben sie sich ein kleines Haus gebaut, das sie als Kapelle und Schule gebrauchen. An jedem Ort haben sie sich, mit unserer Zustimmung, einen aus ihrer Mitte gewählt, der ihnen, so gut es geht, des Sonntags Gottesdienst und Sonntagsschule hält. Wenn jemand getauft werden will, muss er erst hier eine Zeit lang zum Taufunterricht gehen. – So haben wir es vorläufig eingerichtet, wir müssen dann sehen, wie es später wird."

not worth our while to establish a preaching location over there, especially since I don't have a teacher at hand to do this work."[392] In view of the plethora of other Christian congregations, he was of the opinion that his energy would be better spent in areas where there was still a lack of an adequate ministry. It is for this reason that, for a long time, he paid very little attention to the congregation in Zeerust. The parishioners in that town nevertheless continued to remain faithful to the Lutheran Church.

In spite of the congregation growing considerably over the next few years, he had not appointed a teacher for Zeerust. The significant increase in parishioners also captured the interest of other communities. The congregation had become active to such an extent that, within the period of one year, twenty traditional believers had signed up for baptismal classes.[393] It is astonishing that Ferdinand Jensen was not prepared to hold church services in Zeerust, given the growth in numbers and the obvious vibrancy of the congregation. The congregation was obliged to get by without their missionary, holding its own church services and Sunday school. The sacraments, however, continued to be exclusively administered from Dinokana.

Aspirations for independence began gripping the black population in South Africa from the late 19th century onwards. The Africans began resisting the oppressive laws of the Europeans. Neither did this movement stop at the doors of the traditional churches and mission societies. Independent African congregations sought to become autonomous. This movement also found its way into the Lutheran Church. It did admittedly hardly play a role in Dinokana, but the subsidiary congregation in the location of Zeerust was confronted by it. There were men in the congregation who were sympathetic towards the aspirations for independence. They invited the black pastor from the independent Bapedi Church in Rustenburg. The latter, together with his companions, was subsequently also admitted to Lutheran families at Zeerust. They held a church service together with him. A discussion about church affiliation subsequently ensued amongst the women of the location. They took a unanimous vote not to join the Bapedi Church. Consequently the congregation remained a subsidiary of Dinokana.[394] Ferdinand was only informed at a later stage that the visitor from Rustenburg

392 Ferdinand Jensen 05.07.1904 p. 3 – "In Zeerust … wird von so vielen Kirchengemeinschaften gearbeitet, dass es sich für uns nicht lohnt, dort eine Predigtstelle einzurichten, zumal ich für diese Arbeit keinen Lehrer zur Hand habe."

393 Id., 1913 p. 6.

394 Loco citato.

had not achieved anything. This incident proved to be an incisive one for Ferdinand Jensen, causing him to change his point of view. He now also held regular church services in Zeerust.

Other subsidiaries had meanwhile arisen, while others were in the process of becoming such stations, all of which were subsequently regularly visited by Ferdinand Jensen. Most of the new subsidiaries had arisen due to divisions within the tribe. At various times disaffected families moved out in larger groups under the leadership of both Chief Israel Moiloa and Chief Pogiso Moiloa. In each case Ferdinand Jensen went after them and established a subsidiary congregation in various places. This was the case in *Enselsberg/Tshwenyane, Leeuwfontein/Mokgola*[395] and, at a later stage, *Braklaagte/Lekubu.* In 1937 the following outstations were part of Dinokana: *Jacobsdal, Zeerust, Vaalkop, Braklaagte, Leeuwfontein* and *Langgezocht.*[396]

5.3.6 The First Church Taxes

Performing practical work formed part of the Hermannsburg missionary model. The pioneer missionaries were obliged to have learnt a trade before enrolling into the seminaries for their missionary training. Practical know-how and –skills facilitated their start as missionaries in the field. In Dinokana they built the missionary house, the outlines of which can be seen to this day. They built the church and the school. Money was a scarce commodity. The average African did not have any money. He lived off the yields of his garden, the small tilling field that the chief had assigned to him, and by bartering his produce and his livestock with others. The Bahurutshe supported the building of the church and school with material and unpaid work and services. The necessary monetary funds came from a few individuals who were already able to deal with money as a means of payment, as well as from the mission society in Germany.

Once money was in circulation, the Bahurutshe gradually gave up the barter trade. Money was now taking the place of the customary bartering of goods or services. Bartering soon became a rare practise and eventually disappeared totally from public trade. Money was now also introduced to cover the running costs of the mission. Thomas Jensen started to use money in 1874. "Last year I began with the practise of letting those who wanted

[395] Ferdinand Jensen 1910 p. 2.

[396] Id. 1937.

to be baptised or married pay a nominal fee; for baptism 2/6 and marriage 10/."[397] That would suffice for a start. It was a small amount. The parishioners had at that time already grown accustomed to the handling of money. When he proposed the introduction of a fee he wanted the parishioners to pay after the church service, they agreed to that contribution as well.

After just one year he confronted his parishioners with yet another contribution. He requested of them to co-finance his upkeep by paying an annual tax into the church coffers. Here too, he met with no resistance, neither did people leave the congregation, only some remarks were made to the effect that he should also bear in mind that they were poor people. "The whole congregation was prepared to give something straight away, only a number of them asked me to be mindful of the fact that they were really mostly poor people."[398] The amount to be paid was then discussed in the congregational meeting, during which it was decided "... that each member of the congregation should pay 5 shilling = 1 thaler and 1 guilder per annum, the widows excepted. (...) Taking local conditions into account this is not much, to be sure, but nevertheless constitutes an encouraging start."[399] The willingness to co-finance the "budget" was a significant step on the congregation's road to co-responsibility and stabilisation.

It bears mentioning that one reason why Thomas Jensen requested a contribution to be made towards his income was the low salary of the Hermannsburg missionaries. Compared to missionaries of other protestant mission societies, those from Hermannsburg were "poor missionaries". The Hermannsburg Mission Society didn't have the money to pay their missionaries an appropriate salary. Hasselhorn writes: "The salary (of the Hermannsburg missionaries, HB) amounted to between 80 and 90 (British

397 Thomas Jensen 19.07.1875 p. 2. – 1 British pound sterling = 20 shilling; 1 shilling = 12 pence. 2/6 denotes 2 shilling and 6 pence. At current exchange rates from €to Pounds = 1:1,21 that is 46 pence = ca. 0,23 €. – 10/ denotes 10 shilling = 200 pence, at the same exchange rate ca. 1,01 €.

398 Loco citato p. 3. – "Die ganze Gemeinde fand sich auch gleich dazu bereit etwas zu geben, nur einige baten, dass ich doch bedenken möge, dass sie meist nur arme Leute wären." – In this instance the denotation of "poor people" needs to be put into relative perspective. The lament was probably justified, coming from a rural population that relied heavily on favourable weather conditions for their survival, but could also be construed in the sense that the financial burden of the church fee triggered a general feeling of unease in the face of indigence.

399 Thomas Jensen 19.07.1875 p. 3 – "... dass jedes Mitglied der Gemeinde 5 Schilling = 1 Taler und 1 Gulden im Jahr bezahlen solle, die Witwen ausgenommen. (...) Nach hiesigem Verhältnisse ist es zwar nicht viel ist aber doch ein erfreulicher Anfang."

pounds, HB) in nominal terms. In practise, deductions had to be made on a regular basis … as there were insufficient funds. (…) From the 1st of January 1874 the salaries were cut back by a quarter. (…) The missionaries from the Methodist- and Reformed missions received a base salary of 250 (British pounds, HB)."[400] Hasselhorn addresses the actual reason for the introduction of a church fee. The small annual salary was too low anyway, and was barely enough to live on. Now it was cut back even further.

Thomas Jensen had approached the adult members of his congregation with his demand for a steady church fee in a circumspect way. On 3 December 1873 a resolution had already been adopted at the missionaries' conference at Hebron that, starting in 1874, "… each head of the family was to pay the sum of 1 British pound to the church, a widow 10 shilling and a confirmed young man also 10 shilling, only poor widows could be exempted."[401] It was not Thomas Jensen who had effectuated this resolution that was adopted at the conference. In accordance with his parishioners he proposed lower rates to begin with. Thomas Jensen was content with the modest resources of his congregation. The people of the Dinokana congregation agreed to the taxes that would be levied for the first time.

The fact that there were no major objections to the introduction of a church tax was due to several reasons. In the early years the Bahurutshe were compelled to render, not money, but rather labour tasks to the chief, as well as supply him with natural produce. The tribe also had obligations towards the Boers, assuming work on their fields and sometimes having to pay stiff penalties. All powers that be exacted taxes from their subjects. Over time the church had no choice but to adopt a similar approach to manage its affairs. Being accustomed to the services rendered to the chief and the forced labour and taxes imposed by the Boers, the Bahurutshe were prepared to contribute financially to the congregation. The contribution that was expected of them was reasonable. The willingness with which the baptised Christians were prepared to render their financial contribution to cover the congregational costs bears witness to the trust they placed in their mis-

400 Hasselhorn 1988 p. 58f – "Das Gehalt betrug nominell 80 bis 90. In der Praxis mussten oft Abzüge gemacht werden … weil nicht genügend Geld in der Kasse war. (…) Zum 1. Januar 1874 wurde das Gehalt um ein Viertel gekürzt. (…) Die Missionare der methodistischen und reformierten Mission erhielten ein Grundgehalt von 250."

401 W. Behrens 20.01.1874 p. 2 – "… jeder Familienvater 1 englisches Pfund im Jahr an die Kirche gebe und eine Witwe 10 Schilling und ein konfirmierter Jüngling auch 10 Schilling, nur arme Witwen könne man frei ausgehen lassen."

sionary. Thomas Jensen had already developed and consolidated his work in the congregation on a continuous basis for eleven years when the church tax was introduced.

5.3.7 The Foreigners Once Again

At the beginning of the mission work in Dinokana, the congregation consisted of just one family and Reverend Zimmermann. Zimmermann was not married. He had become acquainted with Sehuneloa during the tribal councils and had been able to engage him for the mission work. Moiloa II gave Zimmermann permission to hold his services on the tribal gathering place. Sehuneloa attended these services with his family, and so did a large number of traditional believers. The traditional believers of Dinokana were interested in this novel cause, but were nonetheless hesitant to get baptised during the first two years. They adopted a wait and see attitude. That was not the case where the foreigners who had settled at Dinokana were concerned. There were a number of these living in Dinokana, besides Sehuneloa. He was initially the only baptised Christian. This fact proved to be a privilege where the collaboration with Zimmermann was concerned. This did not escape the notice of the other foreigners and as a result they, too, began leaning towards the missionary. They were the first to enrol in the baptism classes and to be baptised. Zimmermann had arrived at Dinokana on 7 January 1859 and, almost 11 months later, on 27 November 1859, he performed the first baptisms. There was not one Bahurutshe amongst these first Christians to be baptised; they were all foreigners who had relocated to Dinokana.

The first Bahurutshe were eventually baptised while Zimmermann was still at Dinokana. It has been stated previously that, when Thomas Jensen took over, the congregation consisted of 42 baptised Christians, and that two married couples had been expelled from the congregation due to their transgression of the Sixth Commandment. Zimmermann had initiated their sequestration before he left. We do not know their names, but Sehuneloa was not one of them.

After Thomas Jensen had assumed his duties in the congregation, the transgressions of the Sixth Commandment increased. He writes about *Mamba,* also one of the foreigners, who no longer attended the church services. In a small congregation every member who fails to turn up becomes highly conspicuous. Mamba failed to attend for a succession of Sundays.

His unchristian behaviour affected other men in the congregation. A group of four married men had intercourse with other women. Thomas Jensen was told about this licentious conduct. "4 men were particularly guilty: One of them felt like taking a second wife, two others … wanted to swop their wives for a while but the women, who are Christians, would have none of it. (…) The latter three promised to change for the better, so I let them be. (…) But when I questioned Mamba … he simply said no."[402] Thomas Jensen visited Mamba in his hut and urged him to stop lusting after other women. Mamba didn't heed his advice, however, and went away on a trip shortly afterwards. He neither asked the congregation to pray for his safe return, as is customary in a small congregation, nor did he bid farewell to Thomas Jensen and the parishioners. He returned to Dinokana a while later, accompanied by a second wife, proclaiming "… that Satan was indeed more powerful than the Lord Jesus and that is why he wanted to be a servant of Satan again."[403] Then he left Dinokana, never to return again.

Mamba used the term "Satan" in his proclamation. He had adopted this term from Thomas Jensen. Satan represents everything that is evil. The concept itself has undergone a long evolution in religious history. In the Bible this term is used for the first time in the Book of Job (e.g. 1,6; 7; 12). If the name Satan is employed to denote everything that is evil, that which is universally evil subsequently undergoes a process of personification. That is what happened in the case of Mamba and Thomas Jensen. There are other manifestations of evil ascribed to Satan: evil thoughts, evil forces, sorcery and magical practises. The case of Mamba and Thomas Jensen is of a different nature, however. Here Satan is equated with lust that is not placed under God's commandments. Mamba transgressed God's commandment "Thou shalt not commit adultery" by giving free rein to his emotions and taking an additional wife to the one he had.

The provost of the Hermannsburg missionaries also wrote about this case. As opposed to Thomas Jensen, he does not speak of Satan but rather of a "pernicious influence" within the congregation of believers. "Things

[402] Thomas Jensen 1874 p. 49f – "Besonders schuldig waren 4 Männer: Einer hatte Lust gehabt, eine zweite Frau zu nehmen und zwei hatten … mit ihren Frauen zeitweilig tauschen wollen, und die Frauen, die Christinnen sind, wollten es nicht. (…) Die letzten drei geboten Besserung, und so ließ ich sie. (…) Als ich aber Mamba fragte … antwortete er geradezu nein."

[403] Id. 01.10.1867 p. 2 – "… dass der Satan doch starker wäre als der Herr Jesus, darum wolle er auch dem Satan wieder dienen."

are bad as well as good on our Dinokana station. Bad, because the small congregation does not segregate itself enough from the traditional believers in order to make itself entirely holy to the Lord. Our dear Brother Jensen over there often has his hands full, as the pernicious influence on the small congregation from those Christians who have been chased or have run away from Kuruman and settled at Dinokana is such, that a parishioner by the name of Mamba recently proclaimed publicly in front of his teacher and the congregation: God knows that Mamba doesn't believe in God, neither does he love God, therefore Mamba is renouncing his Christian faith today and is returning to the heathens."[404]

We note – as propounded above – that Behrens does not use the term Satan, but rather speaks of a bad and pernicious influence. One may furthermore deduce from this quote that Mamba's apostasy had already previously been registered in Kuruman, where he had failed to adhere to the ordinance of the London missionaries and had therefore fled to Dinokana. In Dinokana he saw himself being subjected to the same rules, which caused him to fail yet again.

It bears mentioning that there were quite a number of foreigners from other tribes who had come to settle at Dinokana. Most of them were from Kuruman, Sehuneloa and Mamba amongst them. Behrens is of the opinion that they had run away from Kuruman. What he means to say is that these individuals had, for whatever reason, been expelled from the Christian congregation and were looking for a new home in Dinokana. These were the people who were accommodated by the Hermannsburg missionaries to form the beginning of a Christian congregation in Dinokana. The Hermannsburg missionaries were at first unaware of the events that had taken place in Kuruman. If the Bahurutshe were not willing to be baptised, and these foreigners offered to help establish the congregation, then they were welcome as far as the missionaries were concerned.

---

[404] Behrens 01.10.1865 p. 4 – "Auf unserer Station Dinokana sieht es schlecht und gut aus. Schlecht, weil die kleine Gemeinde sich nicht genug von den Heiden absondert, sich dem Herrn ganz und gar zu heiligen. Der liebe Bruder Jensen hat oft seine liebe Not daselbst, denn der verderbliche Einfluss von denen aus Kuruman weggejagten oder weggelaufenen Getauften, die sich in Dinokana angebaut haben, wirkt also auf die kleine Gemeinde, dass neulich ein Gemeindeglied, mit Namen Mamba, vor seinem Lehrer und der Gemeinde offen erklärte: Gott weiß, dass Mamba nicht an Gott glaubt, auch Gott nicht lieb hat, darum sagt Mamba heute den christlichen Glauben ab und kehrt wieder zu den Heiden zurück."

The troubles at Dinokana began piling up. One day Thomas Jensen went and sat at his desk and wrote and despatched a letter to Kuruman. A dialogue developed between him and R. Moffat. After having exchanged a number of letters Thomas Jensen prepared to embark on a journey to Kuruman. He did however not specify the reason for his visit to be that he wanted to talk to Moffat about those parishioners of his who had originated from Kuruman, but rather the orthography of the Setswana Bible. The Hermannsburg Mission Society had elected Thomas Jensen onto the panel of the Literature Commission. The Society was in favour of a standardised Bible translation of the various tribal dialects of the Batswana. Thomas Jensen was told to go and talk to Moffat about this. He made preparations "… to travel to Kuruman in order to talk to the old Moffat about the new orthography that the British wanted to impose on us. (…) I had already looked forward to meeting the old Moffat personally, seeing that I had corresponded with him for quite a while already."[405] He started two attempts but had to turn back each time, on the first occasion because of safety concerns due to the war. On his second attempt he was called back home because of sudden illness in his family. Thus it happened that the personal encounter he had been looking forward to for so long never materialised.[406]

There are no records of this correspondence in the archives of the ELM. The assumption can be made, however, that he would have broached the subject of the misconduct of the parishioners who had relocated from Ku-

---

405 Thomas Jensen 01.07.1870 p. 1 – "… nach Kuruman zu reisen, um mit dem alten Moffat über die neue Orthographie zu sprechen, die die Engländer uns aufdrängen wollten. (…) Ich hatte mich schon darauf gefreut, den alten Moffat, mit dem ich schon lange in Briefwechsel stand, persönlich kennenzulernen."

406 The Hermannsburg missionaries, as well as those from the Berlin Mission Society, took issue with the fact that the missionaries of the London Mission Society determined the orthography for the translation of the Bible, a disapproval that lasted into the early years of the 20th century. Behrens jun. writes: 'In October we, the members of the Book Commission, held our conference in Dinokana. The Free State brethren from the Book Commission of the Berlin mission had also come, as well as Solomon Plaatje, a pupil of the latter and the editor of the 'Betshuanaland Gazette'. We deliberated on a common orthography, reaching a compromise on several books that are being worked on. We also addressed a letter to the Bible Society in London concerning the new Bible which is being printed for the London Mission Society, and which we are unable to accept in that form.' [Behrens jun. 1907 p. 16] – A common orthography did however not materialise. The British missionaries were not prepared to share with the Germans their claim to leadership with regards to a primary translation of the Bible for various Batswana tribes.

ruman to Dinokana with Moffat. Such a conversation would not have made much difference, though. An encounter between the two could however have led to greater mutual respect for the differing doctrines of their respective denominations, and to mutual encouragement of the consensus not to tolerate transgressions of the Sixth Commandment. In the end none of this came about.

The congregation at Dinokana grew. The foreigners who adhered to the ordinances of the church and did not break the Sixth Commandment had also contributed to its growth.

Those Bahurutshe who were sympathetic towards the gospel but did not yet want to submit themselves to baptism kept a watchful eye on the foreigners. Gradually they decided to join the congregation. It cannot be established with any certainty which Bahurutshe were the first to receive baptism. Many of their names are similar to those of the tribe of the Barolong. What is certain, however, is that those who first received baptism were not of the Bahurutshe tribe. The congregation that Zimmermann handed over to Thomas Jensen then already counts a number of Bahurutshe amongst its members. During the ensuing years it happened regularly that foreigners were baptised together with Bahurutshe. Then things began to change.

In 1875 there were, for the first time, no foreigners in a group of sixteen young adults in the baptism class. Thomas Jensen writes: "They are all unbaptised young men aged between 18–30 years, and all of them Bahurutsi at that. (...) In the last number of years those who wanted to be baptised have, with only a few exceptions, all been foreigners who reside here."[407] What is remarkable about this group is that they were not only all Bahurutshe, but only young men as well. Thomas Jensen does not comment on this circumstance. One supposition might be that these young men belonged to one or two of the same circumcision age groups and had found their way into the church out of solidarity with one another. Consequently, neither women nor foreigners had signed up for this particular group. A definite trend could be discerned in 1875. An increasing number of Bahurutshe accepted the gospel.

1875 is the year in which Moiloa II died. K. Rüter believes that these sixteen men only agreed to be baptised after the death of their great chief.

407 Thomas Jensen 17.09.1875 p. 1f. – "Die Ungetauften sind alle junge Männer von 18–30 Jahr alt und dazu sind es alle Bahurutsi. (...) Es waren in den letzten Jahren einige Ausnahmen, sonst waren es alle hier wohnenden Fremdlinge, die sich hatten taufen lassen."

She writes: "Up until two days before his (Moiloa's) death on 6 July 1875, there was not one Mohurutshe who had officially converted to Christianity."[408] Rüter thereby attests to the fact that, up to that point, the converted Bahurutshe did not feature as Christians within their tribe. She is however not correct in her assumption that the sixteen men that were baptised on 4 July 1875 were the first Bahurutshe to do so. Thomas Jensen, as well as Zimmermann before him, had previously baptised other Bahurutshe. The large group of sixteen men made a more lasting public impression than the small number of Batswana, Bahurutshe and foreigners who had been previously baptised.

After more and more Bahurutshe were baptised, they also began assuming leadership positions within the congregation, positions that had previously only been held by foreigners. There was a steady stream of people who wanted to leave their traditional belief behind and desired to be admitted to the congregation. There were no mass conversions, as was the case in Bethanie near Pretoria and Phokeng near Rustenburg, where the resident tribes were directly surrounded by Boers. They suffered under the intimidation of the Boers and sought emotional security in the Christian faith, as well as moral protection with the missionaries. The congregation in Dinokana grew slowly but steadily. At the same time, it was less vulnerable to outside influences like the large number of independent churches that sprang up at the turn of the century. But the traditional believers also adhered to their belief system more strongly than they did in Bethanie or Phokeng. To this day the traditional belief system is highly prevalent in Dinokana.

[408] Rüter p. 96 – "Bis zwei Tage vor seinem (Moiloas) Tode am 6. Juli 1875 war kein Mohurutshe offiziell zum Christentum übergetreten."

6 Ferdinand Jensen's Retrospection

Thomas Jensen had died. Ferdinand Jensen had taken over the work in the Dinokana congregation. After having been in the service of the mission at Dinokana for seventy years he reflected on his missionary work. Even though the majority of the tribe had not converted to Christianity, the external appearance of Dinokana had changed completely. The Bahurutshe had adopted the European way of clothing themselves. There was no Mohurutshe who still walked about town half naked or totally naked. They had also, for the most part, aligned themselves with the Europeans in the way they worked. They used ploughs to till the soil. Many houses were now built in a rectangular fashion with bricks or cement stones. The roof was covered with corrugated iron sheets. The houses were furnished with tables, chairs, wardrobes and beds. By being connected to the water supply, each family now had sufficient water to cook, wash and water the garden. The people now kept themselves cleaner. The unpleasant body odour of earlier times was gone. In general terms the living standard had gone up. The children attended one of a number of schools that existed in the settlement, with lessons commencing punctually.

Great changes had occurred within the family as well. The church had contributed to a large extent to this change with its classes and church services. In many families the former habit of complaining and loathing had made way for loving and caring for the sick. One matter was particularly emphasised. A turning point had occurred regarding the subordinate role assigned to women. "The woman was the man's slave who, in spite of having to do all the building- and field work, gathering wood, pounding and grinding the grain and also preparing the food, had no rights or social standing, and was forced to remain silent even if her husband led an immoral and dissipated life. It is especially in this sphere that the Word of God has effected a change. It has put the woman on an equal footing with the man, thereby turning her into his counsel and assistant."[409] This adjustment posed a great

[409] Ferdinand Jensen 1929 p. 2 – "Die Frau war die Sklavin des Mannes, die alle Bau- und Feldarbeiten, das Holzholen, das Stoßen und Mahlen des Getreides und die Zubereitung der Speisen zu verrichten hatte und trotzdem keine Rechte und kein Ansehen besaß und selbst dann schweigen musste, wenn der Mann ein sittenloses, ausschweifendes Leben

challenge to the men. The impetus that had brought them to reason had come from the mission station. They had risen to the challenge and Christian education had become a part of tribal culture. This change of thinking was probably very difficult for many men. The first impetus of change had gone out from the missionaries' proclamation of the gospel. The men had received this new image of marriage during the baptismal classes on the mission station. By and large, as far as married life was concerned, the traditional believers, too, followed the Christian example. "Very few heathens still live in polygamy, marriage has become more humane."[410]

Other changes compelled the men to implement that which had been imparted to them via the mission station. One such change was the fact that they now had to work in a disciplined way on the farms of the Boers, or else do migratory work. In 1866 the first diamonds had been discovered in Kimberley and gold had been mined in the area around Johannesburg since 1886. The men who earned their wages in the mines of Kimberley and Johannesburg had gained new insights, which in turn also contributed towards a change in attitude towards their wives. Ferdinand Jensen comments on the men who worked back home: "[The man] now assumes responsibility for all the more strenuous work like housebuilding and fieldwork. Many tracts of land are being cultivated and worked with more care than previously."[411] The reason why this huge change that posed the greatest challenge for mainly men was accepted lay in the fact that it promoted a better standard of living. For many it didn't matter whether this impetus had come from the mission station or whether it had found its way to Dinokana via the economic changes brought in by the Europeans in the cities.

These changes were however not only accompanied by advantages. The civilised world also had its share of negative headlines. Had it not, with the two Anglo-Boer Wars, already shown its darker side to the Batswana? The Europeans imposed taxes on them. The Boers did not treat them as equals. But now things would get even worse. Many parishioners worked in the houses and gardens of the Europeans, and on the Johannesburg mines.

---

führte. Gerade auf diesem Gebiet hat das Wort Gottes Wandel geschafft. Es hat die Frau dem Manne gleichgestellt und so zur Beraterin und zur Gehilfen desselben gemacht."

410 Loco citato – "Nur wenige Heiden leben noch in Polygamie, die Ehe ist menschlicher geworden."

411 Ferdinand Jensen 1929 p. 2 – "… übernimmt nun alle gröberen Arbeiten wie Hausbau und Feldarbeiten. Viele Landstrecken werden urbar gemacht und sorgsamer beackert als vormals."

Once a month they came home to their families in Dinokana and paid their missionary a visit at the weekend. They told Ferdinand Jensen that Europeans and Africans were unable to find common ground. The Europeans were drawing dividing lines between the races. Black people were discriminated against. They were allowed to work under white supervision, but ate in separate locations during their lunch break and lived and resided on the peripheries of the white suburbs. In the white areas they were deprived of their civil rights. The structures of Apartheid were beginning to become apparent. Even though there were as yet no official laws to that effect, black people were nonetheless treated in a discriminatory and derogatory manner. That did not bode well. Hatred and contempt took hold amongst the black miners. How long would they let themselves be oppressed in this way? The insurrection against this oppression started in Johannesburg, dragging on for several years. In the end, and in spite of the tightening of laws by the South African Europeans, the policy of Separate Development could not be upheld. Apartheid was abolished in 1990.

Back to Dinokana. The modern, development-related trend had only partially transformed the Bahurutshe. The traditional belief system continued to be the central for the non-Christians. The circumcision school continued as before. It had however taken on a slightly more liberal character, compared to the harsh structures of previous years. Ferdinand Jensen wrote: "The castigations and atrocities have become less severe in nature."[412] He cited chief Gopane as an example. We recall that Moiloa II had appointed Gopane as his successor but that the tribe had favoured Ikalafeng instead, and that Gopane was subsequently obliged to move out after the arbitrary ruling by the British. The chief that succeeded Gopane, a young man of forty years who had been baptised by the Hermannsburg missionaries, decided that he wanted to get circumcised. By the virtue of his office he was awarded his own hut on the circumcision mountain. Ferdinand Jensen believes that he was neither castigated with beatings, nor was his woollen blanket torn off his body in those cold winter nights.[413] As far as the traditional believers were concerned, what was deemed to be essential in this regard was the fact that they were able to get the chief on their side and could refer to him as a "real man".[414]

412 Ferdinand Jensen 1930 p. 4 – "Die Züchtigungen und Quälereien sind milderer Art geworden."

413 Loco citato.

414 Traditional believers took pride in their circumcision. An uncircumcised man, usually a

Traditionalists always welcomed it when their chief underwent the initiation school. This was now a rare occurrence, however. Since the gospel had been proclaimed in Dinokana there hadn't been a chief who had undergone circumcision. That did not imply, however, that the chiefs averse to the traditional belief system. On the contrary, they were sympathetic towards traditional believers, letting them have their way and lending them their support. Ferdinand Jensen deals with the chiefs at Dinokana in his résumé, in which he writes: "One should recall … modern heathendom and, if nothing else, the attitude of the chiefs who have shown themselves almost without exception to be the enemies of Christendom. Of the six potentates who have ruled the Bahurutshe since 1859, it was only … the old man Moiloa who sided with the 'moruti' and the congregation. All others have either been fanatical opponents of the Church, promoting instead their heathen customs, or else they have, in spite of being baptised, secretly adhered to heathendom. (…) Is it then not miraculous that, despite these antagonistic and destructive influences, over 5,000 names could be entered into the baptism register."[415] Ferdinand Jensen recalls the negative impressions the various chiefs have left on him. He finds the positive aspect of his retrospection to lie in the number of baptisms.[416]

It's no wonder that the chiefs were obliged to make allowances for the traditional believers. The vast majority of the Bahurutshe had not converted to Christianity. They continued to adhere to their traditional belief and, as such, had an influence on the tribal councils. Every chief was compelled

---

baptised Christian, was referred to as *mosimane* = a condescending, belittling term for a small man who was not really a man, whereas a circumcised man was referred to *monna* = accentuating an actual, real man.

415 Ferdinand Jensen 1929 p. 4f – "Man denke … an das moderne Heidentum und nicht zuletzt an die Haltung der Häuptlinge, die sich fast ausnahmslos als Feinde des Christentums gezeigt haben. Von den sechs Herrschern, die seit 1859 das Volk der Bafurutshe regierten, war der alte Moiloa … der einzige, der sich auf die Seite des 'Moruti' und der Gemeinde stellte. Alle anderen sind entweder fanatische Gegner der Kirche und Förderer der heidnischen Bräuche gewesen oder solche, die, obgleich sie getauft waren, es doch heimlich mit den Heiden hielten. (…) Ist es da nicht wunderbar, dass trotz dieser feindlichen und zerstörenden Einflüsse über 5.000 Namen in das Taufregister eingetragen werden konnten."

416 Standing in contrast to the chiefs listed by Ferdinand Jensen who only attended church on rare occasions, the conduct of the residing chief at the time of the writing of this book, Monnamere Moiloa is, in some respects, comparable to that of Moiloa II. He was a member of the men's group of the congregation and regularly attended the church services.

to listen to them. The Bahurutshe lived in a protected space. The Boers resided at quite a distance from them and had no influence on the internal matters of the tribe. It was the chief's obligation to strive for harmony and equilibrium within the tribe. If he failed to do that he ran the risk of the traditional believers secretly agitating against him and eventually dethroning him. Such conduct was not to be expected of the Christians. If, according to Ferdinand Jensen, the chief was subsequently more sympathetic towards the traditional believers than he was towards the Christians, this was probably the subjective Christian perspective of a missionary. We should also not forget all the good things that various chiefs did for the Christians. Ikalafeng had built the new church, for example, towards which the traditional believers were also asked to make contribution. He had also decreed for the prayer service for rain to be held in the church, which the traditional believers were also obliged to attend. Ferdinand Jensen cites Moiloa II and wishing he had a chief of a similar disposition. But Moiloa II was an exception. First-generation chiefs of similar stature could be found in Phokeng and Bethanie. In keeping with the trend of the time, subsequent chiefs acted in a more neutral way. They would be supportive of Christian concerns on one occasion, and of those of traditional believers on another.

Even if the traditional believers continued to play a major role in Dinokana, the number of baptised Christians should nonetheless not be underestimated. During a period of seventy years 5,000 Bahurutshe were baptised in Dinokana. The patient and sustained service rendered by the Dinokana missionaries had borne fruit. Zimmermann and Thomas Jensen had changed the face of Dinokana. Ferdinand Jensen had followed in their footsteps. The Bahurutshe began to feel proud of their missionaries. Only a few of the tribal leaders converted to Christianity. There had been no baptisms of entire families. The congregation had grown due to many individual conversions.

Over the years the ratio between the traditional believers and the Christians remained roughly the same. Reverend Schlag, who ministered to the congregation in the 60s, writes towards the end of the 20th century: "Today there reside about 14,000 people [in Dinokana], of which around 4,000 belong to the Lutheran Church. But well over half of them are not Christian."[417] Other than Ferdinand Jensen, Schlag is only referring to Dinokana.

[417] Schlag 1999 p. 10 – "Heute leben dort etwa 14.000 Menschen, von denen etwa 4.000 der lutherischen Kirche angehören. Aber weit über die Hälfte sind keine Christen."

In the number of baptised Christians mentioned by Ferdinand Jensen, those on the outstations are included as well. According to Schlag's estimation one could ostensibly make the assumption that, apart from the 4,000 Christians, there are around 10,000 traditional believers in Dinokana. This is however not the case. Other churches and church communities are also meanwhile operating in Dinokana. Large numbers should always be approached with some circumspection. As Schlag's numbers also constitute merely an estimated figure, one can nonetheless derive a possible trend from them. One may gather from this trend that, even today, there are a large number of Christians in Dinokana but also still a large number of traditional believers.

7 In Conclusion

Over a period of eighty years, the tribe of the Bahurutshe was missionized by three Hermannsburg missionaries. The Hermannsburg Mission Society established its first mission station in the Transvaal, they held church services and built churches. The first generation of African Christians distanced themselves from the traditional belief system. Christianity had taken root. Thomas Jensen constructed the first school building in the Transvaal. The congregation grew and gained in reputation in the eyes of society and was, by its public congregational celebrations, also often at the centre of tribal life.

In the end the missionaries' dedication was however not able to totally conquer the traditional belief. The circumcision school continued as before. Medicine men and, at a later stage, also female practitioners continued to clandestinely practise their craft, sometimes misusing it. Ancestral belief, demonstrated by the cairn, remains a visible indication of traditional belief. Their demi-gods, who constitute an exception within the other Batswana tribes, continue to form part of tribal memory, even if they are not worshipped openly.

The Bahurutshe themselves have hitherto not published anything by way of a comprehensive depiction of their history. Many things from the past have already been forgotten. Oral tradition is only able to partially depict certain aspects. It is therefore important to delve into the archives and consult the reports of the missionaries of the 19th and 20th century, not only to read about their successful mission work but also to view the tribe in which they spent their entire lives as a single entity. This includes, over and above the missionizing endeavours, a socio-cultural existence lived with and amongst each other, the ordeals faced in crisis situations, as well as the contentious engagement with the traditional belief system. The missionary reports contain traditions, narratives and historical facts that touch on these aspects. They lie far back in the past, to be sure, but it is only through a knowledge of the past, of the historical connections, that will allow us to deal appropriately with the present. It is for this reason that knowledge of the historical context of the last two centuries will also continue to remain relevant to the Bahurutshe themselves, for the present as well as the future.

The three missionaries F. Zimmermann, Thomas Jensen and Ferdinand Jensen have, together with the respective chiefs of their time – with Moiloa II leading the way – lived through difficult times with the Bahurutshe. Amongst these was the tribal transition from a migratory way of life to a more sedentary one, the transition from subsistence farming (self-sufficiency) to an industrialised society, as well as the acceptance of the tensions that exist between traditional belief and the Christian faith and steering them into a manageable direction.

Zimmermann wanted to work closely with the tribe. He concerned himself with the culture of the tribe and espoused the rights of the Bahurutshe. Thomas Jensen's way was to build up the congregation. He asked to be told the elements of traditional belief and sought to find a way of appropriate confrontation. Ferdinand Jensen was proficient in the Setswana language like no other missionary. This enabled him to gain a deep insight into the world view of the Batswana. He communicated with proverbs and expedited the process of inculturation. Before the arrival of the Hermannsburg missionaries, various missionaries of other mission society had, within a short period of time, attempted to establish themselves amongst the Bahurutshe. They were unsuccessful and were obliged to leave the tribe again after a short period of time.

The Bahurutshe had initially not been the focus of the Hermannsburg missionaries. This was to change by happenstance or rather by the providence of God. Once this was accepted, mission work began in Dinokana on a continuous basis, which was particularly shaped by the patient and constructive style of the two Jensens. The way in which they missionized the Bahurutshe, gave them advice and support and lived amongst them for the rest of their lives was a contributing factor in enabling the tribe, which resided in a remote area away from large cities, to maintain its homogenous identity, shielding it from stressful external influences.

Ferdinand Jensen, through his close contact with the spiritual élite of the population, succeeded in understanding the traditional religious and culturally transmitted values of the Bahurutshe and to transfer tenable elements thereof into the Christian congregation. His collected literary estate, which has been released recently lies ready to be reappraised in the UNISA archives.

The author concludes this book with a text from the vast number of Ferdinand Jensen's collected proverbs. It is a Bahurutshe proverb of wisdom which, when looking back on historical events, may be food for thought.

> *Ditshaba e rile re sa aga mmogo re a be re tshaba go tshegana*
>
> When all the tribes were still living together we were afraid to laugh at each other.[418]

[418] Ferdinand Jensen, *Sprichwörter der Bahurutshe* No. 15.

8 Appendix

8.1 Personal Observations by the Author

There were a number of circumstances which led me to write this book. I heard the name Dinokana for the first time during my missiological studies in Hermannsburg. Signs with the names of old mission stations had been hung above the doors of our study rooms. I shared a room bearing the name "Dinokana" with Dieter Schütte and Johann Wichern for a while, a name that initially meant nothing to me.

My journey into the mission then led me to the Batswana in South Africa, however. While doing mission work amongst the Bahurutshe Boo-Manyana in Motswedi, I had regular contact with the Bahurutshe Boo-Moiloa in Dinokana, which was roughly sixty kilometres away. While other congregations already had African pastors, Dinokana, being the first Hermannsburg mission station in the Transvaal, remained a bastion of the mission for the time being. The last two Hermannsburg missionaries who served in that congregation were Fritz-Carsten Töllner and his wife Margret, and Harald Thönicke with his wife Ruth. I visited these two families frequently. In those days the network of roads was not as well developed as it is today. There were two dirt roads and a bush track leading from Motswedi to Dinokana.

The main Bahurutshe tribe settled at Dinokana in 1848. During the course of history of the previous two centuries a number of secessions took place. All break-away factions, who for their part instituted their own chief, subsequently settled in the vicinity of Dinokana, most of them thirty to eighty kilometres to the north or north-east. Dinokana continued to remain the cradle of all subsequent Bahurutshe tribes. The newly formed tribes maintained close relations with the historical roots of their kin and with the former Bahurutshe chiefs of whom they were descended.

I was unable to address and deal with the complex situation of the various breakaways, their secession history and the establishment of the newly formed tribes elsewhere. I concentrated my research exclusively on the main tribe of the Bahurutshe-Boo-Moiloa of Dinokana. This provided me with sufficient material which was, for the most part, admittedly only discovered due to my research efforts. Parts of these research results had hitherto been unknown in Hermannsburg. The Bahurutshe themselves had already forgotten many events from their recent past.

I spent the first ten years of my missionary service amongst the Bahurutshe. The longer I stayed, the more I began developing an interest in the history of this tribe. I lived in a rural area with little variety, had no television, didn't subscribe to any newspaper, led a simple life and strove to adapt to the Bahurutshe's way of life. This almost inevitably led to the circumstance that I got to know and understand the local people, their culture and traditional belief system better as time went by. At a later stage I wanted to further deepen my knowledge and understanding and enrolled in a study course at the University of South Africa. This book comprises roughly a third of my doctoral thesis, and has been reworked and augmented with additional material to be used as a separate presentation.

For the German publication of this book I visited the chief in Dinokana, Monnamere Moiloa, on three separate occasions and had conversations with the tribal council of elders. I informed the ladies and gentlemen of the tribal council of my undertaking and discussed certain sections of my manuscript with them. I was sorry to hear that Chief Monnamere Moiloa had died in 2007, a few months after my last visit in Dinokana. He was 57 years old. In his memory I have added a picture of him at his inauguration in the addendum.

My gratitude goes to the following persons who gave me permission to publish their pictures: Monnamere Moiloa, the tribal council of Dinokana, Werner Jensen, Erika Wenhold, Helmut Reinke and Heinrich Schlag.

With the Setswana proverb *"motho ke motho ka batho ba bangwe"* I fondly recall all those countless Bahurutshe whom I encountered over the past forty years and who have shaped and accompanied me in my life. The literal translation of this proverb is: "A human is human through other humans", its figurative meaning being: "A person evolves through his or her fellow humans. A human is shaped by his or her fellow humans." What is remarkable is that this proverb arose within the collective society depicted in this book.

In my research I have done my best, but there is always something to be added or to be viewed from a different perspective. That work is now left to the Bahurutshe themselves.

8.2 Biographies

8.2.1 Thomas Jensen

Thomas and Ferdinand Jensen were father and son. They spent their entire professional life in Dinokana. Between them they lived with the Bahurutshe for 99 years and accompanied and counselled the tribe in its chequered history during this time.

Thomas Jensen was born on 24 April 1829 on the island of Alsen in Denmark.[419] He became a mariner and, being on a sailing ship in 1850, went ashore in Natal and stayed. Since he spoke German he attended the German church services held by the Berlin missionary Posselt in Pietermaritzburg. He told Posselt that he had no intentions of going back to sea and that he was looking for work in Natal. Posselt was acquainted with a Boer named van Rooyen who had several children and was on the look-out for a private tutor for them. In those days the school system was not that advanced yet, and teachers were not required to have had any training or a university degree. Anybody could be employed as a teacher who deemed him- or herself suitable for the post. Posselt advised Thomas Jensen to go and introduce himself to van Rooyen.[420] Thomas Jensen took his advice and was employed as private tutor in 1852 on van Rooyen's farm in the Umvoti district.

The Hermannsburg missionaries established their mission station in the same district. He began to regularly attend the church services there and had discussions with the missionaries about the differences between Reformed and Lutheran church doctrine. The Boers belonged to the Reformed Church. As did van Rooyen, who had expounded the Reformed church doctrine to him. The Hermannsburg missionaries were Lutherans. He debated the Lutheran church doctrine with them, and was eventually persuaded by it. After having been a private tutor with van Rooyen for five years, Thomas Jensen left his employ. He had taught seventy Boer children during this time.

The Hermannsburg missionaries had won him over to their mission work. He writes: "The thought now also arose in me that I wanted to become a missionary."[421] He studied at the mission seminary in Hermanns-

419 Thomas Jensen, *Kurzer Bericht* p. 1.

420 Id. 1861 p. 6; 8.

421 Loco citato p 11 – "Nun entstand auch in mir der Gedanke, Missionar zu werden."

burg from 1857 to 1861. In 1862 he returned to Natal, sailing on the ship Kandaze that Louis Harms had had constructed for his missionaries and colonists.

In Natal he now began learning Zulu as he had initially been ear-marked for the Zulu mission. The mission society sent him to Emakabeni,[422] where he only remained for a short while, however. After the Hermannsburg superintendent Hardeland had suspended the missionaries in the Transvaal, Thomas Jensen was amongst those missionaries who were to be placed on the orphaned mission stations. After only one year of working amongst the Zulu people in Emakabeni he embarked on the journey to Botswana, together with the missionaries Chr. Backeberg, W. Behrens and K. Lohann. He had been instructed to fill the vacancy at Dinokana.

He comments on his arrival in Dinokana: "We arrived here in December, shortly before Christmas (10.12.1863, HB)."[423] Thomas Jensen married Karoline Witte from Hermannsburg/Germany. He had met her during his study years but was not allowed to depart for Africa with her. Louis Harms had meanwhile changed the stipulations for those who were missionaries for life. He abandoned his stance that missionaries should remain celibate and allowed them to get married. He subsequently sent the future wives after them to Africa.

For the time being, though, the missionaries had to prove themselves in their work and learn the language of the indigenous people. Then their fiancées could come and join them. That was also the case with the Jensens. Karoline Witte followed Thomas Jensen to Dinokana in 1865.

The Jensen's first two children died, the first one in utero, the second one in infancy. On the stillbirth Thomas Jensen comments: "On the 8th of May my dear wife was delivered of a stillborn daughter. The whole process was so difficult, however, and lasted so long (70 hours) that we really feared for her life as there was no medical help nearby, but the good Lord, who is the best physician, helped us through it."[424] After the couple had lost two children, they adopted two others. They subsequently had two of their own children as well. Karoline Jensen died on 5 November 1905, and Thomas

---

422 Thomas Jensen 1874 p. 25.

423 Loco citato p. 17 – "Im Dezember kurz vor Weihnachten kamen wir hier an."

424 Id. 28. 06. 1866 p. 4 – "Meine liebe Frau hat am 8. Mai von einer toten Tochter entbunden. Es ging aber so schwer dabei vor und dauerte so lange (70 Stunden), dass wir um ihr Leben sehr besorgt waren, weil keine ärztliche Hilfe in der Nähe war, aber der liebe Gott, der der beste Arzt ist, hat geholfen."

Jensen followed her on 9 February 1908. Both are buried in the cemetery at Dinokana, across the church hall.

8.2.2 Ferdinand Jensen

Ferdinand Heinrich Wilhelm Jensen was the third child to be born to Karoline and Thomas Jensen on 20 February 1871, in Rustenburg,[425] a town lying roughly 180 km to the east of Dinokana that had grown into a sizeable Boer settlement by that time. A European physician had his practise there. After their previous experiences the parents had made the decision to place the birth process under the watchful eye of the physician in Rustenburg.

Ferdinand Jensen spent 8 years of his childhood in Dinokana.[426] He played with the Bahurutshe children and learnt to speak Setswana fluently. He went to school in Morgensonne, which was a German private school. It was established in 1876 by Hermannsburg missionaries and was primarily aimed at missionary children from the tribal area of the Bafokeng. The school was situated about 25 km to the northwest of Rustenburg. On 20 June 1887 Ferdinand travelled to Germany. Having arrived in Hermannsburg he laments: "Morgensonne was very disadvantageous to me. Sometimes, and for long periods of time, I would not have any tuition in German, only in English."[427] In Hermannsburg he attended a private school, learnt a trade in a joinery and studied at the missionaries' seminary from 1890–1895. He subsequently returned to South Africa.

His father had asked for help on the mission station. The work in Dinokana had borne positive fruit and Thomas Jensen had established subsidiary stations on the outlying settlements of the congregation. He could no longer manage all the work by himself. The mission administration in Germany complied with his father's request.

The regional mission council in South Africa had however ear-marked another vacant post for Ferdinand Jensen. He was to teach at Morgensonne, the school he had attended, on a temporary basis. Following that, he was to assume a lecturing post at the teaching seminary of the Hermannsburg mission in Bethel.[428] These plans proved to be unsuccessful, however. An

[425] Ferdinand Jensen 1891 p. 1.

[426] Id. Curriculum Vitae dated 14. 08. 1890 p. 1.

[427] Loco citato p. 2 – "Morgensonne war mir sehr nachteilig. Oft hatte ich längere Zeit keinen deutschen Unterricht, nur englischen."

[428] Ferdinand Jensen 02. 01. 1897 p. 3.

illness and a serious accident prevented him from doing his work for two years. He recuperated with his parents in Dinokana. It then so happened that, because no missionary was available for the neighbouring station of Limao in Botswana, Ferdinand Jensen was transferred there in 1898. Because he was still single and wanted to get married, he regularly commuted from Limao to his parents in Dinokana. His fiancée was Magdalene Achilles from Wahrenholz. Just like his father before him, Ferdinand had also met his fiancée during his study years in Hermannsburg. Louis Harms had died in the meantime but his brother Theodor Harms, who succeeded him as mission director, upheld the same principle of subjecting the prospective missionary wives to a probation period of a minimum of two years. Only then were they allowed to travel to their country of destination. The wedding of Magdalene Achilles and Ferdinand Jensen took place in Dinokana on 5 May 1898.[429]

A short time after his wedding Ferdinand Jensen returned from his work in Limao to Dinokana. Meanwhile, other neighbouring stations remained vacant. Ferdinand Jensen was to minister to all of them by visiting them in turn. He was able to reside with his family in Dinokana but, being a young missionary, was nonetheless always on the road. The following mission stations had been assigned to him: *Harmshope* (later renamed *Ramotswa*) with its subsidiary of *Lekophung; Melorane* with its subsidiaries of *Sikoane* and *Dinokaneng/Enselsberg;* the congregations of *Motswedi*[430] and *Maanoane/Gopane.*[431] During this period of travelling ministry, Jensen's wife remained at Dinokana. The couple had three children.

After the death of his father he was released from his travelling ministry duties. He assumed his post at Dinokana and remained the resident missionary at this station till the day he died. In 1911 Ferdinand Jensen was appointed superintendent for the Marico District.[432] Several other mission stations had meanwhile been established. The Hermannsburg Mission Society had divided its Transvaal stations into two superintendentures. The Marico District was one of them. Owing to his superior language skills

429 Id. 1898 p. 1.

430 Id. 12. 10. 1901 p. 1f.

431 Ferdinand Jensen 1930 p. 2.

432 Pape p. 85.

he was elected to the Literature Conference of the Hermannsburg Mission Society.[433]

Ferdinand Jensen died on 7 July 1941, and Magdalene Jensen on 28 May 1959. Both are buried alongside Jensen's parents. The father, Thomas Jensen, had been missionary in Dinokana for 44 years while the son, Ferdinand Jensen, ministered to that congregation for 45 years, which includes his short sojourn in Limao and his period of travelling ministry, which he conducted from Dinokana.

8.3 Chiefs and Missionaries

8.3.1 Reigning Chiefs of Dinokana

Moiloa II, born 1795, died 6.7.1875
Sebogodi II, born between 1815 and 1820, died 9.7.1877
(Interim chief *Gopane* reigned from 1875 – 1882)
Ikalafeng Moiloa, born in 1850 at Dinokana, died 24.6.1894
Pogiso Abraham *Moiloa,* born 1883, enthroned on 6.4.1906, died 17.10.1918
Israel *Keobusitse Moiloa*
Alfred, *Ramokhutswane Moiloa*
Pogiso II, Abraham *Moiloa*

8.3.2 Pastors and Missionaries in Dinokana from the period 1859–1940

8.3.2.1 Stationary Missionaries

1859 – 1863 Ferdinand Zimmermann
1865 – 1907 Thomas Jensen
1905 – 1941 Ferdinand Jensen

8.3.2.2 Temporary Pastors and Missionaries

1869 Heinrich Köller
1885 and 1886 Christoph Schulenburg
1886 Ernst Wehrmann
1898 – 1904 Ferdinand Jensen
1920 and 1928 Israel *Mangope*

[433] This group of missionaries occupied themselves with the translation of biblical books, the Lutheran catechism as well as hymns. They also edited the school- and prayer books compiled by individual missionaries, as well as the liturgical book.

1921; 1928; 1932 and 1936 Kornelius *Sephoti*
1933 Zacharia *Lekaba*
1933 August Witthöft
1933 Abel *Legotlo*
1933 Heinrich Lange
1938 Ernst Lange
1940 Thomas *Ntsimane*

8.4 Supplementary Pictures and Picture Credits

8.4.1 Additional Pictures from Dinokana

Chief Monnamere Joseph Godfrey Moiloa and his wife Ntebogang Theodocia on his inauguration on the 11th of June 1983 at Dinokana

Men attending a lekgotla *in Dinokana*

A common round hut built in traditional style, surrounded by a typical clay wall to screen the inner yard

Clay-built, thatch-covered granary hut in Dinokana

Front view of a rectangular thatch house; the windows, door and retaining wall have been decorated with ochre-coloured paint. The people are pastor L. Mogase and family members of the court.

An ox wagon with women on their way home after a day's work in the fields

Repairing an ox wagon wheel in the open cartwright

Harvest time in Dinokana

The pottery of Mrs Nyenye

*Ox wagons at the fountain (*sekhutlo*) on Confirmation Day, which everybody celebrates out in the open*

Ruins of the former settlement of the Bahurutshe in Ga-Ditshwene (Boer name: Enselsberg) on the farm Bultfontein

The grave of a tribal leader, piled with stones into a cairn, on the farm Bloemfontein in Elselsberg/Ga-Ditshwene, denoting a visible place for descendants to sacrifice.

Orthography: The spelling of names of persons, places and rivers in the quotations is retained in the way that the missionaries wrote them in accordance with the knowledge that was available to them in those days. In the text, these names have been brought in line with modern orthography, e.g. *Batswana* instead of *Bechuana; Bahurutshe* instead of *Bafurutshe, Baharutzi, Bahu; Setswana* instead of *Sichuan*; *Moiloa* instead of *Mohilo*; *Mokgatlhe* instead of *Mokatla; Mzilikazi* instead of *Mosilikatsi*; *Zulu* instead of *Zoola; Dinokana* instead of *Linokana, Ga-Ditshwene* instead of *Kaditshwene, Tshwenyane, Kurrechene; Mathebe* instead of *Matebe* etc.

Quotations: The Hermannsburg pioneer missionaries wrote their reports in the old German Sütterlin script. All quotations from these reports have been transcribed into standard modern German. Where explanatory words were deemed to be necessary, these have been put in parentheses by the author. Great care was taken in adjusting the outdated spelling to that of modern times.

If several quotations are cited from the same source, these have been denoted by the Latin phrase *loco citato*. If this phrase appears more than twice in succession, the name of the author is mentioned once again. If the same author is quoted twice in succession, this is denoted with *id. = idem* (the same).

8.6 Church Service Today

The church service, as it is conducted today amongst the Batswana and therefore also amongst the Bahurutshe, has undergone some changes. Ever since the missionaries passed the administration of the church into African hands, the forms of worship have been reviewed. Around forty years ago the process was started to incorporate a whole range of African cultural elements into the church services. In Germany, the attendees of the regional church services (Landeskirche) would usually remain seated in their pews throughout the service. They might stand up once for a prayer. The organ is played from the gallery. The church choir also stands at the back. The pastor is normally still the only person ministering from the altar. This outer form now seems to be outdated. Many church-goers expect to find the general change in lifestyle to also be reflected in the form of worship. An age that is orientated towards activity and optical and acoustic stimuli is no longer reflected in the church service. It is especially non-churchgoing members of the public who, upon attending a conventional church service, find it lacking in this regard.

The German structure of the form of worship as it is practised in the regional church (Landeskirche) can still be discerned in the African church services of the Lutheran church. However, the changes that bring an African worship service to

life and that have been contextualised to accommodate African culture are very conspicuous indeed.
In African culture there exists one intrinsic phenomenon that brings about all these changes. This basic phenomenon entails that every African person who attends a church service is obliged to make a visible appearance in some or other way. He or she must be seen and put in an appearance. In doing so, a person is being acknowledged and strengthened in his or her self-confidence. The fact that a person can let him- or herself be seen in this way is testimony to their clear conscience and good heart. In African culture every kind of concealment can be viewed with suspicion. Secrets have no place in a worship service. God has revealed himself. He does nothing in secret. In a worship service he is being revered as "the Lord". With the Batswana, this takes on the following form: Each member of the congregation belongs to a choir. There is the children's choir, the confirmand choir, the youth choir, the church choir, the women's choir, the men's choir, the choir of the church elders and the congregation choir. The latter accommodates all those churchgoers who, for whatever reason, do not belong to any of the group choirs.
Dancing and singing, each choir makes its way to the altar, from where it will sing its hymn to the assembled congregation. Choruses are sung when the collection is held, too, during which all church-goers move around the altar in groups. This custom of moving around the altar existed in Germany as well. From the way that many old churches were constructed, one can still deduce that this was the intention all along. This custom has been abandoned, maybe due to the affluent society we increasingly find ourselves in, which has led to a certain lethargy. To this day, this form of moving around the altar in African worship services is viewed as being symbolic for approaching the holy triune God, without being able to comprehend him. The African worship service is characterised by a great deal of movement. Nobody will fall asleep or experience a feeling of boredom. Guests must also be seen. They are asked to stand up or to go to the front and say a few words. Guests are warmly welcomed with a shake of the hand. They are celebrated as they enhance the fellowship and bring good tidings.
This form of worship demands quite an amount of time, of course, of which there is an abundance. In the context of African culture time forms an integral part of living one's life in togetherness within the community. The phenomenon of this way of life is carried over into the worship service.

9 Bibliography

9.1 Original Reports by the Missionaries

1. Reports by the French missionaries in the archives of the Paris Mission Society.

(French translation done by Annette Lange)
Journal des Missions Evangeliques. Septiem Annee 1832, pp 5–26. Paris.
Journal des Missions Evangeliques. Huitieme Annee 1833, pp 5–28. Paris.
Journal des Missions Evangeliques. Extraits de lettres des missionaires Rolland et Pellissier, Latto, 5 novembre 1832. Paris.
Journal des Missions Evangeliques. Lettre de missionaire Lemue, Motito, 1er janvier 1835. Paris.

2. American Missionaries of ABCFM Archive, New York.

Grant, A. Cape Town, 14. 03. 1835; 21. 05. 1835.
Lindley, D. Kuruman, 28. 12. 1835; Lindley Journal (from 22. 01. 1836–14. 04. 1836); Mosika, 29. 08. 1836; Grahamstown, 10. 05. 1837.
Lindley, H.J./Venable, A.E./Wilson, A.E, Mosika, 18. 08. 1836.
Venable, H. Journal dated 22. 1.-18. 05. 1836; Venable Journal dated 31. 05.-02. 08. 1836; Ginani, 24. 08. 1837; Oct./Nov. 1837.
Wilson, A., Mosika, 15. 03. 1836; Mosika, 27. 05. 1836.
Wilson/Venable/Lindley, Grahamstown, 06. 05. 1837.

3. English Missionary LMS Archive, London.

Inglis, W. reports: 23. 03. 1840; 31. 03. 1847; 15. 10. 1847; 06. 09. 1849; 16. 10. 1852. CWM/LMS Archive London, in SOAS Library: Africa/Incoming Correspondence.

4. Hermannsburg Missionaries ELM Archive Hermannsburg.

Behrens, W. sen.: 01. 10. 1865; 20. 01. 1874. ELM archive Hermannsburg: A-SA 1.310a.
Behrens W. jun. Annual Report 1907, A-SA 42–1b 1893–1908.
Jensen, Th. July 1861: Lebenslauf des Missionszöglings Thomas Jensen. ELM Archive Hermannsburg: Personal File.
Jensen, Th: 4.8.1864; 29.6.1865; 29.12.1865; 28.6.1866; 30.9.1866; 1.10.1867; 1.7.1870; 31.12.1870; 3.1.1872; 2.7.1973; 2.1.1875; 19.7.1875; 10.7.1876; 5.7.1878; 13.7.1879; 2.1.1883; 2.1.1884; 2.1.1885; 5.2.1889; 21.5.1889;

2.1.1891; 29.6.1891; 12.1.1892; July 1896; 7.1.1898; 19.6.1903. ELM Archive Hermannsburg: A-SA 42–18a.
Jensen, Th. 1874: Chronicle of Linokana in 1874 (Geschichte der Station Linokana bis 1874). ELM Archive Hermannsburg: A-SA 42–18b.
Jensen, F.: 7.7.1905; 1909; 1912; 1913; 1921; 1924; 1929; 1930; 1931; 1937. ELM Archive Hermannsburg: A-SA 42–18a.
Jensen, F. 9.1.1922 (Superintendent's Report). ELM Archive Hermannsburg: A-SA 1.315.
Köller, F.H. 24.6.1871. ELM Archive Hermannsburg: A-SA 42–18a.
Penzhorn, Chr. 1874: Chronicle of Saron Station (Geschichte de Station Saron vom 14.8.1874). ELM Archive: A-SA 42–36a.
Zimmermann, F. 1874. Chronicle of Linokana from Foundation in 1858 until 1864 (Geschichte der Station Linokana von der Gründung 1858 bis 1864). ELM Archive Hermannsburg: A-SA 42–18a.

5. UNISA Archive, Pretoria.

Jensen, F. Collected Papers: Files A, B, C, D, E, F.

9.2 Secondary Literature

Aland, K. (ed) 1983. Luther Deutsch – Die Werke Martin Luthers. Vol. 3. Der neue Glaube. Göttingen: Vandenhoek und Ruprecht.
Bammann, H. 1990. Koinonia in Afrika – Bei Bruno Gutmann (Tansania) und den Hermannsburger Missionaren im Südlichen Afrika. Bad Liebenzell: Verlag der Liebenzeller Mission.
Bammann, H. 1997. Consecration of the New Church at Motswedi on the 26–10–1997, In: B Klein, pp 3–22.
Bammann, H. 2004. Inkulturation des Evangeliums unter den Batswana in Transvaal/Südafrika – Am Beispiel der Arbeit von Vätern und Söhnen der Hermannsburger Mission von 1847–1940. Nürnberg: Verlag für Theologie und Religionswissenschaft.
Bammann, H. 2014a The Bafokeng – History, culture, religion and education in perspective from the first three Hermannsburg missionaries until 1940. Berlin/Zürich: LIT Verlag.
Bammann, H. 2014b Geistererscheinungen und magische Inszenierungen aus phänomenologischen Fallstudien im Kontext des südafrikanischen Weltbildes. Hermannsburg: Ludwig-Harms Haus Verlag.
Bammann, H. 2015a Bethanie in Transvaal/North West Province of South africa from 1846 to 1940 (Abridged version with an extension). Brits: Brits Printers.
Bammann, H. 2015b The Bakwena-ba-Mogopa of Bethanie – Their culture, and religion – Two gifted Hermannsburg missionaries evangelise among the

Batswana and establish a new village in South Africa. Hermannsburg: Ludwig-Harms Haus Verlag.

Barber, H./Berger, L. 2004. Field Guide to the Cradle of Humankind – Sterkfontein, Swartkrans, Kromdraai and Environs World Heritage Site. Cape Town: New Holland Publishing.

Beck, R 1997. Monarchs and Missionaries among the Tswana and Sotho. In Elpick/Davenport pp. 107–120.

Boeyens, J. 2008. In Search of Kaditshwene. Appendix D in Langwieder/Scheepers pp. 3–17.

Breutz, P. 1953a. The Tribes of Marico District. Ethnological Publications No. 30, Pretoria: The Government Printer.

Breutz, P. 1953b. The Tribes of Rustenburg and Pilanesberg District. Ethnological Publications No. 28, Pretoria: The Government Printer.

Breutz, P. 1989. A History of the Batswana and Origin of Bophuthatswana. Thumbprint Margate/Natal.

Blaiki, W. 1881. Das Leben David Livingstones. Gütersloh: Verlag Bertelsmann.

Briggs R./Wing J. 1970. The Harvest and the Hope – The Story of Congregationalism in Southern Africa. Johannesburg: The United Congregational Church.

Butler, A. 1987. Kuruman Moffat Mission: A Historical Survey. Kuruman: Moffat Mission Trust.

Campbell, J. 1815. Travels in South Africa. London.

Carruthers, V. 1990. The Magaliesberg. Bergvlei: Southern Book Publishers Ltd.

Coertze, R. 1971. Die familie-, en opvolgingsreg van die Bafokeng van Rustenburg – met verwysing na prosesregtelike aspekte. Pretoria: Sabra.

Cole, D. 1955. An Introduction to Tswana Grammar. London: Longmans Green and Ltd. Co.

Comaroff, J. 1985. Body of Power, Spirit of Resistance – The Culture and History of a South African People. Chicago: University Press.

Couzens, T. 2003. Murder at Morija. Johannesburg: Random House Ltd.

Davenport, R. 1997. Settlement, Conquest and Theological Controversy: The Churches of Nineteenth-Century European Immigrants. In: Elpick/Davenport pp. 51–67.

De Beer, B. 1975. Agter die Magalies. Fonainebleau: Postma Publikasies.

Elbourne, E./Ross, R. 1997. Combating Spiritual and Social Bondage: Early Mission in the Cape Colony. In: Elpick/Davenport pp. 31–50.

Elpick/Davenport (eds.), Christianity in South Africa – A Political, Social and Cultural History. Claremont: David Philip Publishers, pp. 107–120.

Elpick, R. 1977. The Benevolent Empire and the Social Gospel: Missionaries and South African Christians in the Age of Segregation, in Elpick/Davenport (eds.): Christianity in South Africa – A Political, Social and Cultural History. Claremont: David Philips Publishers, pp. 347–369.

Fiedler, K. 1983. Christentum und afrikanische Kultur – Konservative deutsche Missionare in Tansania, 1900 – 1940. Gütersloh: Verlagshaus Gerd Mohn.

Gercke, A. 1965 (ed.): Hermannsburg – Die Geschichte eines Kirchspiels. Celle: Verlagsanstalt Pohl.

Gollbach, F. 1992. Leben und Tod bei den Tswana – Das traditionelle Leben- und Todesverständnis der Tswana im südlichen Afrika. Berlin: Dietrich Reimer Verlag.

Grobler, J. 1997. Jan Viljoen, the South African Republic and the Bakwena, 1848–1882. In: South African Historical Journal 36, pp. 240–255.

Haccius, G. 1913. Erlebnisse und Eindrücke meiner 2. Reise in Südafrika 1912–1913. Hermannsburg: Verlag der Missionshandlung.

Harms, L. 1886 Katechismuspredigten. Dritte Auflage. Hermannsburg: Verlag der Missionsdruckerei.

Harms, Th. 1922 Louis Harms's Leben. Neunte Auflage. Hermannsburg: Verlag der Missionshandlung.

Harms, H. 1999. Concerned for the Unreached – Life and Work of Louis Harms – Founder of the Hermannsburg Mission. Addis Ababa and Hermannsburg: Co-published by Missionshandlung Hermannsburg and Mekana Yesus Seminary.

Häselbarth, H. 1972. Die Auferstehung der Toten in Afrika – Eine theologische Deutung der Todesriten der Mmabolo in Nordtransvaal. Gütersloh: Verlagshaus Gerd Mohn.

Hasselhorn, F. 1987. Mission, Land Ownership and Settler's Ideology. Johannesburg: The South African Council of Churches.

Hasselhorn, F. 1988. Bauernmission in Südafrika – Die Hermannsburger Mission im Spannungsfeld der Kolonialpolitik 1880–1939. Erlangen: Verlag der Ev. Luth. Mission.

Heinrich, H. 1998. Ludwig Harms und die Katechismusfrage – untersucht vor dem Hintergrund des Hanoverschen Katechismusstreits. Jahrbuch der Gesellschaft für Niedersächsische Kirchengeschichte. Mager, I. (ed.), Vol 96, pp. 197–228.

Hermannsburger Missionsblatt, 1854ff. Established by L. Harms. Hermannsburg: Verlag der Missionshandlung.

Hodgson, J. 1997. A Battle for Sacred Power: Christian Beginnings among the Xhosa. In: Elpick/Davenport pp. 68–88.

Hofmeyr, J./Pillay, G. 1994 (eds.): Christianity in South Africa. Pretoria: HAUM Tertiary.

Holub, E. 1880. Von der Kapstadt ins Land der Maschukulumbe. Wien.

Jeffreys, M./Jensen, F. 1947. Note on the Bafurutshe. Revision of 'A short History of the Native Tribe in the Transvaal', published in 1905 by the Transvaal Government, Pretoria. Revised again in 1912, from notes supplied by Rev. F. Jensen and the Native Commissioner, Zeerust. African Studies 6 (4):78–90.

Jensen, F. 1929. Das Heldenlied (Seboko, Plur. Dipoko) der Betschuanen. Neue Allgemeine Missionszeitschrift: 371–375.
Jensen, F. 1904. The Baharutze. File 6 item 176, translated by M. Aalberd.
Jensen, F. (?) Sprichwörter der Bahurutshe. Hermannsburg: Mission Archive A-SA IV 510.
Jensen, F. 1910. Litirafalo tsa Bahurutshe le likgosi tsa bona. Moshupa – Tsela No. 3–8 pp. 20–61.
Kalo, O. (ed.) 2005. African Christianity: An African Story. University of Pretoria: Department of Church History.
Kirby, P. (ed.) 1948. Robert Moffats Visit to Mzilikazi in 1835. Bantu Studies Monograph Series No.1. Witwatersrand: University Press.
Kistner, W. 1948. The anti-slavery agitation against the Transvaal Republic 1852–1868. Groningen: Nord Nederlandse Copieerinrichting.
Klein, B. (ed.) 1977. Commemoration Booklet for the Opening of the New Church – 26th October 1997. Motswedi Immanuel Lutheran Parish.
Kotze, D. 1950. Letters of the American Missionaries 1835–1838. Cape Town: Van Riebeeck Society.
Langwieder, G./Scheepers, J. 2008. Great Kaditshwene Ruins – The Lost City of the Bahurutshe. Rustenburg: Unpublished Manuscript.
Lange, H. 1949. Vierzig Jahre im Mariko-Buschfelde – Eine Missionsstation. In: Und die Vögel des Himmels wohnen unter seinen Zweigen. Wickert, W. (ed.) pp. 182–199.
Lemmer, J. 2004. Vreemde Stories uit Afrika. Pretoria.
Lestrade, G. 1926. Some Notes of the Bogadi System of the Bahurutshe. South African Journal of Science. Vol. XIII pp. 937–942.
Lewis-Williams, J./Pearce, D. 2004. San Spirituality – Roots, Expressions and Social Consequences. Cape Town: Double Storey Books.
Livingstone, D. 1985. Zum Sambesi und quer durch Südafrika. Pleticha, H. (ed). Stuttgart: Thienemanns.
Lüdemann, E. 2005. Communion in Christ – Through Difficult Times and in Renewed Hope. Hermannsburg: Evangelical Lutheran Mission in Lower-Saxony.
Manson, A. 1990. The Hurutshe in the Marico District of the Transvaal, 1848–1914. Cape Town: University.
Manson, A. 1992. Changing Forms of Resistance: Braklaagte and Leewfontein 1906 – 1996. University of the Witwatersrand: Unpublished Manuscript.
Maree, W. 1966. Uit Duisternis Geroep – Die Sendingwerk van die Nederduits Gereformeerde Kerk onder die Bakgatlavolk van Wes-Transvaal en Betsjoeanaland. Pretoria: N.G. Kerk-Boekhandel.
Mbiti, J. 1971. Concepts of God in Africa. London: S.P.C.K. Holy Trinity Church.
Mgadla, P./Volz, S. 2006. Words of Batswana – Letters to Mahoko a Bechwana 1883–1896. Cape Town: Van Riebeeck Society.

Mignon, A. 1996. The 19th Century Lutheran Mission in Botswana. Gaborone: Government Printer.

Mills, W. 1997. Millennial Christianity, British Imperialism and African Nationalism, in Elpick/Davenport (eds). Christianity in South Africa – A Political, Social and Cultural History, pp. 337–346. Claremont: David Philips Publishers.

Molokoe, B. 2000. Bophuthatswana and its Impact on the North West Province, 1974–1998. University of North West: Unpublished Doctoral Thesis.

Mulemfo, M. 1996. Palaver as a Dimension of Communal Solidarity in Zaire: A Missiological Study on Transgression and Reconciliation. Missionalia, 24(2) pp. 129–147.

Von der Ohe, A. 1965. Alte Sitten und Gebräuche. In: Gercke pp. 91–94.

Pape, H. (ed.) 1986. Hermannsburger Missionare in Südafrika – Ein Beitrag zur Südafrikanischen Missionsgeschichte. Vol. I. Edenvale.

Purnell, M. 1995. Long Walk to Freedom – The Autobiography of Nelson Mandela. Johannesburg: Macdonald Purnell Ltd.

Rüter, K. 1995. Social Strategies in African Conversion to Christianity – The Experience of the Hermannsburg Mission in South Africa 1854–1879. University of Hannover: Unpublished Master's Thesis.

Schapera, I. 1939. Marriage Life in an African Tribe. London: Faber and Faber Ltd.

Schapera, I. 1971. Rainmaking Rites of Tswana Tribes. Cambridge: African Studies Centre.

Schapera, I. 1976. The Tswana. London: International African Institute.

Schapera, I. 1978. Bogwera – Kgatla Initiation. Mochudi: Phuthadikobo Museum.

Schlag, H. 1999. Tladi e bogale e sa tswa marung – Ein vernichtender Blitz kommt nicht aus den Wolken (Tswana-Sprichwort). Vision Mission. Zeitschrift des Missionsseminars Hermannsburg. No. 6, pp. 10–13.

Schlag, H. 2001. Afrikanische Religiosität. (1. Teil) Vision Mission No. 11, Zeitschrift des Missionsseminars Hermannsburg, pp. 25–36.

Schlag, H. 2002. Afrikanische Religiosität (2. Teil). Visio Mission No. 14, Zeitschrift des Missionsseminars Hermannsburg, pp. 19–29.

Schroeder, F. 1992. Missionare und Pioniere, Fairland/South Africa: Lugo Printing and Publishing C.C.

Schütte, H. 1973. Aus dem Leben unserer Voreltern: Müller/Schöneke und Schröder/Buthmann – Aus den alten Hermannsburger Missionsblättern, Tagebüchern, Berichten, Briefen und mündlichen Erzählungen gesammelt. Izotsha: Umhlangeni Literature Centre.

Setiloane, G. 1976. The Image of God among the Sotho-Tswana. Rotterdam: A. A. Balkema.

Shillington, K. 1985. The Colonisation of the Southern Tswana 1879–1900. Braamfontein: Ravan Press Ltd.

Smith, E. 1957. Great Lion of Bechuanaland – The Life and Times of Roger Price, Missionary. London: Memorial Hall.

Strauss, P. 1994. The Boer Immigrants and their Church. In: Hofmeyr/Pillay (eds.) pp. 93–122.

Sundermeier, T. 1988. Nur gemeinsam können wir leben – Das Menschenbild schwarzafrikanischer Religionen. Gütersloh: Verlagshaus Gerd Mohn.

Tlou, T./Campbell, A. 1986. History of Botswana. Gaborone: Macmillan Botswana Publishing Co. Ltd.

Thönicke, H. 1975 (ed.) Berichte und Statistiken aus dem Hermannsburger Missionsblatt (1959–1935) über die südafrikanische Missionsstation Dinokana (Transvaal). Unpublished manuscript.

Voges, H. 2000. Die Arbeit (der Hermannsburger Mission und des Ev.-Luth. Missionswerkes) im Südlichen Afrika. In: Lüdemann, E. (ed.) Vision: Gemeinde weltweit – 150 Jahre Hermannsburger Mission und Ev.-Luth. Missionswerk in Niedersachsen. Hermannsburg: Verlag der Missionshandlung, pp. 233–356.

Volz, S. 2006. From the Mouth of our Countrymen – The Careers and Communities of Tswana Evangelists in the Nineteenth Century. University of Wisconsin: Unpublished Doctoral Thesis.

Von Wimmersperg, A. 1999. The Rev. John Campbell's Water Colour Sketches of Kaditshwene (a late 'Iron-Age' Tswana City) and its people, the Bafurutshe. Cape Town: University.

Wallis, J. (ed) 1945. The Matabele Journals of Robert Moffat 1829–1860. London. Chatto and Windus.

Willan, B. 2001, Sol Plaatje – A Biography. Johannesburg: Ravan Press.